GLOBAL FINANCIAL NETWORKED GOVERNANCE

Global Financial Networked Governance provides a careful analysis of the Financial Stability Board (FSB) and the standard-setters under its umbrella to show how such government networks harness the power of public reputation to herd their members into compliance.

The FSB's track record in coordinating global financial regulatory reform is uneven. Some items on its agenda have seen the rapid evolution of globally coordinated regulatory standards and their implementation by all member states, sometimes even ahead of the stipulated timelines. In contrast, other initiatives have stalled at different stages of the policymaking process, global coordination is lacking, deadlines have been missed, and it is currently unclear when the post-crisis financial reform project will come to completion, if ever. In this book, the author asks the question: why has the FSB succeeded in some areas of its global financial regulatory coordination work and not in others? The book traces the global policymaking process in three major issue areas: banking regulation (Basel III), over-the-counter (OTC) derivatives, and ending too-big-to-fail. Through a combination of careful process tracing and rigorous testing against alternative explanations, it challenges the existing literature by revealing that the institutional pathway of policymaking is the main predictor of FSB progress. It shows that government networks on their own have succeeded in implementing globally coherent safety standards. In contrast, legislation and legislators in key G20 countries have limited the power and effectiveness of the FSB. The author analyzes the causes and effects of this phenomenon and suggests a novel institutional solution to the effectiveness-legitimacy dilemma that global governance forums face, combining the advantages of functional specialization and electoral accountability.

This book will be of great interest to graduate students; academics working at the intersection of economics, political science, and international law; students of the FSB in particular; and policymakers in global economic governance.

Peter Knaack is an Adjunct Professorial Lecturer at the School of International Service at American University, in Washington, DC, USA. He also serves as a senior research fellow at the Global Economic Governance Programme at the University of Oxford, UK; as a research associate at the Centre for Sustainable Finance at SOAS University of London, UK; and an associate at the Council on Economic Policies, a Swiss think tank. His research focuses on global financial governance. He has written and published on the political economy of global financial standard-setting, digital financial inclusion, green finance, and China's financial system.

Ripe Series in Global Political Economy

Series Editors: Susanne Soederberg *(Queen's University, Canada)*, Adrienne Roberts (*The University of Manchester, UK*), Samuel Knafo (*University of Sussex, UK*) and Naná de Graaff (*Vrije Universiteit Amsterdam, the Netherlands*).

For almost two decades now, the *RIPE Series in Global Political Economy* published by Routledge has been an essential forum for cutting-edge scholarship in International Political Economy, which we understand to be a broadly defined area of research that may cut across other disciplines. The series brings together new and established scholars working in critical, cultural and constructivist political economy. Books in the *RIPE Series* typically combine an innovative contribution to theoretical debates with rigorous empirical analysis.

The *RIPE Series* seeks to cultivate:

- Field-defining theoretical advances in International Political Economy.
- Novel treatments of key issue areas, such as global finance, trade, and production, both historical and contemporary.
- Analyses that explore the political economic dimensions of relatively neglected topics, such as the environment, gender, race, and colonialism from both Western and non-Western perspectives.
- Accessible work that will inspire advanced undergraduates and graduate students in International Political Economy.

Capital Claims: Power and Global Finance
Edited by Benjamin Braun and Kai Koddenbrock

Global Financial Networked Governance
The Power of the Financial Stability Board and its Limits
Peter Knaack

For more information about this series, please visit: www.routledge.com/RIPE-Series-in-Global-Political-Economy/book-series/RIPE

GLOBAL FINANCIAL NETWORKED GOVERNANCE

The Power of the Financial Stability Board and its Limits

Peter Knaack

Routledge
Taylor & Francis Group
LONDON AND NEW YORK

Designed cover image: © Getty Images

First published 2023
by Routledge
4 Park Square, Milton Park, Abingdon, Oxon OX14 4RN

and by Routledge
605 Third Avenue, New York, NY 10158

Routledge is an imprint of the Taylor & Francis Group, an informa business

British Library Cataloguing-in-Publication Data
A catalogue record for this book is available from the British Library

ISBN: 978-1-032-26805-7 (hbk)
ISBN: 978-1-032-26807-1 (pbk)
ISBN: 978-1-003-29000-1 (ebk)

DOI: 10.4324/9781003290001

Typeset in Bembo
by Apex CoVantage, LLC

To my family:
Horst, Helga, and Sarita

CONTENTS

ACKNOWLEDGMENTS

In the ten years that have passed from the inception to the completion of this book, a number of people have provided indispensable support. My research on the FSB and global economic governance started with my dissertation at the University of Southern California, where I studied economics and international relations. I am indebted to the members of my doctoral committee, Saori Katada, Manuel Castells, and Joshua Aizenman, who helped me frame the topic, supported me in my research efforts, and provided me with excellent guidance and inspiration. Simon Radford, Sean Wong, Chin-hao Huang, Iva Bozovic, Cynthia Macias, Jessica Liao, Cintia Quiliconi, and Rook Campbell formed the community of intellectual peers who served not only as sounding boards but who also made my days as a graduate student much more enjoyable than they would otherwise have been.

I continued my research and turned the dissertation into a book manuscript while working as a postdoctoral fellow at the University of Oxford. Emily Jones, Ngaire Woods, Tom Hale, Duncan Snidal, Alexandra Zeitz, Natalia Naqvi, and Ivaylo Iaydjiev graciously dedicated their time to provide feedback during a manuscript workshop at the School of Government. I am especially indebted to Emily for being a truly empathetic, supportive, and inspiring boss. My gratitude also goes to Stefano Pagliari, Eric Helleiner, Kevin Young, Lucia Quaglia, Elliot Posner, Abe Newman, John Vickers, Wang Yong, Jiajun Xu, Andrew MacDonald, Sharinee Jagtiani, Bob Keohane, Allan Dafoe, Thorsten Beck, Jean-Baptiste Velut, and Julian Gruin, who in a series of meetings and conferences helped me sharpen my thinking on global networked governance in general and the FSB in particular. Over 100 financial experts in 11 jurisdictions spent their time answering a young nerdy researcher's questions about global financial regulatory reform without getting anything in return. Their generosity is duly acknowledged.

Eleni Tsingou kindly read my book proposal and submitted it to peer review for the Routlegde/RIPE series in Global Political Economy. I am grateful for the extensive feedback provided by three anonymous reviewers and to the Routledge team for their editorial work. Any errors and misinterpretations remain my sole responsibility.

Myra Sinnott offered both a serene location on an island in Maine for my book revisions and a house renovation project to clear my mind from margin requirements for non-centrally cleared OTC derivatives. Painting real walls can be a wonderful counterbalance to changing letters on a computer screen. I recommend both activities in tandem. And I am particularly grateful to Sarah Holswade, without whose cheerful and enduring support this book would have never happened.

1

THE FINANCIAL STABILITY BOARD – A MIXED TRACK RECORD AT THE CENTER OF GLOBAL FINANCIAL GOVERNANCE

The security glass shattered a few minutes before noon. After relentlessly pounding the storefront windows of the Royal Bank of Scotland on Threadneedle Street, protesters stormed the offices, dancing through the broken windows and smashing telephones and computers to vent their anger. Around 5,000 people had gathered on four departure points in central London to lay siege to the Bank of England, each march led by one of Four Horsemen of the Apocalypse. An unnamed protestor sprayed the slogan "Stop the Bullshit" on the walls of Britain's central bank, a first in the 323-year history of the institution. Professor Chris Knight, senior research fellow in anthropology at University College London and one of the protest organizers, dressed in a black suit and top hat, brandished an "Eat the Bankers" sign as he talked to reporters about the velvet revolution that was about to start that day. Police used truncheons and batons to beat back the protesters each time they surged forward, and a local newspaper vendor died from a heart attack after being pushed over by police officers.

The G20 Meltdown March occurred on 1 April 2009. Dubbed "Financial Fool's Day" by the organizers, the day of protest coincided with a meeting of leaders from 19 major countries and the European Union, the so-called Group of 20. It was the second G20 summit since the outbreak of the global financial crisis, an event that made financial fools out of bankers, supervisors, and economists alike. Barack Obama, then brand-new president of the United States, met Prime Minister Gordon Brown at Downing Street and spoke of the "sense of urgency" needed to confront the financial crisis. At the time of the summit, all advanced economies were in deep recession, unemployment was rising fast, and developing countries around the world had to slash their growth projections due to a sharp reduction in global demand. In the epicenter of the crisis, tent cities mushroomed on public squares as US middle-class families had to foreclose on their houses because they were unable to meet debt obligations. An inquiry commission on the financial

DOI: 10.4324/9781003290001-1

crisis established by the US Congress noted that "nearly $11 trillion in household wealth has vanished, with retirement accounts and life savings swept away" (FCIC, 2011, p. xv).

Today, while economic growth rates and stock market prices have recovered (and tanked again due to the nonfinancial crisis caused by COVID-19), the repercussions of the global financial crisis are still manifest. Andy Haldane, then chief economist of the Bank of England, estimated the net present value of persistent losses to global GDP due to the crisis at $60–200tr, which is between 1 and 2.5 times global output in 2010 (Haldane, 2010). It may have been pure coincidence that public anger at the G20 Meltdown march was directed at the Royal Bank of Scotland, but the firm is a fitting example of the lingering consequences of the crisis. Once a star performer with operations in 50 countries, RBS had to be bailed out in October 2008 at the expense of taxpayers. Even in 2022, after a wave of restructuring and a name change to NatWest Group, the British government is still the majority shareholder of the loss-making bank, and the only consequence its CEO faced for his actions was to be stripped of his knighthood by the Queen (Wintour, 2012; Wallace, 2016; Crow, 2020).

The Birth of the Financial Stability Board

The G20 summit in London in April 2009 marked not only the zenith of the global financial crisis but also the beginning of an ambitious new project in global financial governance. Facing the magnitude of the financial disaster, policymakers in the leading economies pronounced their willingness to overhaul the global regulatory framework, increase bank resilience, end too-big-to-fail, and bring financial markets under tighter regulatory control. They created the Financial Stability Board (FSB) to facilitate policy coordination across borders and ensure G20 members will stick to their commitments.

The FSB is a peculiar organization. It was not created by international treaty, it is not an intergovernmental organization (IGO), and its members are not nation-states. Based in Basel, it is merely an association under Swiss law. And neither its charter nor the agreements it forges are legally binding. In other words, the organization is – by design – flying under the radar of international public law. But as the handmaiden of the G20 in financial affairs, the FSB plays a central role in global financial governance.

Just like the G20, the FSB was born from the ashes of a less transparent and less powerful organization. The original G20 was created in 1999 as a forum for finance ministers and central bank governors to coordinate financial regulation after the Asian Financial Crisis revealed gaping holes in global financial governance. In the same year, financial regulators from 11 high-income jurisdictions gathered with representatives from financial standard-setting bodies, the Bretton Woods Institutions, and the OECD under the umbrella of the Financial Stability Forum (FSF). The FSF was created to coordinate and promote the adoption of prudential standards to make the global economy less prone to financial turmoil.

But the organization had no founding charter and never more than a 7.5 full-time equivalent staff to carry out that work (Helleiner, 2010). In November 2008, the G20 was elevated to a central node of global economic governance, a forum where heads of state would consult with each other and coordinate their actions. And on "Financial Fool's Day" in London half a year later, the FSF was renamed FSB and given much greater powers to help G20 leaders implement their financial regulatory reform commitments (Pagliari, 2013b). Just like its predecessor, it is housed at the Bank of International Settlements (BIS), the central bank of central banks (Seabrooke, 2006), where it occupies (maybe not by accident) the floor above the Basel Committee. The BIS also supports the budget of its 33-member-strong Secretariat, although many staff members are seconded from FSB member organizations.

The FSB is a government network (Slaughter, 2004). Unlike an IGO, it does not have member states. Instead, its Plenary brings together 59 representatives from finance ministries, central banks, and financial market supervisors from 24 jurisdictions and the EU, along with delegates from international financial institutions and standard-setting bodies. In addition to the Plenary and several Standing Committees, the FSB hosts an ever-changing number of working groups for specific topics of relevance to global financial regulatory governance. These are an essential element of FSB operations because they allow members to address disagreements and solve cross-border problems behind closed doors, one step removed from outside scrutiny and the pressures of international politics that come with it. The FSB reports regularly to the meetings of G20 finance ministers and central bank governors and to heads of state at the annual G20 summit. All decisions in the Plenary are made by consensus, and rather than signing an agreement, FSB members unilaterally pledge to meet the targets, follow the principles, and implement the standards they agree on. Each member also pledges to undergo a variety of peer reviews, where financial supervisors from other jurisdictions check the domestic legal and regulatory framework to assess whether it is consistent with the global standard. Any shortfalls or inconsistencies are first discussed within the peer review team, giving the reviewed party a chance to address concerns. Subsequently, the peer reviews are taken to and approved by the Plenary to be published for everyone to see. None of the procedures described here are of legal relevance, and none of them are common in the intergovernmental world of global economic governance that revolves around international public law, voting rights, and other formal instruments of interest aggregation. Yet this book argues that they provide the FSB with more virility and power than the traditional IGOs that dominated global economic governance in the 20th century.

The first chapter of this book shines a light on the FSB from an institutional design perspective. First, it looks at its track record in implementing the G20 commitments during the first decade of its existence. The pattern of successes and shortcomings on the global financial reform agenda reveals the power of the FSB and its limits. But rather than looking at it as a unique organization, this book understands the FSB as an instance of a government network, an institutional design that is of significant and growing importance in many areas of global governance. It argues that the strengths and weaknesses of the FSB are indicative of a wider range of government networks such as the Basel Committee, which also features prominently in this book. This chapter teases out what exactly government networks are, how they operate, how they can steer powerful stakeholders from around the world towards a common cause, and the constraints they face in this pursuit. Both the power of the FSB as a government network and its limits are illustrated in two subsequent sections of this chapter. The first dives into a dispute between FSB members from Asia and the West on how to govern non-bank finance. It assesses how the organization leverages the power of reputation to nudge its members into compliance without recourse to any legal tools. While this dispute marked a defining moment in the organization's history, the biggest challenge to the FSB does not come from within. As a subsequent section will show, FSB members from the executive branch and regulatory agencies are constrained by parliamentarians in their respective jurisdictions. Legislators are reluctant to endow regulators with the powers to coordinate policy in the FSB, reluctant to remove obstacles to cross-border cooperation, and reluctant to implement FSB decisions domestically. The chapter provides telling examples of such legislative reluctance. And it offers an explanation for the criticism leveled by legislators against the FSB in particular and government networks in general. After noting a few methodological considerations, the chapter then concludes with an outline of the book.

The Track Record of the FSB

In the first decade of its existence, the FSB made an impressive effort at galvanizing policy coordination both across borders and across financial sectors and the authorities that supervise them. But its track record is uneven. Some items of its work agenda have seen the rapid evolution of globally coordinated regulatory standards and their implementation by all member jurisdictions, sometimes even ahead of the stipulated timelines. In contrast, other reform initiatives have stalled at different stages of the policymaking process, global coordination is lacking, deadlines have been missed, and it is currently unclear when G20 members will fully meet their reform commitments, if ever. Why has the FSB succeeded in some areas of its global financial regulatory coordination work and not in others?

This book sets out to provide an answer to this question. It assesses the power of the FSB and its limits by tracing the global policymaking process in three major issues on its agenda: prudential banking regulation (Basel III), over-the-counter (OTC) derivatives, and ending too-big-to-fail (TBTF). Prudential banking regulation is the success story of the financial reform project. In 2010, only a year after global leaders called for stricter prudential rules for global banks, the Basel Committee (a government network that is an FSB member) agreed on a new global standard. Basel III has seen rapid implementation by all FSB members, and banks have increased their capital and liquidity buffers in record time, making them more resilient to economic shocks.

In the area of OTC derivatives regulation, the FSB track record is mixed. In the first years after the crisis, it struggled to coordinate policy efforts, and FSB members missed all deadlines on the implementation of agreed standards, while key jurisdictions started bickering over the extraterritorial reach of their national set of rules. In the second half of the 2010s, the FSB was able to address some cross-border frictions and orchestrate its member government networks to issue globally coherent standards that will govern the plumbing of the OTC derivatives market. But cross-border inconsistencies and implementation gaps remain. And supervisors still don't have access to the information necessary to make a global assessment of risk accumulation in this vast market.

The never-ending too-big-to-fail story contains a similar mix of policy successes and challenges. Cross-border cooperation to govern the recovery and failure of systemically important financial institutions (SIFI) is still shaky, and market participants continue to believe that public authorities will be on the hook if one of them fails. But thanks to FSB coordination work, SIFIs have enlisted a growing array of private creditors as shock absorbers, and thus taxpayers are more sheltered from their failure than before.

Figure 1.1 shows the uneven track record of the FSB as extracted from the progress report submitted by the organization to G20 leaders in November 2020, a bit over a decade after its creation. It measures implementation among the 24 member jurisdictions of the FSB, which is comprised of all G20 members plus Spain, the Netherlands, Hong Kong, Switzerland, and Singapore. By end-2020, all FSB members have adopted and implemented capital and liquidity buffers for banks with cross-border activities in line with Basel III. In other areas, reform progress is mixed. Jurisdictions are in an implementation phase when regulators are requesting comments on rule proposals or when rules are partially effective. Finally, jurisdictions fall into the "no action" category when rules have not been proposed and published for consultation yet.

The empirical research that underlies this book discovers a peculiar pattern of successes and shortcomings in the FSB work program over the first decade of its existence. This pattern manifests in policy areas with vastly different market mechanisms, distribution of interest, and power dynamics.

The first item on the G20/FSB agenda is prudential banking regulation. Banks were at the center of the global financial meltdown, exposing the serious shortcomings of prudential regulation around the globe. G20 leaders were quick to commit to a thorough overhaul of prudential regulation to make banks more resilient. They put a government network that is an FSB member organization, the Basel Committee on Banking Supervision (BCBS), in charge of devising a new global prudential standard that builds on the lessons learned from the crisis. Ahead of the end-2010 deadline set by the G20, the BCBS published Basel III, a new prudential banking standard. All Basel Committee member states implemented Basel III capital requirements domestically two years later. Despite a generous phase-in period that extends to 2019, banks have adjusted quickly. All large, internationally active banks in Basel member states met the new capital requirements by end-2015, with

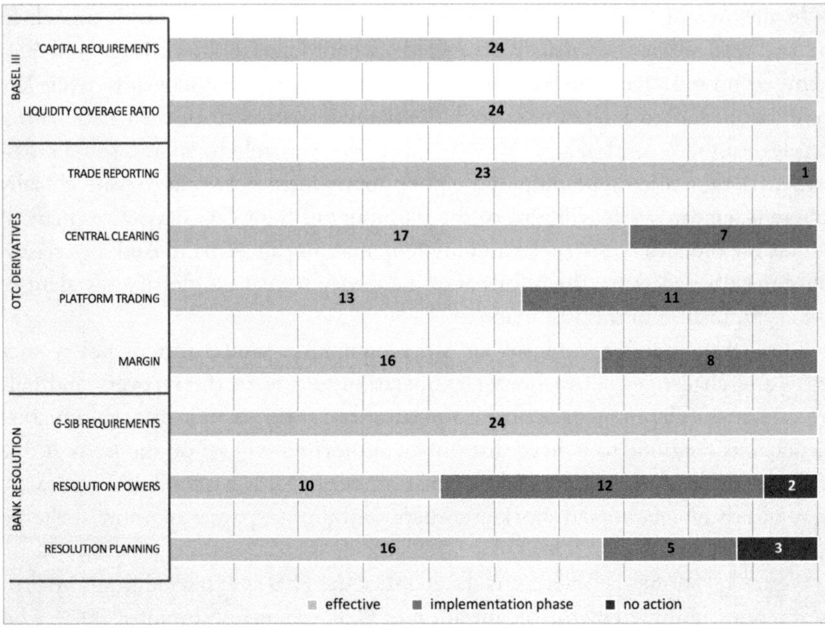

FIGURE 1.1 The Track Record of the FSB

Source: FSB (2020b)

the smaller ones meeting the targets one year later (BCBS, 2016b). Furthermore, 81 nonmember states have taken regulatory action to adopt Basel III standards in their jurisdiction (E. Jones, 2014; E. Jones & Zeitz, 2017). The Basel Committee has also developed global standards for novel regulatory tools, but policy deliberations started at a later stage. The liquidity coverage ratio requirement was issued in January 2013 and phased in from 2015 onwards but has nevertheless been implemented by all member jurisdictions already. The development of a global leverage ratio and a net stable funding ratio started even later, and the Basel Committee has revised certain technical details of its standard to increase cross-border consistency in 2017. It also issued global guidelines for interest rate risk in the banking book and rules regarding bank exposure to derivatives (counterparty credit risk exposures, capital requirements for bank exposures to central counterparties). This book covers these newer standards and recent revisions only at the margin, but the current state of progress in this area suggests that it follows the trajectory of capital requirement implementation (BCBS, 2014f, 2016b, 2020a).

The second item on the G20/FSB agenda contrasts with the success of prudential banking regulation. Turmoil in OTC derivatives markets exacerbated the global financial crisis, complicating state efforts to stabilize financial markets. Even though it had attracted regulatory concern before, this multi-trillion-dollar market was largely unregulated before the crisis. In 2009, G20 leaders declared their joint decision to bring the OTC derivatives market under regulatory control. They committed to having all eligible OTC derivatives contracts traded on platforms, centrally cleared, and reported to so-called trade repositories. Contracts that were not centrally cleared would be subjected to higher capital and margin requirements. By 2015, five years after these commitments were made and three years after the implementation deadline has passed, not a single jurisdiction had fully realized the reform goals. While domestic implementation in the leading jurisdictions is reaching completion today, derivatives regulation is fragmented along jurisdictional lines. Legal obstacles encumbered the emergence of global standards for platform trading, central clearing, reporting, and margin requirements, and even though some of them have been removed in recent years, remaining cross-border inconsistencies undermine the effectiveness of the entire OTC derivatives reform package. For example, central counterparties are established in several countries, but most are not authorized to offer direct or indirect clearing services to clients from other jurisdictions. There is no global standard that would subject a given derivatives product to identical clearing or platform trading requirements independent of location. Until 2016, the United States and the European Union, the two leading jurisdictions with the biggest market shares, were embroiled in a political negotiation over extraterritorial authority and the mutual recognition of standards that each side developed unilaterally. In recent years, the FSB orchestrated its member government networks in charge of securities (IOSCO) and market infrastructure (CPMI) to develop global standards that govern central counterparties, and it created a new technical language (the LEI system) that makes the intricate network of OTC derivative trades legible. In doing so, it was able to overcome previous coordination failures both across borders and between regulatory authorities in the same jurisdiction. But in an environment of uncertainty and absence of global harmonization, other jurisdictions adopted a wait-and-see approach, trying to minimize the expected incongruence between the domestic rules and whatever would emerge as a dominant global standard.

The third and final item on the G20/FSB agenda examined here concerns systemically important financial institutions (SIFI) and banks (SIB) in particular. The financial crisis revealed that the bankruptcy of some financial institutions can threaten the entire financial sector because they are large, complex, embedded in an intricate web of contracts with other financial firms, and hard to replace – in short, they are too big to fail. Because financial market actors expect them to be bailed out by the government in a future crisis, SIBs can finance themselves at lower cost, and they are able to engage in riskier behavior, a phenomenon that is called moral hazard. G20 leaders declared their willingness to identify global SIFIs, subject them to higher loss absorbency requirements, and engage in global cooperative efforts to facilitate their orderly wind down if necessary. Progress in this issue area is mixed. FSB members agreed on a global standard to measure systemic importance and on corresponding additional capital requirements for global SIBs ahead of an end-2011 deadline. In the same year, the FSB published a global standard on effective resolution regimes for TBTF banks. It requires member jurisdictions to work together in crisis management groups, share information, and supervise plans for the recovery or resolution of banks. Ahead of the 2015 deadline, global SIBs were identified, and additional capital requirements implemented in all jurisdictions where they operate. On the other hand, member jurisdictions are lagging in implementing the global standard on effective resolution regimes. Crisis management groups struggle with overcoming legal obstacles to sharing information and coordinating credible resolution plans. In sum, regulators have forced large global banks to adhere to globally coordinated requirements that increase their resilience against shocks, but they have not convinced anyone that cross-border bank resolution would not be a messy uncoordinated process that makes bailout a preferred option, again. In other words, banks are less likely to fail but still too big to fail.

Overall Argument

Why does a reform package agreed upon by the same group of world leaders under identical temporal circumstances and coordinated by the same organization exhibit such a staggering variation on a spectrum between failure and success?

This book employs a combination of careful process tracing, over 100 elite interviews conducted in 11 jurisdictions on four continents,[1] and rigorous testing against alternative explanations to show that the *institutional pathway of policymaking* is the main predictor of FSB performance. Specifically, reform areas that are handled in government networks such as the FSB and the standard setters it coordinates reach relatively rapid and consistent completion. In many cases, the regulators and members of the executive branch that participate in government networks are able to overcome cross-border differences and provide globally coherent solutions for financial governance problems. Using a variety of informal methods and soft law instruments such as working groups, committees, peer reviews, and the publication of implementation progress ahead of politically sensitive G20 meetings, government networks have the power to galvanize cross-border cooperation in the absence of any legal punitive threats.

Conversely, in areas where the legislative branch of government is involved, FSB work on global financial reform remains incomplete, and cross-border inconsistencies are common. Legislators – even those dedicated to strict regulation aimed at safeguarding financial stability – have been reluctant to remove legal obstacles to international cooperation. They have refused to endow regulators with sufficient authority to engage with their peers abroad, and they have made legislative changes for financial regulatory reform without consulting other G20 member jurisdictions, leading to cross-border inconsistencies in the rules that govern a global market. In other words, national law and national legislators limit the power of the FSB, representing the foremost obstacle to the completion of its global regulatory reform program.

To illustrate how the power of government networks and its limits plays out in the decade-long evolution of global financial regulatory reform at the G20 and the FSB, Figure 1.2 sketches the institutional pathways of reform along five stages of

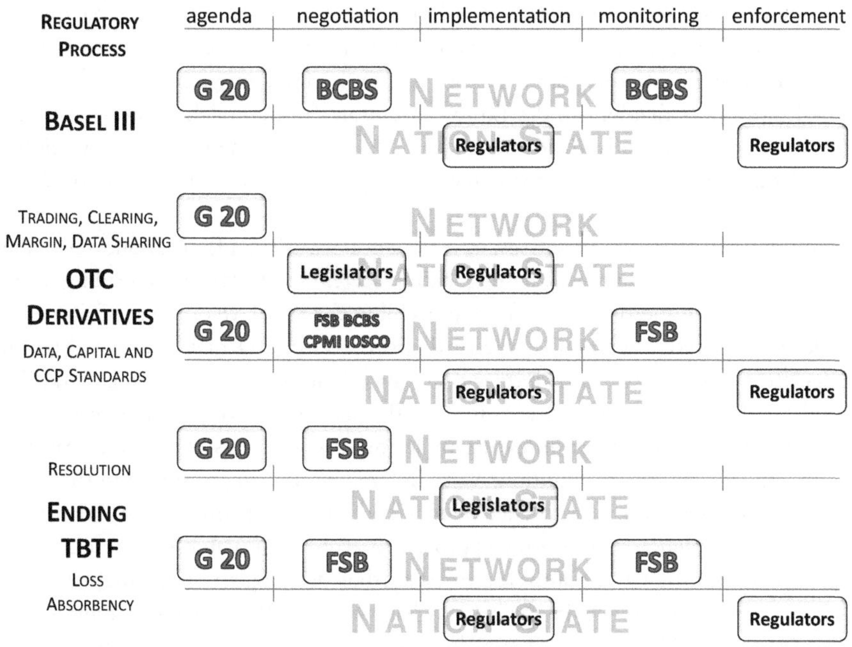

FIGURE 1.2 Institutional Pathways of Global Financial Regulatory Reform

Source: Author's visualization

the regulatory process (Abbott & Snidal, 2009). After an issue of regulatory concern has been put on the agenda, policymakers then engage in the negotiation of a standard. Once negotiators reach agreement, the authorities are responsible for implementation, monitoring, and enforcement of a given standard.

The figure shows that even though all reform initiatives analyzed in this work were put on the agenda by G20 leaders in 2009, they evolved along different institutional pathways in the negotiation and implementation stages. Those initiatives that were negotiated in government networks and implemented with little or no involvement of legislative bodies are reaching successful conclusion within or ahead of the timelines stipulated by the G20. On the other hand, all reform initiatives that involved legislative bodies exhibit shortcomings, either because legislators have not removed existing legal obstacles to global coordination or because they have not provided regulators with sufficient authority to engage in cross-border cooperation.

The success of prudential banking reform (Basel III) can be attributed to the decisive action of a government network, the Basel Committee. New banking standards were negotiated among regulators in the BCBS and implemented in most jurisdictions with marginal involvement of legislative bodies. In some jurisdictions, minor legal changes had to be made; in others, regulators merely implemented the new standards by publishing domestic rules. The government network is also in charge of monitoring implementation and assessing whether it meets global quality guidelines. To date, the only jurisdiction that failed the global consistency test is the one where legislators played a major role in domestic implementation, namely, the European Parliament in the European Union. In spite of the European quagmire, jurisdictions within and outside the G20 are implementing the new global standard, and the private sector is meeting regulatory requirements ahead of the deadline.

In the area of OTC derivatives, government networks under FSB purview were weak and inconsequential at the negotiation stage. Legislators in the leading jurisdictions gave domestic regulators responsibility for the development of domestic rules without considering the role of the FSB. Without a mandate to engage in regulatory harmonization with their peers abroad, domestic regulators drafted rules unilaterally. Cross-border externalities of the new regulatory system were considered only afterwards, culminating in acrimonious debates over extraterritorial authority and mutual recognition. With different sets of rules written in the leading jurisdictions and in the absence of effective FSB-led harmonization, other G20 members adopted a wait-and-see approach to avoid a mismatch between globally dominant and their own domestic rules, further delaying the implementation of OTC derivatives reform. In the second half of the 2010s, the FSB strengthened its role as a problem-solving forum to address disagreements across borders and across regulatory authorities. Together with member government networks that set standards for securities markets (IOSCO) and market infrastructure (CPMI), the FSB was able to produce concise and coherent standards for the resilience, recovery, and resolution of central clearing counterparties. The FSB also created a new standard-setter, the so-called Global Legal Entity Identifier Foundation (GLEIF) that governs and issues the "barcodes" that makes derivatives trades legible. Yet derivatives trade reporting remains fragmented along jurisdictional lines, and regulators struggle to obtain a global picture of systemic risk accumulation in this market.

The FSB showed more protagonism in promoting a harmonized response to ending TBTF. It established a forum for regulators and finance ministers to negotiate a novel global standard of key attributes for bank resolution that was subsequently endorsed by the G20. Nevertheless, legal obstacles hinder the implementation of this global standard. Legislators are reluctant to remove legal impediments to cross-border insolvency procedures, such as the recognition of foreign bail-in, nor have they advanced much in providing regulators with sufficient authority to engage in meaningful cooperation agreements with their peers abroad. At the same time, the FSB was successful at creating a new global standard for loss absorbency requirements of TBTF banks called TLAC. The standard was developed in a government network and speedily implemented in all FSB member jurisdictions. TLAC also proved instrumental in fostering renewed cross-border cooperation, and authorities in key member jurisdictions rolled back unilateral measures they had taken before. One reason why the TLAC initiative is a success story of global financial reform is that the FSB took inspiration from the Basel Committee, channeling its work along an institutional pathway that sidelines legislator and concentrates on members of the executive and regulators that sit at the table of the government network.

Why would legislators be unwilling to empower the FSB and similar government networks? The answer lies in a combination of institutional constraints and bureaucratic turf wars that I term *legislative reluctance* (see Chapter 2). Government networks in finance and other issue areas bring together regulators and members of the executive branch of government, but legislators are not involved. By relying on unilateral pledges, diffusion of global standards and nonbinding instruments such as memoranda of understanding, government networks can reduce contracting and sovereignty costs while providing greater flexibility for network members. This quality is of great utility for governments, especially in areas of rapid change and uncertainty such as finance (Zaring, 1998; Abbott & Snidal, 2000; Berman, 2004; Brummer, 2010; Jordana, 2017). That the agreements forged by government networks are not legally binding does not mean that they are ineffective, as this book will show at length. Rather, such agreements often incorporate a rigorous peer review structure, addressing collective action problems by raising the reputational cost of noncompliance (Raustiala, 2002, 2005; Ho, 2002; Kent, 2007; Underhill & Zhang, 2008; Keohane & Nye, 2003; Kahler & Lake, 2009).

While many supporters of government networks attribute their effectiveness to the freedom from legal compliance concerns, this book argues that its strength lies in its institutional design: Agreements forged in government networks can circumvent domestic power holders, namely, legislators, to a large extent. Unlike agreements under international public law, decisions made in government networks do not require ratification. In areas of regulatory cooperation such as finance, domestic implementation of global standards rarely takes legal form. Instead, the new rules are issued by regulatory agencies, subject to a comment period, and enter into effect when they are published in the national register (Gibson, 2013).

The reluctance of legislators to empower government networks like the FSB can be understood when analyzing the relationship between the branches of government from a bureaucratic politics perspective (Allison & Halperin, 1972). As bureaucratic actors, legislators seek to maximize the scope of policies they are responsible for, as well as the resources such responsibilities demand. Yet a larger and sociological perspective shows that the process of globalization has eroded the turf of legislators vis-à-vis regulators and the executive branch.

In the eyes of Manuel Castells, the key feature of the multifaceted process of globalization is the transformation of the dominant form of human organization from vertically structured hierarchies to transnational networks (Castells, 2000, 2004). This rise of the network society also includes global governance arrangements. Non-state actors from business or civil society organize across borders to take on economic governance functions in ways that create a new world of transnational neopluralism (Cerny, 2010). Early on, scholars expressed concern that transnational business networks would shift the balance of power vis-à-vis nation-states in their favor (Strange, 1996). But states have adjusted to the structural transformation of the network society, in two ways.

The first relevant phenomenon is the transformation from the postwar interventionist to the modern regulatory state (Majone, 1997). The rise of regulatory agencies as a state response to the increasingly complex and interconnected challenges of a globalized economy has eroded legislators' authority over economic decision-making. Regulatory agencies are one step removed from their political headmasters, attached to the executive branch and legislators by arm's-length agreements. Often they are overseen by a bipartisan "special commission," granting it further insulation from the party-political dynamics of the legislative branch (Berg & Horrall, 2008; Gilardi et al., 2006; Jordana et al., 2011; Way, 2005).

The second structural transformation concerns global governance. Over the past few decades, states have forged transgovernmental networks that allow states to cooperate in disaggregated fashion (Keohane & Nye, 1977). As Slaughter (2004) notes, "These 'organizations' do not fit the model of an organization held either by international lawyers or political scientists: they are not composed of states and constituted by treaty; they do not have legal standing; they have no headquarters" (p. 43).

Delegation to international agencies of any kind involves sovereignty sharing, but sovereignty losses associated with government networks are borne unevenly by different branches of government. Legislators see their area of authority circumcised, whereas the executive and regulators are able to retain or even gain policy-making power when engaging in government networks

The rise of regulatory agencies has reduced the power of legislators domestically, and the shift of policymaking authority away from the domestic to the transgovernmental level has further eroded their turf. Because parliamentarians have no seat at the table of government networks, they have little incentive to facilitate domestic implementation ("rubber stamping") of the agreements that were made without their input. Legislative reluctance can thus be understood as the result of geographic and temporal myopia ingrained in the institutional design of national parliaments and the erosion of power they are facing due to the dual transformation from the interventionist to the regulatory state and from national to transgovernmental policymaking. Regulators are forging ties in government networks, and the executive branch is increasingly involved, but legislators are lagging behind, unwilling and incapable of engaging in government networks themselves.

A few qualifications are in order to avoid misunderstandings and point out caveats. The reluctance of legislators to empower the FSB and similar government networks is not driven by lack of good faith or any desire to subvert the G20-led global financial reform process. Legislators around the world are concerned with the citizens they represent, and they are developing the policies they believe are most congruent with their mandate. Concerns over the institutional ability of parliamentarians to be meaningfully involved in international affairs are at least as old as the Federalist Papers (Jay, 1788). The phenomenon identified here is also not associated with any party, ideology, or identification with special interests. For example, legislative initiatives presented in the US Congress have aimed to either strengthen or relax regulatory stringency and the scope of extraterritorial authority regarding OTC derivatives regulation. What the proposals from either side of the aisle have in common though is that they do not sufficiently contemplate coordination with policymakers in other jurisdictions. Moreover, the notion of institutional constraints as one of the drivers of legislative reluctance only applies to issues of global governance. There is no contradiction between a certain myopia concerning global public goods and a clear vision for national issues. Most policy challenges to date remain confined to the national realm, and legislators are in an optimal position to develop responses that are congruent with the public interest within national borders.

The notion that parliaments, a key institution of democracy, have hindered the G20/FSB global reform project inevitably raises normative concerns. After all, global networks of technocrats in financial regulation have not only been criticized for a lack of accountability to the people, they have also failed to prevent, let alone foresee the global financial crisis. The final chapter of this book engages in detail with the normative implications of the empirical analysis offered here. It builds on the understanding that policymakers around the world face a trilemma of financial stability, financial integration, and national financial policies (Schoenmaker, 2011). If only two of these goals can be obtained concurrently, a fragmented world of financially stable, sovereign nation-states similar to that of the postwar years can be one desirable option. However, this book seeks to show that financial regulation can be coordinated at the global level without sacrificing democratic accountability, at least in principle. The analysis offered here indicates that the parochialism of parliamentarians is not a function of electoral pressures or relatively short time horizons, since members of the executive branch face similar constraints. Instead, the book will argue that elected officials will have an incentive to engage in cross-border coordination if they are accountable to an entire nation, not a small geographically defined sliver of it, and if they are experts. The concluding chapter will advocate for a new global regulatory governance design that rests on (1) a strict insistence on subsidiarity (as most policy challenges today are still best dealt with at a national level) and (2) the creation of expert councils that are elected to represent an entire nation in government networks.

While government networks are particularly powerful in the area of global financial regulation, we may expect state principals to employ this institutional design in other fields of global governance such as climate change and artificial intelligence (Biermann et al., 2012; Bulkeley et al., 2014; Whytock, 2005; Bostrom, 2013). Chapter 2 engages with this question, exploring sector similarities and the potential of government networks in addressing the burning global governance challenges in these two nonfinancial sectors.

The FSB as a Government Network

Government networks play important roles in cross-border cooperation in a wide array of policy areas, ranging from aviation (Bermann, 1992), human rights (Cardenas, 2003), and data privacy (F. Bignami, 2004; Newman, 2008) to antitrust (Damro,

2006; Whytock, 2005). Arguably though, nowhere is the tension between government networks and legislators clearer than in the realm of financial regulation.

The financial sphere can be understood as the spearhead of globalization because financial networks have transcended national borders faster than other sectors of the economy. In a speech, the Bank of England's Andy Haldane shows how savings and investment flows were largely contained within the nation-state from the Great Depression until the 1980s. Haldane (2014) states, "For much of the 20th century, global finance was more patchwork than network" (p. 5). This changed dramatically over the last three decades as capital flows went global, unfettered by national barriers. Haldane concludes,

> The international monetary and financial system has undergone a mini-revolution in the space of a generation as a result of financial globalisation. It has become a genuine system. This has altered fundamentally the risk-return opportunity set facing international policymakers: larger-than-ever opportunities, but also greater-than-ever threats.
>
> *(Haldane, 2014, p. 14)*

Because financial policymaking entails substantial cross-border externalities and because it requires specialization, the benefits of delegation to international institutions are considerable. In fact, some of the oldest international agencies can be found here, such as the World Bank and the IMF. However, the Bretton Woods Institutions and the FSB represent very different kinds of agencies. The former were designed as classic intergovernmental organizations, created by an international treaty and with carefully calibrated (and contested) voting rights. The FSB, in contrast, is a government network, and decisions in its main organ, the Plenary, are made by consensus (see FSB members in Figure 1.3). According to principal-agent theory, this would increase agency autonomy and open the potential for considerable agency slack (Cortell & Peterson, 2006).

Why does the institutional design of what Treasury Secretary Geithner called the "fourth pillar" of global economic governance at the time (US Treasury, 2009) differ so much from the other three pillars? This section argues that the FSB is designed as a government network because it is considered an optimal design by state principals. In contrast to traditional international organizations, the FSB harnesses the benefits of delegation while drastically reducing agency losses. At the height of the global financial crisis, heads of state chose to revamp the FSF rather than elevating the IMF (including the IMFC) with its thousands of employees to the central site of G20 financial reform coordination (Blustein, 2012; Kharas & Lombardi, 2012; Knight, 2014). In contrast, the FSB has less than 50 staff, many of whom are seconded from agencies in member jurisdictions. In addition, the Charter of the FSB ties the agency closely to the prime forum of interstate cooperation, the G20 (Donnelly, 2012; FSB, 2009, 2012b).

The institutional design of the FSB is that of a quintessential government network. As mentioned previously, it was not constituted by international treaty,

FIGURE 1.3 The Financial Stability Board

Source: Author's summary

and it has no member states. Instead, it brings together financial regulators and supervisors from a small number of jurisdictions. This disaggregation of the state in global governance is not new. Half a century ago, Keohane and Nye (1977) highlighted the operations of "transgovernmental" channels as a defining characteristic of complex interdependence. Transgovernmental here means that individual agencies and departments transcend the government as a unit to connect across borders. They do not represent their country, and they have no independent status in international law or politics. Slaughter (Slaughter, 2004, p. 33) calls them the "political equivalent of the informal economy." Much of the literature in recent years has focused on a subset of this institutional design, namely, transgovernmental regulatory networks that involve only regulatory agencies, not other parts of the executive branch (Bach & Newman, 2014; Jordana, 2017). This book adopts Slaughter's (2004) wider definition of government networks, not only because it befits the FSB, but also because the distinction between regulators-only networks and those that also involve line ministries does not prove to be decisive for the analysis offered here.

The FSB design builds on that of existing government networks in the field of global financial governance. While the Bretton Woods institutions are IGOS, all standard-setting bodies in finance are government networks. The oldest among them, the Basel Committee, has provided key blueprints for the tool kit and organizational procedures of the FSB (W. R. White, 1997; Tarullo, 2008). As the standard-setting body for the banking sector, it is a member of the FSB, along with the government networks that govern insurance, securities, accounting, and other relevant sectors. The connection between the Basel Committee and the FSB is tight. Several leading officials and technical staff of the FSB had previously served in the BCBS. Housed just one floor apart in the BIS, the Basel Committee was involved in all three FSB reform areas covered in this book. It took the lead in developing Basel III (Chapter 3) and has coordinated extensively with other standard setters under the FSB umbrella when working in related areas such as capital requirements for derivatives exposures (Chapter 4). Chapter 5 on ending TBTF illustrates an instance where the FSB takes inspiration from the Basel Committee in re-energizing reform work that was bogged down by legal obstacles.

Two institutional design differences between the FSB and the standard setters it coordinates are noteworthy. The first concerns finance ministries, which have no seat at the table of standard-setting bodies. The decision to extend membership beyond regulatory agencies goes back to the creation of its predecessor, the FSF, in 1999. Reisenbichler (2015) shows that the great powers quibbled over whether the organization was to be dominated by regulators or ministry officials. The outcome was an FSF driven by finance ministries in line with US preferences, not the regulatory forum European states would have favored. When G20 leaders created the FSB from the ashes of the FSF in 2009, they retained its composition of financial supervisory agencies, central banks, and finance ministries. The second institutional design difference to standard-setting bodies concerns its connection to political leadership. While standard setters do not have to report to heads of government, the Charter of the FSB makes it explicitly accountable to the G20.

The FSB uses the full range of soft law instruments at the disposal of a government network. It hosts an evolving array of working groups and forums for formal and informal policy deliberation among members. It has coordinated the development of global standards and best practices among the standard-setting bodies that are FSB members. And it has published global standards of its own (such as the Key Attributes, see Chapter 5).

The most noteworthy instruments in the FSB toolbox is the use of peer reviews to nudge member jurisdictions into compliance (Weber & Staiger, 2014). Unlike its predecessor, the FSF, the FSB has published peer reviews both on a single issue area and on individual member jurisdictions across issue areas. In order to harness the power of reputation through peer review, the FSB has devised a Coordination Framework for Implementation Monitoring in 2011. It assigns monitoring responsibilities between the internal implementation monitoring network, the Standing Committee on Standards Implementation, and external standard-setting bodies that are FSB members. The monitoring framework combines peer pressure within the government network at an early stage with public pressure at the time of the annual G20 progress report publication (FSB, 2011b).

The FSB has adopted this peer review procedure from the standard-setting bodies that are FSB members. Their experience reveals that the power of naming and shaming can even overcome legislative reluctance in some instances. An official at a standard-setting body recalls,

> We called out the outliers when there were people who were laggards and a little bit slower in adopting the rules. And I think that process, I can tell you, it was very effective because there'd be a scramble, a legislative scramble in the last couple of months in many countries to get their rules in place, because they knew that we'd be publishing the results.
>
> *(International Regulator 5, personal communication, December 18, 2014)*

Some scholars contend that even though countries are barred from vetoing their peer review in the Plenary before publication, FSB members are guided by a deep-rooted norm of mutual deference and thus might be unwilling to call out reform laggards (Helleiner, 2014a, p. 140ff). Even from a rationalist perspective, it is conceivable that avoidance of naming and shaming is a long-term "cooperation" strategy among states.

However, the FSB reform progress reports that this book relies on extensively do not support this conjecture. The empirical picture is consistent with the assessment of an international regulator who states that,

> There is plenty of calling a spade a spade about countries that have not implemented things by the deadline. And yes, there were discussions with all those countries, and most of them like any child with their homework had got their excuses for why, you know, that you should look at it in a slightly different way, but that doesn't mean that what they say the answer should be is what's reproduced in that table.
>
> *(International Regulator 6, personal communication, December 19, 2014)*

That even powerful states have chosen to meet their FSB commitments comes as a surprise to some scholars of international politics. Yet reputation appears to be a salient consideration among the major powers at the FSB. A former US Treasury representative notes that

> given that FSB negotiations are a repeated process, a country's credibility and influence within the group is in part determined by its willingness to implement the policies agreed. Failure to implement today may translate into reduced influence in international negotiations tomorrow.
>
> *(Sheets, 2017, p. 8)*

In the first decade of the FSB's existence, the utility of peer reviews in leveraging the power of reputation to make members comply with their unilateral pledges has not gone unchallenged. The following section zooms in on a regulatory dispute between financial authorities from the West and Asian jurisdictions.

Contestation Within the FSB and the Power of Reputation

The arguably largest test for the FSB to date arose when its members disagreed over how to understand and regulate the vast sector of nonbank credit intermediation (NBCI). Representatives from developing countries have criticized the FSB for casting NBCI in a pejorative light of "shadow banking" and excluding financial inclusion considerations from a global regulatory approach to it. Chinese regulators in particular put forth a series of innovative arguments to suggest changes to the shadow banking frame that would take developing country prerogatives into account. Yet regulators from Western advanced economies refused to adjust their conception of shadow banking and its implications for financial governance. In the face of such recalcitrance, Chinese authorities made their disagreement public and reduced the degree of cooperation with the FSB shadow banking work. In response, the FSB engineered a strategic shift in its peer review process, harnessing the power of reputation to punish noncooperation by member jurisdictions. The evolution of this dispute provides a rare case to assess the power of the review process in an area where epistemic authority over the regulatory discourse at the FSB is contested (Seabrooke, 2014; Seabrooke & Henriksen, 2017).

As is laid out in greater detail in Knaack and Gruin (2020), Chinese authorities started disputing the Western frame of NBCI as shadow banking in the mid-2010s. They argued that NBCI is a welcome source of capital for otherwise financially excluded parts of the economy and that NBCI regulation should be proportional to development stages rather than "globally consistent" (PBOC, 2013). Advanced economies should adopt a stricter regulatory stance while low- and middle-income countries can harness shadow banking for the development of the financial system and the economy at large (Ba, 2010; Sheng & Soon, 2016; Yan & Li, 2014, p. 280ff). Regulators from other Asian jurisdictions (both FSB members and not) echoed that sentiment (Gruin et al., 2018). They employed one of the regional FSB Regional Consultative Groups (RCG) to voice their disagreement with the dominant FSB frame – to no avail (more on this in Chapter 6).

Unable to change the FSB shadow banking frame, Chinese and Indian authorities chose to reduce cooperation with the peer review and report only NBCI activities they deemed part of shadow banking. Moreover, they made their epistemic disagreement with the FSB public. A footnote in the appendix of the 2016 peer review states that "the Chinese authorities did not agree with the classification of certain entity types as shadow banking" (FSB, 2016b, p. 93). Indian regulators added a footnote with the same content. This juncture represents a telling instance of the power of government networks: The FSB has no recourse to legal instruments and cannot force member jurisdictions to comply with its principles and standards, even though they were issued with consensus among its members. In the case of NBCI, no standards were formulated at all, the government network was merely engaging in a monitoring exercise.

In the absence of legal authority, the FSB harnesses the power of reputation in two ways: First, as mentioned in the previous section, states have an incentive to build a reputation as a reliable actor vis-à-vis other states because it is likely to facilitate cooperative behavior in the future (Axelrod & Keohane, 1985a). The reputational costs of noncompliance are especially high for newcomers to an international organization (Downs & Jones, 2002). Second, in the financial realm in particular, states seek to build reputation vis-à-vis market participants as a low-risk investment destination (Flandreau & Flores, 2012; Tomz, 2012). The FSB peer review is designed to employ both reputational mechanisms to dis-incentivize noncompliance. FSB members subject their national regulatory approach to external scrutiny by their colleagues abroad and make their collective assessment publicly available. Laggards or deviant jurisdictions risk being labeled as such.

Reputation vis-à-vis regulatory peers is relevant not just to facilitate cross-border cooperation in the future but also to avoid regulatory escalation: Even though FSB members have not publicly declared any willingness to negotiate a global NBCI standard, the FSB work on shadow banking is explicitly designed to "strengthen oversight and regulation" (FSB, 2012e). Financial regulators are aware that scrutiny by their peers will likely increase over time, especially if their domestic NBCI sector is large and growing. An international regulator recalls, "China and India, their regulators were so sensitive about labelling certain activities shadow banking. Because if you label it shadow banking you have a requirement to have tools for it" (International Regulator 17, personal communication, December 19, 2017). Again, such a "requirement" has not taken shape as a global standard. To date, the FSB merely refers to a "regulatory toolbox" that supervisory authorities in member jurisdictions are encouraged to use.

But financial authorities from developing countries cannot rule out the possibility that regulators in the "dominant centers" act as first movers in standard-setting again, as they have in areas such as banking and money laundering (Simmons, 2001a). A UK regulator confirms that this kind of regulatory escalation is not an unlikely scenario:

> Politics is just one layer underneath. If you have Europe and the US coming up with some sort of standards, they will probably expect other countries to do the same. Or they will criticize the countries that don't follow in some shape or form.
>
> *(UK Regulator 5, personal communication, November 7, 2017)*

Even in the absence of a global standard, uncooperative jurisdictions risk being criticized publicly by the IMF when it undertakes its regular Article IV surveillance.

Reputation vis-à-vis international investors may be a concern of comparable salience. Financial observers can be expected to pay attention to FSB reports as they update their risk assessment of the Chinese (and Indian) market. Estimates of the size and composition of China's shadow banking system are fraught with problems of over- and under-counting and consequently range widely, but analysts agree that it is larger in absolute terms than that of other emerging markets and growing at a faster rate than any other jurisdiction (FSB, 2017b, 2018b). Chinese regulators have a clear incentive to be seen both by their peers in the FSB and international investors as having a firm regulatory grasp on any potential risk emerging in the nonbanking sector and to allay concerns of threats to financial stability.

In the face of such threats to reputation at the international level and FSB resistance to changing its shadow banking frame, Chinese regulatory authorities had an incentive to drag their feet in the peer review process, understating the extent of the domestic shadow banking system and voicing polite disagreement while stopping short of a public fallout with the FSB. Unsatisfied with such lukewarm engagement, the FSB Secretariat decided to adjust the peer review process in ways that strategically excludes the status quo as an option (Oatley & Nabors, 1998).

Until 2016, member jurisdictions had considerable leeway in defining which parts of their nonbank financial sector would be *included* as shadow banking. Since 2017, the FSB has begun with a conservative estimate that considers all NBCI as shadow banking by default. Financial authorities have to assess NBCI activities in their jurisdiction against a sophisticated set of economic functions with associated systemic risk benchmarks and need to justify why they should be *excluded* from the shadow banking measure. Definitional disagreement as in the Chinese and Indian case would thus lead to a very large shadow banking measure, an outcome that national regulators would want to avoid for the reputational reasons outlined in the previous section. This strategic change in status quo thus puts the burden of proof onto FSB members, as an international regulator explains,

> The process means that if I'm China and I'm saying "well, I really don't think this needs to be shadow banking, I'm not going to call it shadow banking," the other people around the table can say [bangs fist on the table] "Prove it to me. That needs to stay in shadow banking unless you have the data and you can convince the majority of us that there's something extraordinary about your money market fund or your open-ended funds that warrants it being excluded."
>
> *(International Regulator 17, personal communication, December 19, 2017)*

This episode of epistemic contestation regarding NBCI ends in 2017, when the PBOC representatives in the FSB Plenary change their stance, opting to fully cooperate with peer review again. Since President Xi Jinping pronounced financial security as a key priority for the nation (Xinhua, 2016), China's shadow banking sector has been subjected to heightened supervisory scrutiny and tighter regulation as part of what Chinese analysts have dubbed a "regulatory storm" (Wu, 2017). There is no evidence to date that Chinese regulators have changed their stance because they have been successfully persuaded by their Western peers that developmental concerns should be anathema to NBCI regulation. Beijing's turnaround is more likely to be attributed to a variety of domestic drivers that merit analytical attention beyond the scope of this book (see for example Naughton, 2017).

But this episode showcases how the FSB can leverage the power of reputation to nudge wayward jurisdictions to increase their degree of cross-border adherence to its workflow. It is just one of the methods in which a government network can foster compliance in the absence of any legal instrument (more on effectiveness in Chapter 6). It also shows one process in which representatives from the executive branch and regulators deal with policy differences under the umbrella of the FSB.

Legislative Reluctance

While regulators and members of the executive branch of G20 governments can use the channels outlined previously to address their differences regarding global financial governance, legislators have a seat at the FSB table. Yet the operations of the FSB overlap with legislators' sphere of authority (Rosenau, 2005). Backer (2011) provides a revealing summary of FSB activities: "It does not legislate but produces law; it does not govern but it produces standards" (p. 791). In the post-crisis reform areas under study in this book, legislation and legislators have constrained the power of the FSB. As the empirical chapters will show in detail, legislators are reluctant to empower regulators to coordinate rulemaking in the FSB, reluctant to implement decisions made in the FSB, and reluctant to remove preexisting legal obstacles to cross-border regulatory cooperation in the FSB and the standard setters it coordinates. This book argues that such legislative reluctance is the main reason why global financial reform in the FSB is not as advanced as regulators and G20 leaders would prefer.

The tension between the FSB and national legislators does not come as a surprise to all. At the outset of the financial regulatory reform process, Dani Rodrik asserts, "It is hard to imagine that America's Congress would ever sign off on the kind of intrusive international oversight of domestic lending practices that might have prevented the subprime-mortgage meltdown, let alone avert future crises" (Rodrik, 2009).

Congressional unease with the operation of government networks in finance reaches back to the mid-1980s. A few years after the foundation of the Basel Committee, legislators from the House Banking Committee requested the nonpartisan Government Accounting Office (GAO) to inform Congress about the involvement of US regulators in the organization. The GAO report of 1986 states that "the Chairman of the House Banking Committee was concerned about the lack of knowledge of the Basle Committee's activities, and Congress subsequently passed legislation providing for GAO to review the status of international coordination of bank supervision" (GAO, 1986, p. 2).

As the FSB became the focal institution for the coordination of financial regulatory reform in the wake of the 2008 crisis, representatives of domestic interest groups increasingly voiced their resistance. In a response paper to a consultation document on bank resolution, the leader of an American civil society group calls the creation of the FSB a "bankers' coup" that undermines national sovereignty. The author asks, "Where did the FSB get these sweeping powers, and is its mandate legally enforceable?" (Brown, 2014). The FSB faces similar criticism from the right wing of the political spectrum. In a blog post titled "What Happened to American Sovereignty at G-20?", Barnewall (2009) lashes out against foreign regulatory intrusion.

In May 2014, leading members of the House Financial Committee sent a letter to the US agencies that are FSB members. The authors assert that the FSB designation process of a systemically important financial institution is nontransparent and "not accountable to the American people." Pointedly, the committee members state, "The last thing we should to do [sic] is surrender U.S. sovereignty on financial regulatory matters to an international 'old boy's club' that deliberates in secret" (US House Committee on Financial Services, 2014a, p. 2f). One of the signatories of the letter, Jeb Hensarling, condensed the opinion of many parliamentarians in the following words:

> Neither the Treasury, the Fed, nor the SEC has ever reported to Congress about its participation, nor have they ever asked for Congress' approval to participate in the global organization. . . . Great risks . . . lurk to U.S. financial stability and competitiveness in a shadow regulatory system in which Treasury and the Federal Reserve may have ceded U.S. sovereignty over financial regulatory matters to a secretive, unaccountable coalition of European bureaucrats.
>
> *(US House Committee on Financial Services, 2014b, p. 2)*

Congress leveled another attack against FSB work on ending TBTF in April 2015, when Richard Shelby, chairman of the Senate Banking Committee, asserted that "the FSB is not a U.S. regulator, and it is not accountable to Congress or the American people" (Jopson & Binham, 2015). This move was triggered by the potential designation of asset management companies as systemically important (FSB, 2017a), but it reflects widespread irritation among Congress members regarding the authority of the Financial Stability Oversight Council (FSOC), a domestic regulatory body created by the Dodd-Frank Act and its connections to the government network. A Wall Street Journal article argues that

> the FSOC has consistently moved to implement the FSB's decisions without telling Congress, or the public, that it regards the FSB's decisions as binding. There's a reason for this lack of candor. Congress has never endorsed the idea that FSB decisions are binding on U.S. agencies. . . . The result would unravel the separation of powers and the role of Congress in the U.S. constitutional system.
>
> *(Wallison & Gallagher, 2015)*

When the FSB designated two US companies as global systemically important insurers, legislators questioned the implementation of this regulatory decision by FSOC:

> Nowhere does existing law authorize any U.S. regulator to cede its authority to a foreign council like the FSB. American regulators should surely participate in international forums and work with their counterparts to protect the stability of the global financial system. But, our regulators must take the lead in writing the rules that govern the American financial system, subject to Congressional direction. Not only is this legally required, it also ensures that the entities writing our rules actually place American interests first.
>
> *(Rothfus, 2017)*

After the Republican Party's decisive election victory in 2016, House Finance Committee vice-chairman Patrick McHenry addressed Janet Yellen, the Fed's chair at the time, with a letter that is worth quoting at length:

> I am writing regarding the Federal Reserve's continued participation in international forums on financial regulation. Despite the clear message delivered by President Donald Trump in prioritizing America's interest in international negotiations, it appears that the Federal Reserve continues negotiating international regulatory standards for financial institutions among global bureaucrats in foreign lands without transparency, accountability, or the authority to do so. This is unacceptable.
>
> *(McHenry, 2017)*[2]

One year later, six senators sent another letter to President Trump, Treasury Secretary Mnuchin, and top financial regulators, stating the following:

> We are concerned that the FSB has been driving a significant amount of U.S. policymaking regarding financial regulation. We strongly urge you to shift the emphasis from global standards imposed on U.S. entities to ensuring that our federal regulators take into account first and foremost the interest of U.S. affected entities and U.S. consumers.
>
> *(Cotton et al., 2018)*

Members of Congress did not limit themselves to words. Legislative proposals that reassert Congressional authority over financial regulators have been introduced both in the House of Representatives and the Senate. The draft bills under consideration include the Regulations from the Executive in Need of Scrutiny (REINS) Act, which would make all material new rules subject to congressional approval, the Regulatory Accountability Act, and the Financial CHOICE Act, which would repeal the parts of the Dodd-Frank Act that enable cross-border regulatory coordination (*H.R.26–115th Congress (2017–2018)*, 2017; *H.R.5–115th Congress (2017–2018)*, 2017; *H.R.5983–114th Congress (2015–2016)*, 2016; Zaring, 2016).

While Republicans in Congress have been more vocal in criticizing the FSB, this issue crosses party lines. In April 2015, Senators Heller and Tester introduced a bipartisan bill to increase congressional oversight over the interaction of US representatives with global standard-setting bodies (*Text – S.1086–114th Congress (2015–2016)*, 2015). In late 2017, the Senate introduced a new bill that is designed to provide "regulatory relief" for large financial institutions. It is co-sponsored by 11 Democrats, most of whom are facing elections in their home states in the coming months (Warmbrodt, 2017). And as Chapters 4 and 5 will show in greater detail, the Democrat-driven 2010 Dodd-Frank Act itself falls short of FSB recommendations to provide regulatory agencies with a mandate to cooperate across jurisdictional lines.

Tellingly, the executive branch does not share the sovereignty concerns of legislators in the United States. The Trump administration lashed out against international organizations on many occasions, but it never publicly supported legislator's criticism of the FSB. Treasury Secretary Mnuchin even "stressed the importance of cooperation between the United States and other G-20 and Financial Stability Board members to achieve our common goals of addressing financial stability risks, fostering efficient global financial markets, and promoting a global level playing field" (US Department of the Treasury, 2017). Similarly, Trump appointees at the Federal Reserve (Jerome Powell and Randal Quarles) and the CFTC (J. Christopher Giancarlo) have continued and even deepened American involvement in the FSB (Cocheo, 2017; Rubin, 2018).

Legislative disapproval of the authority of government networks is not confined to the United States. On the other side of the Atlantic, members of the European Parliament, a legislative body that is transnational in nature, started questioning the authority of government networks when European banking regulation was found to be inconsistent with Basel III standards (see Chapter 3). A comment by a European regulator captures the tension between government networks and parliaments well:

> It is all very nice that people hook up in G20, that is at least that these are heads of states, fine but you have the FSB or other organizations which are regulators and then they say, "Oh, we are going to do this." But you cannot just take this home and have it rubber stamped by our parliament. I mean we all live in a democracy, right?
>
> *(EU Regulator 6, personal communication, November 14, 2014)*

In April 2016, the European Parliament issued a "Report on the EU role in the framework of international financial, monetary and regulatory institutions and bodies" (European Parliament, 2016). It "stresses the need for the Commission, representing the whole Union in an international body . . . to be held more directly accountable to citizens; [and] stresses the importance of the role of Parliament in this process" (art. 11). The report further asserts that "national parliaments and the European Parliament should not be reduced to a role of mere rubberstamping but must be incorporated, actively and comprehensively, into the whole decision-making process" (art. E). Legislators seek to expand their authority by formalizing a so-called "financial dialogue" in which the commission would be obliged to coordinate its position with the Parliament in "the run-up of major international negotiations" (art. 19). The resolution was approved by 68% of the European Parliament. It found supporters among party groups across the political spectrum, with the exception of the Nordic Green Left and right-wing groups led by Nigel Farage and Marine Le Pen, who believe the European Parliament itself undermines the power of national legislatures (European Parliament, 2016). It is telling that even though legislators in the European Parliament do not often find cross-party consensus, this report was endorsed by legislators from all mainstream parties. A European Parliamentarian (whose party supported the resolution) comments on the report: "It's a traditional power grab thing. Give a bigger role to the Parliament" (EU Legislator 1, personal communication, November 26, 2017).

The previous array of actions taken by legislators on both sides of the Atlantic merely serves to exemplify and illustrate the most conspicuous forms of legislative reluctance vis-à-vis the FSB. As Chapter 2 will explain in greater detail, the shift in policymaking authority away from legislators with the rise of the regulatory state and government networks is a structural phenomenon. The unease of legislators with this long-term trend manifests in active and passive forms. Both the examples of active resistance in the preceding paragraphs and the lack of legislative action identified in subsequent chapters are different sides of the same coin in that they respond to the same incentive structure that legislators are facing due to the erosion of their turf.

The empirical chapters will provide a more detailed analysis of the power of the FSB and its limits in three issue areas, namely, prudential banking regulation, OTC derivatives, and ending too-big-to-fail. But before doing so, a few methodological considerations are in order.

Method

Measuring and analyzing the progress of global financial regulatory reform is not an easy undertaking. The three main challenges any scholar of the FSB in particular and the G20 reform progress in general is facing are benchmarking, case selection, and endogeneity. This section deals with each in turn.

Any type of progress needs to be measured against a benchmark, but the existing literature has struggled to agree on a benchmark in the field of global financial reform at the FSB. Some scholars have assessed financial reform against their own expectations or those of prominent commentators (Admati & Hellwig, 2013; Lall, 2012). Some measure global financial reform progress by the extent to which new policies depart from the pre-crisis status quo (Helleiner, 2014a; Moschella &

Tsingou, 2013; Pagliari & Wilf, 2018). Others focus on the difference in authority and capacity of the FSB and its pre-crisis predecessor, the FSF (Griffith-Jones et al., 2010; Pauly, 2010; Blustein, 2012). This book takes a different approach. It uses the reform goals in specific areas of financial regulation as they are stated in G20 summit declarations as benchmarks. The reform commitments for all issue areas under analysis here were clearly pronounced at the G20 summits in London and Pittsburgh in 2009. That they were agreed upon by the same group of state leaders in a relatively short time period facilitates comparison across issue areas. Thus, reform progress is measured in this book as the gap between reform commitments as stated by G20 leaders and de facto implementation by end-2020.

At the height of the global financial crisis, G20 leaders were eager to show their determination to stabilize the financial system and accelerate global economic recovery. They launched a wide range of policy initiatives, including governance reform of the international financial institutions and measures to improve citizens' access to financial services. Over the years, new initiatives were added, and the G20 agenda has expanded continuously (Knaack & Katada, 2013).

This book concentrates on G20 agenda items that strictly concern financial regulation and thus fell under the purview of the FSB. But even in the narrower field of financial regulatory reform, the list of policy measures is long, including issues such as the reform of credit rating agencies, insurance companies, and executive compensation. But from the outset, the G20 placed banking regulation, over-the-counter (OTC) derivatives, and ending too-big-to-fail (TBTF) as the top three reform issues on its agenda. The FSB identifies shadow banking as the fourth main item on the global agenda in its progress reports, and an earlier section in this chapter provided an analysis of reform progress in that area. But FSB work on shadow banking started several years later, which complicates any comparison with the other three main reform areas (FSB, 2017d; Knaack & Gruin, 2020).

Other policy areas such as credit rating agencies, hedge fund supervision, and executive compensation remain on the sidelines of the FSB work agenda. This might not be a random selection, as such issues might have been dealt with in a satisfactory fashion without the involvement of government networks. Whether this is the case and whether it introduces bias to the present analysis are questions that certainly deserve scholarly attention. Reform initiatives such as the global introduction of a bank levy never made it to the FSB because they failed to garner support from key G20 members. The issue areas selected in this study appeared on the G20 agenda in 2009. It is thus possible to undertake a more rigorous comparison among

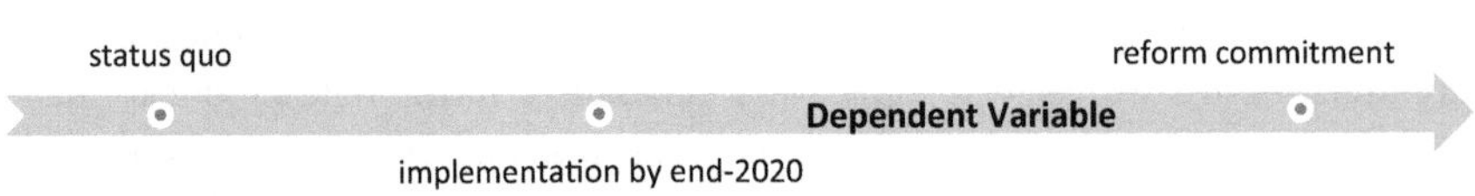

FIGURE 1.4 Measuring the FSB Track Record

Source: Author's visualization

these three issues rather than incorporating policy items that were removed from the agenda or that appeared more recently. Moreover, progress across these three issue areas differs substantially, allowing for important variation in the dependent variable. Nevertheless, the appearance and disappearance of policy items on the G20 agenda are unlikely to be random, raising concerns of endogeneity and selection bias.

Endogeneity is an issue that many scholars of international relations face. For instance, Downs et al. (1996) rightfully criticize the managerial school of compliance (Chayes & Chayes, 1993) for being overly optimistic about cross-border cooperation, arguing that states may choose to engage only in issue areas of little substance, which would make compliance both easy and irrelevant. The same critique applies to scholarship that seeks to extract the independent effects of international law on state behavior (Keohane, 1997). Endogeneity and selection effects are manifest in the G20/FSB reform project too. The 2009 commitments were made in London and Pittsburgh at a time when the US Congress negotiated its key piece of post-crisis financial legislation, the Dodd Frank Act. Heads of state in the leading jurisdictions certainly considered the domestic feasibility of financial reform policies before choosing which ones to commit to publicly at G20 summits. But arguably, this sort of endogeneity would imply a bias towards greater compliance. This book in turn seeks to explain why the FSB succeeded in meeting G20 commitments in some (but not all) of these issue areas even though G20 leaders regarded them as politically feasible in the wake of the crisis.

The FSB and its role in global regulatory governance are complex phenomena, and the peculiar pattern of success and challenges its work program exhibits a decade after the global financial crisis deserves an explanation. This book proposes a new government network approach to do just that, but the literature has developed a variety of competing explanations. Before setting out to discuss old and new approaches to understanding financial reform progress in particular and global governance in general, a few methodological considerations are in order.

Global financial regulatory reform fits Bennett and Elman's (2007) characterization of a complex, relatively unstructured, and infrequent phenomenon. Not only is the object under study a rare, unusual event, but it also involves a very reduced number of actors. Global financial reform at the FSB is driven by the G20, a group that unites the national governments of 19 nation states and the European Union. The reforms are coordinated by the Financial Stability Board that has a slightly larger membership than the G20. Five jurisdictions, namely, Singapore, Spain, Switzerland, Hong Kong, and the Netherlands have representation in the FSB but not directly in the G20, bringing the total number of FSB membership to 24. However, much of the financial regulatory reform agenda in Europe is driven by the European Union, and the legal characteristics of the financial regulatory reform package severely curtail the discretion of EU member states in its implementation. Consequently, the European Union is regarded as a single jurisdiction by many scholars of financial regulation and the FSB itself. Brexit is changing the member count again. The EU regulatory framework applied to the United Kingdom until the end of 2020 in accordance with the Withdrawal agreement between the two parties, but the country has regained full regulatory control over itself in 2021.

This book models the actors and institutional structures relevant to the process of global financial regulatory reform not as independent variables but rather in an interactive process that unfolds across borders and over time, avoiding the pitfalls of methodological reductionism (Oatley, 2011). Because understanding the political economy of policy work inside the FSB requires special attention to temporal development, sequencing, and complex interaction effects between institutional and actor-level variables, process tracing stands out as the most adequate method of inquiry. At the core of process tracing lies a fundamental ontological difference between causal effects and causal mechanisms. Conventional statistical methods seek to maximize parsimony by identifying linear or curvilinear relations between certain causal variables and the outcome. Causal mechanisms such as learning, institutional conversion, and path dependency in contrast highlight the complexities of the causal process (Falleti, 2006).

Taking inspiration from Posner's (2009) elucidating work on transatlantic regulatory politics, this study employs systematic process analysis (Hall, 2006) as its methodological core. Hall's approach starts with the selection of rival theories that could explain the outcome of the event under study. The second step of this process is to derive predictions from the theoretical frameworks that should be as "brittle" as possible, that is, distinguishable from the predictions of other theories and falsifiable by the data available. The third step involves empirical observation with a special emphasis on the process that leads to the outcome. Each theory relies on a particular causal mechanism to explain the outcome. Congruence analysis allows the researcher to verify whether the empirical chain of events is compatible with such causal mechanisms. Thus, even when rival theories predict the same outcome, a systematic process analysis is able to validate and falsify the claims they make regarding which process leads to this outcome.

This book develops five competing explanations from state-of-the-art literature in international political economy. It subjects each to a congruence analysis relying on a combination of archival data and interviews with financial regulators, politicians, private sector advocacy groups, and civil society representatives from eleven jurisdictions in Europe, Asia, and the Americas.

Outline of the Book

This introduction is followed by five chapters. Chapter 2 contains the core intellectual building blocks that inform this book. It assembles insight from scholarly work in international relations, law, sociology, and political economy to situate the emergence of the regulatory state and the rise of government networks in the larger process of structural transformation that is globalization. The chapter then compares the institutional design of government networks to that of traditional IGOs, outlining key concepts that help explain the power of government networks in the realm of 21st century global economic governance. After showing, in theory and in practice, how a government network can exert power, the chapter turns to its limiting factors. It develops a theoretical perspective on why legislators as bureaucratic actors have an incentive to curb the power of government networks. The subsequent section then draws from the international political economy literature to distill five competing explanations for FSB performance. The final part of the chapter looks at two other tricky areas of global governance from an institutional design perspective. Focusing on climate change and artificial intelligence, it assesses the benefits and drawbacks of government networks as an institutional blueprint to address the massive challenges humanity is facing in each area.

The empirical analysis of the FSB track record in global financial reform is presented in three subsequent chapters. Chapter 3 analyzes the evolution of prudential banking regulation. It shows how a government network, the Basel Committee, was able to forge consensus on macroprudential issues that were barely debated prior to the crisis. Furthermore, the chapter argues that the main reason for the successful implementation of Basel III is that it largely eschews legislative interference. In fact, the one jurisdiction that provided parliament with a major role in implementing Basel III, the European Union, has failed the regulatory consistency test that is part of the Basel Committee peer review process. The empirical record is then tested against alternative explanations.

Chapter 4 turns to OTC derivatives regulation. It shows how the FSB failed to forge a government network with the composition and powers necessary to facilitate the development of global standards in this issue area. Instead, the United States and the European Union developed standards unilaterally. It connects the protagonism of national legislatures and the absence of a strong government network to shortcomings in the global reform of OTC derivative regulation. The chapter then traces the emergence of new initiatives under the FSB umbrella in the late 2010s and assesses their advances and limits. Based on this empirical material, it tests the government network hypothesis against competing explanations.

Chapter 5 covers two reform initiatives that fall under the same rubric of ending TBTF. It shows how a government network succeeded in finding global consensus on a definition of systemic risk and unprecedented policy measures to address it. The rapid advances in identifying SIFIs and subjecting them to higher loss absorbency requirements contrast with a second bundle of policy measures: bank resolution. Even though the FSB forcefully promotes global cooperation to facilitate the orderly wind down of global banks, reform progress in this area is lagging behind. Again, this hypothesis is tested against competing explanations. The chapter also covers a more recent initiative to end TBTF by developing a new global loss absorbency standard for failing banks. It shows how the FSB imitated the institutional pathways of policymaking in the Basel Committee to make its loss absorbency standards effective.

The final chapter engages with the normative concerns the empirical analysis of the book raises. It looks at the desirability of policy options that are constrained by a financial trilemma. The chapter then looks at two quality indicators of government networks, namely, effectiveness and legitimacy. Finally, it argues that while the institutional design of government network is more effective than its critics would admit, significant improvements in legitimacy can be made. It advocates for the incorporation of elected experts in global governance, an institutional innovation that may combine the benefits of technocratic sophistication and electoral accountability.

Notes

1 Argentina, Australia, Brazil, China, European Union, France, Germany, Hong Kong, Malaysia, Singapore, United Kingdom, United States (plus several visits to the FSB itself).
2 The notion of unaccountable bureaucrats in foreign lands finds further elaboration in a recent book that situates the FSB inside a secret network of financial elites that seek world money, world taxation and world order (Rickards, 2016). Arguably, each respectable international financial institution is the subject of a conspiracy theory, and the FSB has achieved this venerable feat within the first decade of its existence. Congratulations.

2

THE POWER OF A GOVERNMENT NETWORK – AND ITS LIMITS

The Financial Stability Board has an impressive track record of galvanizing policy coordination across borders and across institutions in a global effort to make the financial system safer. Yet after a decade of operations, the gaps between the financial reform commitments of its members and the reality of their implementation indicate that there are limits to what the government network can achieve. And the pattern of successes and shortcomings that has emerged in a decade of FSB operations is not random. What can we learn from the FSB track record about the power of a government network and its limits?

This chapter gathers insight from international relations, law, sociology, and political economy to assemble a theoretical framework that sheds light on what empowers and what limits government networks as a key forum in global economic governance. It situates the institution in a profound historical and structural process of transformation from hierarchy to network as a dominant organizational principle under the conditions of globalization. Drawing inspiration from theoretical work on networked governance, it understands the rise of the regulatory state and the subsequent rise of government networks as consecutive efforts of governments to exert public control over globally interconnected markets.

The chapter then takes a deep dive into institutional design choices in global governance to parse out why state principals may prefer government networks over traditional intergovernmental organizations (IGOs) such as the Bretton Woods Institutions. It discusses the advantages of government networks in facilitating collective decision-making, lowering sovereignty and negotiation costs, addressing time inconsistency problems, and circumventing domestic veto players, while minimizing agency slack.

Against the concerns of "hard law traditionalists," the chapter shows how the soft law instruments employed by government networks can have teeth. It distinguishes between form, substance, and structure of international agreements to highlight

DOI: 10.4324/9781003290001-2

how government networks substitute legal form for a sophisticated review structure in order to facilitate and enforce substantive agreements across borders. In particular, it draws from half a century of theoretical work in international political economy to parse out how and why the power of reputation can be harnessed to nudge parties to an international nonbinding agreement into compliance. It is the peculiar combination of peer review, publication of regulatory reports, and reputational concerns vis-à-vis other states and market actors alike that gives power to government networks in global economic governance.

But the very institutional design features that empower government networks also pose limits to their effectiveness. The rise of the regulatory state and networked governance has empowered some parts of the state but not others. Indeed, the emergence of government networks as key institutions of global economic governance generates tension within the nation-state. This is because some branches of government are in a better position than others to adjust to and benefit from a transnational network logic of organization. The state has undergone successive rounds of restructuring that have wrested control away from legislators in order to adjust to a globalized economy. The power imbalance between the executive and legislative branch grew with the rise of the regulatory state towards the end of the 20th century. The subsequent emergence of transnational networks among members of regulatory agencies and the executive branch has further attenuated legislative control over policy areas. The result is a turf battle within the state over the authority to govern economic activity. This book innovates from existing accounts by conceiving of legislators as bureaucratic actors in their own right. From the perspective of bureaucratic politics, legislators are understood as actors that seek to maximize resources and reputation. They are concerned with maintaining or expanding the scope of policies under their purview as well as their autonomy as decision-makers (Allison & Halperin, 1972). Because ceding authority to government networks implies losing influence vis-à-vis the executive branch and regulatory agencies, the legislative branch shows signs of reluctance towards cross-border cooperation. This phenomenon becomes understandable when situated in the context of a larger structural transformation of the state under conditions of globalization. The section concludes that legislative reluctance, both in its active and passive forms, poses limits to the power of government networks.

The analysis of this chapter inevitably leads to a normative question: Is networked global governance desirable? In other words, are parliamentarians justified in resisting the unfettered operations of government networks? Chapter 6 seeks to address this concern by discussing two quality indicators of networked governance: effectiveness and legitimacy. But before exploring these important normative matters, this chapter provides the theoretical foundations necessary to assess the power of government networks and its limits.

This book makes a novel theoretical contribution by making sense of the FSB's mixed track record from a perspective of government networks and legislative reluctance. But this government network approach is certainly not the only possible explanation. The penultimate section of this chapter draws from the literature in international political economy to distill five competing theories that could also explain the performance of the FSB. Employing Hall's (2006) systematic process analysis, the section outlines the central inferential logic of each competing approach and derives predictions regarding the FSB reform track record. The predictions of the government network approach proposed in this book and the five competing explanations should be as brittle as possible, that is, distinguishable from each other and falsifiable by the empirical data at hand. Because the predictions of each approach are as specific as the empirical chain of events in each reform area under study, the section cannot provide an exhaustive comparative assessment. Readers are kindly asked to consult the competing explanations sections at the end of each empirical chapter for that. But this chapter develops the theoretical foundations of the five competing explanations and offers a bird's-view assessment over their relative inferential power.

The final section of the chapter applies the theoretical tools gathered in this book to two other issue areas that face burning global governance questions, namely, climate change and artificial intelligence (AI). First, it reviews the current institutional design of climate change governance and shows how policymakers have already moved away from intergovernmental hard law traditions. AI governance is still very much in its infancy, especially at the global level. The chapter argues that a global governance arrangement for this technology will be needed soon and that a government network may be a more suitable institutional design than a traditional intergovernmental organization. It also highlights a series of commonalities between finance and AI, arguing that advanced AI algorithms may have more in common with financial derivatives than nuclear bombs. The chapter concludes my making the case for the creation of a government network to govern the development and deployment of AI on a global scale.

Globalization: From Hierarchy to Network

The rise of government networks did not occur in a historical or institutional vacuum. Rather, it is deeply embedded in the institutional evolution in global economic governance since World War II. Global economic governance has had a peculiar trajectory in modern history, varying widely in scope and degree of institutionalization. One would expect global governance institutions to expand in perimeter and depth as a response to deepening cross-border economic integration, yet the empirical evolution of the global economy and institutions to govern it do not exhibit a linear relationship. Nevertheless, we can identify a simultaneous structural transformation in the organizing principle underlying both markets and governance institutions that has taken shape over the last half-century. This section provides a brief overview over the modern evolution of global economic governance and identifies the transformation from hierarchy to network as the key structural feature of globalization.

Abbott and Snidal (2001, p. 346) define global governance as "the formal and informal bundles of rules, roles and relationships that define and regulate the social practices of state and nonstate actors in international affairs." This is a very wide definition that attempts to encompass the entire spectrum of cross-border institutions. Indeed, governance arrangements vary in scope (regional, global), institutional form, and stakeholders (public, private) according to the nature of the issue area to be governed. A first useful step is thus to narrow the area of interest to global economic governance.

Humans have engaged in cross-border economic exchange for millennia, but for almost the entirety of this time period, the global governance institutions that guided this exchange were minimal. No World Trade Organization was necessary to ensure the functioning of the Silk Road, for example; instead, the rules of the market coordinated human behavior. Even today, although it is embedded in a social, legal, and political environment, the market is the default institution of global economic interaction (Polanyi, 1944; Ruggie, 1982). The need for global governance arises from the externalities of human interaction across national borders that are not internalized by market forces. There is a wide variety of externalities that call for corresponding global governance arrangements.

The first organizations designed to handle global governance tasks have been created during the wave of globalization that preceded the current one. Cross-border flows of capital, goods, and labor peaked in the decades before World War I, and intergovernmental organizations such as the International Telegraph Union (1865) and the European Rail Union (1890) were established to regulate the expanding cross-national trade, communication, and transportation infrastructure. In this situation, regulators faced network externalities: the biggest obstacle to exchange was the lack of standardization. Once all economic actors would adhere to a single standard, transaction costs would be greatly reduced, and the resulting efficiency gains would enhance human welfare. Therefore, the nature of strategic interaction was that of a coordination game (Abbott & Snidal, 2001). Early functionalists (Mitrany, 1944) interpreted this phenomenon as a sign that increasing economic interdependence generates a demand for global governance arrangements that will ultimately facilitate the convergence of state preferences (Matthew & Zacher, 1995; Murphy, 1994; Rosamond, 2000). However, functionalist accounts of global governance have been criticized for relying on a false dichotomy between technocratic administration and power politics. Seemingly neutral standard-setting and administrative tasks have significant distributional consequences. As a consequence, actors bargain hard for the choice of one among a variety of possible governance structures. The functionalist approach is ill equipped to fully incorporate the politics underlying this process (Fearon, 1998; Frieden, 2016). In a world where no particular regulatory standard is objectively welfare-enhancing and where regulatory cooperation has distributive consequences, theories that highlight the political dimension of global governance promise to entail a greater degree of explanatory power. Kahler and Lake (2003) emphasize the intrinsic link between form and substance of global governance structures:

> Since institutions shape the politics of choice and the outcomes observed, concerned parties will attempt to align governance structures with their

> interests. That is, the politics of designing, building, and overturning institutions of governance at all levels is really about policy choices. Thus, debates about supranationalism, decentralization, the respective roles of public and private sectors, and accountability are often struggles over institutions that will produce results favoring some groups or interests at the expense of others. Contests over governance are contests over policy.
>
> *(p. 20)*

The interwar years saw a sharp reversal of economic interdependence. Interestingly, it was at a historic low point of global integration at the end of World War II that most institutions of global economic governance of relevance today were established. The temporal evolution of global governance institutions thus attenuates the causal link functionalists make between economic interdependence and institutional development (Kahler & Lake, 2009). Nevertheless, the current wave of globalization has been accompanied by both the strengthening of existing governance institutions (in trade) and the creation of new ones (in finance). From a systemic vantage point, the evolution of global finance and its governance over the last half century is situated in a greater structural tension between state hierarchies and transnational networks that Castells (2000) identifies as the fundamental driver of globalization.

Castells' theory starts with the observation that modern societies are structured around hierarchical bureaucracies. Resources and subjects are integrated in vertical structures that are dominated by a social elite and delimited by national borders. From political parties and trade unions to corporations, government, and the media, nationally bound hierarchies represent the dominant and pervasive structural organizing principle in the modern era (Castells, 2004). The multidimensional and complex shift away from vertical structures and the emergence of horizontal networks is what Castells describes as the rise of the network society. This process started as the result of three independent processes in the late 1960s and early 1970s: the information technology revolution, the economic crisis of both liberal market and planned economies, and the blooming of cultural social movements (Castells, 1998, p. 336ff).

Shaken by economic crisis in the 1970s, advanced capitalist economies underwent a profound structural transformation. Political leaders lowered cross-border barriers to production and trade by liberalizing and privatizing large sectors of the economy (Abdelal, 2006), while technological advances reduced transaction costs, allowing companies to operate as transnational networks (Dicken, 2007). The rise of the network enterprise in an increasingly informational, global, and networked economy over the last four decades had profound repercussions for the global division of labor. Corporate transnational networks emerged as the dominant organizational principle for the accumulation of wealth and power, and nowhere has this structural transformation been clearer than in the financial sphere (Bruszt & McDermott, 2012; Castells, 2000, pp. 77f, 503; Cerny, 2010; McKeen-Edwards & Porter, 2013).

The power imbalance between globally networked capital and local labor precipitated the demise of trade unions and the contraction of the welfare state in many advanced economies. Indeed, scholars have described the tension between increasingly global economic forces and territorial political authority as the overall demise of the nation-state (Gill, 1992; Horsman & Marshall, 1994; Ōmae, 1995; Schachter, 1998; Strange, 1996; Wriston, 1993). Having retreated from economic activity as a result of successive rounds of privatization and liberalization and constrained in its range of policy measures in a globally interdependent economy, the nation-state is indeed facing significant challenges. It encounters increasing difficulties in delivering the public goods that citizens have come to expect from the state: protection from economic shocks, redistributive justice (Piketty, 2014), and management of the economy in accordance with societal preferences that are aggregated in legitimate democratic procedures (J. M. Chwieroth & Walter, 2017). As Castells notes, "National governments in the Information Age are too small to handle global forces, yet too big to manage people's lives" (Castells, 1997, p. 273).

In order to resolve this crisis of political legitimacy, Castells (2009, p. 38ff) argues that the nation-state seeks to reconstruct power by transforming itself into a network state. The author identifies three such transformations: networks of states such as the EU, NATO, or ASEAN, supranational organizations such as the WTO or the ICC, and the devolution of power to regional governments or NGOs. The analytical lens Castells applies here is too narrow for two reasons. First, the distinction between networks of states and supranational organizations lacks relevance because both are based on intergovernmental agreements that entail the sharing of sovereignty to a specified degree. Second, the author oversees a more relevant phenomenon, the rise of government networks.

Unlike the IGOs mentioned previously, government networks are not constituted by international treaty, they do not produce legally binding agreements, and they have no identity under international public law. Yet as this book will show, government networks can be effective in devising rules that match the operation of multinational financial firms in scope.

Faced with the powerful logic of transnational networks in the global economy in general and finance in particular, the state thus has started to embrace a similar structural transformation, moving away from the hierarchical, territorially bound bureaucracies on which it was built. The emergence of transnational government networks can be understood as a structural response to the rise of the network economy (Slaughter, 2004).

The sharing of sovereignty in government networks promises to return some degree of regulatory power over the global economy. As an alternative, policymakers in powerful core jurisdictions may choose to resort to coercion or extraterritorial legal or regulatory provisions, with mixed results (Kaczmarek & Newman, 2011; Newman & Posner, 2015). But in comparison, engagement in government networks is a policy choice that is available to more governments and one that promises a more comprehensive return of authority from global markets to public institutions, at least in principle.

The Rise of the Regulatory State

The evolution of the state from territorially bound hierarchy to transnational network can be understood as a two-step development that is deeply intertwined with the larger process of globalization. It originates in the transfer of responsibility over the management of the economy from the central government bureaucracy to regulatory agencies at a domestic level. In the postwar era, intervention in the market economy for the purpose of strategic economic guidance and redistribution of wealth was an important function of the state. But from the 1970s onwards, with the model of the interventionist state in crisis, a major transformation took place. Large-scale privatization and liberalization led to a retrenchment of the centralized government bureaucracy. Deregulation might not be the most fitting term for this process because privatized sectors were quickly re-regulated. However, rulemaking authority in a growing number of economic sectors changed hands from the central government to regulatory agencies. It is this transformation of central government functions from taxing and spending to rulemaking and the outsourcing of these functions to agencies that Majone (1997) identifies as the central characteristics of the regulatory state.

Regulatory agencies have been in existence throughout the 20th century, and the United States is regarded by Levi-Faur (2005) as the oldest regulatory state. However, the last three decades of the century saw a rapid proliferation of regulatory agencies around the world due to policy diffusion, increased competition among nation-states, and the growing importance of the European Community over its member states (Berg & Horrall, 2008; Elkins & Simmons, 2005; Gilardi et al., 2006; Jordana et al., 2011; Jordana & Levi-Faur, 2005; Majone, 1997; Meseguer, 2005; Way, 2005).

The rise of regulatory agencies implies a shift in authority away from legislators in three key dimensions. First, unlike the core state bureaucracy, the central task for regulators is not redistribution and service delivery but to address market failures. Because the cost allocation of a regulation is much harder to discern than that of redistributive intervention, the policy area of regulators is often regarded as "apolitical." Second, regulatory agencies are one step removed from their political headmasters, attached to the government in arm's-length agreements. They are often overseen by a bipartisan "special commission," granting it a certain degree of insulation from the party-political dynamics of the legislative branch. While political principals have several interventionist tools at their disposal to discipline agencies, monitoring and ensuring that agency behavior is commensurate with their interests is inherently costly. Administrative procedures such as notice and comment help to reduce but cannot fully eliminate the information asymmetry inherent in this principal-agent relationship (McCubbins et al., 1987). Third, regulation requires a high degree of technical knowledge, putting a premium on expertise. This in turn provides regulators with a greater degree of power and discretion than other administrators. Expertise is also the defining identity trait that allows regulators to transcend national borders and perceive themselves as members of a transnational epistemic community.

In sum, the demise of the interventionist state and the proliferation of regulatory agencies have changed the equilibrium between the different branches of the state profoundly. Regulatory policymaking is largely incompatible with the logic of political parties that obtain, via democratic elections, a mandate to undertake redistributive actions in line with their ideological preferences within a specific time frame. While not completely autonomous, regulators are one step removed from party politics.

In addition, the policies of regulatory agencies are rarely subject to explicit legislative approval. Therefore, the rise of the regulatory state represents a shift of policymaking authority away from parliament. Summarizing their empirical work on the proliferation of regulatory agencies, Jordana et al. (2011) conclude, "The old Weberian bureaucracies are changing" (p. 19). While the shift in the power balance between regulators and legislators with the emergence of the regulatory state has generated tension (Heltman, 2015), it still remained within the confines of the nation-state. This changed when regulators started forming transnational networks, further stripping legislators of policymaking authority.

The Rise of Government Networks

The postwar wave of globalization has engendered a tendency towards ever greater cross-border integration, highlighting the transnational nature of a large share of economic transactions. Policymakers have considered several governance designs that could match the global scale of the network economy. The most obvious one is to scale up the operations of the nation state, with its institutional procedures of interest aggregation and contestation within a single center of authority to the global level. Yet as Slaughter notes,

> World government is both infeasible and undesirable. The size and scope of such a government presents an unavoidable and dangerous threat to individual liberty. Further, the diversity of the peoples to be governed makes it almost impossible to conceive of a global demos. No form of democracy within the current global repertoire seems capable of overcoming these obstacles.
>
> *(Slaughter, 2004, p. 8).*

Another option would be to orchestrate private and public actors under the leadership of an IGO (Abbott et al., 2017; Abbott & Snidal, 2009, 2010). During Kofi Annan's tenure as secretary general, the United Nations has pursued such a strategy in creating so-called tripartite global policy networks. But this governance design has received criticism for enmeshing democratically elected governments with non-governmental actors that are either driven by profits (business) or passion (NGOs), thus blurring the distinction between public legitimacy and private power. Slaughter (2004) identifies "the need to exercise authority at the global level without centralized power but with government officials feeling a responsibility to multiple constituencies rather than to private pressure groups" (p. 257) as the trilemma of global governance.

Government networks have emerged as the one solution to this governance trilemma. They connect states in disaggregated fashion, providing the venue enduring and repeated interactions among government officials in a given special policy area. The pioneering work of Keohane and Nye (1977) depicted transgovernmental relations as an essential addendum to further the power of intergovernmental organizations. Today's government networks however exist both under the umbrella of and completely independent of IGOs. Even though many are comprised of officials from regulatory agencies only, as the narrower term "transnational regulatory networks" (Porter, 2010; Verdier, 2009) suggests, officials from the executive and judicial branch of government also form and participate in government networks.

A look at the legal instruments of government networks helps illuminate their prevalent modus operandi. Classic intergovernmental organizations are firmly embedded in international law: They are established by virtue of an international treaty that enters into effect once a predetermined number of signatory states ratify the treaty. The IGO then provides the institutional environment in which representatives of member states engage in often onerous and protracted negotiations for rules that again become legally binding after ratification by a certain number of member states (Sands & Klein, 2001; Shaw, 2008).

In contrast, government networks rely on three main instruments: promotion of standards and best practices, regulatory reports (including peer reviews), and information sharing and enforcement cooperation. Rather than treaties, agreements take the form of a memorandum of understanding (MoU). These documents are not legally binding and do not require ratification (Brummer, 2010). Because of its peculiar modus operandi, Slaughter (2004, p. 33) characterizes government networks as the "political equivalent of the informal economy, alongside formal international institutions."

The advantages of this kind of cooperation are obvious. Government networks address the demand for intergovernmental cooperation but significantly reduce sovereignty costs: Retaliation issues are less salient, and there is little delegation of authority to international bodies, as this chapter will discuss in greater detail. Furthermore, the relative absence of ratification procedures deprives domestic players of veto power, and unexpected coalitions between domestic interest groups and supranational authorities can be ruled out. In addition, negotiation costs are relatively low too because the drafting stage is less time-consuming, and global nonlegal agreements can be amended or changed more easily than international treaties. As Slaughter (2004, p. 49) puts it, "Widespread use of Memoranda of Understanding (MOUs) and even less formal initiatives has sped the growth of transgovernmental interaction exponentially, in contrast to the lethargic pace at which traditional treaty negotiations proceed." This quality of government networks is especially valuable when establishing an international regulatory framework for a sector marked by complexity and uncertainty and with a fast rate of technological change and innovation, such as finance (Brummer, 2010, 2012, 2014; Naím, 2009).

Government networks provide state leaders with two additional advantages vis-à-vis IGOs: they exhibit a low degree of agency slack. And they can foster substantive policy change among member states even in the absence of any legal instruments. The following paragraphs will discuss each in turn.

International relations scholars have developed a variety of theoretical approaches that seek to explain the institutional evolution of interstate cooperation. Building on Keohane's (1984) fundamental insight that international institutions facilitate interstate cooperation, scholars at the beginning of this century examined the uneven expansion of legalization and judicialization of international institutions. They wondered why international arrangements differ in the degree to which rules are legally binding, their precision, and delegation (Abbott et al., 2000; Goldstein et al., 2000). This set of questions gave rise to a research program on the rational design of international institutions. Scholars discovered that institutional design follows from the nature of the governance problem states seek to resolve. More specifically, distributional consequences of agreements, enforcement problems, the number of counterparties, uncertainty over the policy environment, and the verifiability of state actions are found to shape the institutional design of interstate cooperation in significant ways (Abbott & Snidal, 2001; Duffield, 2003; Koremenos, 2008; Koremenos et al., 2001).

The rational design research program was further developed with subsequent work on the determinants for delegation and agency in international organizations. Hawkins et al. (2006) start with a sharp analytical framework that identifies delegation to an international agency as one of three outcomes of a decision tree (see Figure 2.1). They then transpose principal-agent theory from the domestic to the international level in order to explain under what conditions states choose to delegate the tasks of interstate cooperation to agencies.

The choice of delegation to an agency can be understood as the result of a rational calculation whereby the principal weighs the benefits of delegation against expected agency losses. There are multiple benefits from delegation: Because agencies are more specialized than principals, they have a greater ability to collect information, provide expertise, and deliver certain services. Agencies also have an advantage at managing policy externalities and dealing with the dilemmas of coordination and collaboration that arise when states work together. They can also serve as an agenda-setting agent that provides focal points for interstate negotiations, facilitate collective decision-making, and provide a forum for dispute settlement. Maybe most importantly, an agency can provide policy credibility in ways that a principal cannot. This is a consequence of the well-known time inconsistency problem: A state cannot credibly assure the outside world that it will not renege on a policy that entails short-term costs and long-term benefits as political conditions change. Time-inconsistency is a central argument for central bank independence, but it applies in similar ways to most areas of economic policymaking (Gilardi, 2005; D. G. Hawkins et al., 2006; L. Martin, 2006; P. M. W. Tucker, 2018).

The cost of delegation is agency slack. Because information is costly, the principal cannot efficiently obtain full knowledge of the policy environment of the

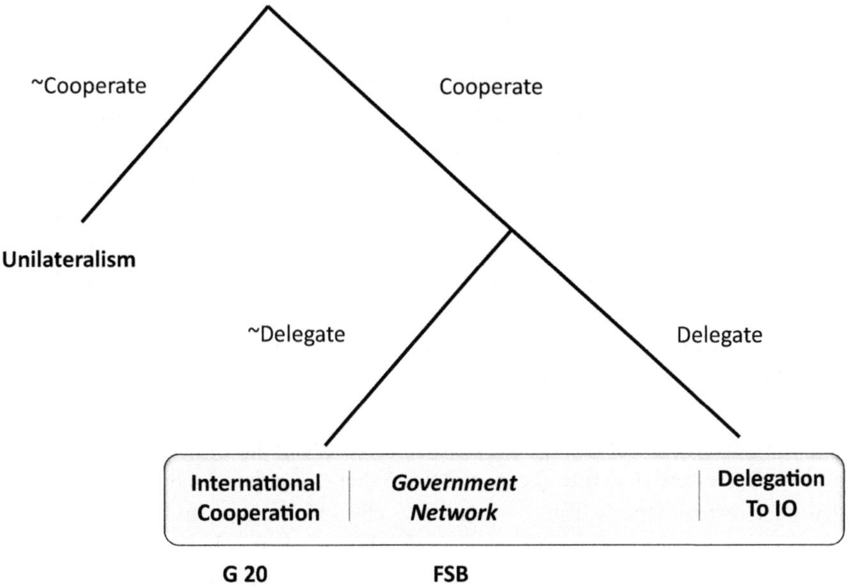

FIGURE 2.1 Decision Tree for States

Source: Adapted from Hawkins et al. (2006)

agency, its actions, and the consequences of its actions. The agency can take advantage of this information asymmetry and pursue its own goals even when they do not match the principal's preferences. The scope for agency slack varies with a host of institutional features such as voting rules, the heterogeneity of preferences among principals, and monitoring procedures (Estache & Wren-Lewis, 2009; Laffont & Tirole, 1991).

While international relations scholars have been successful at applying principal-agent theory to the international level, they did not integrate an important institutional design into their framework. Government networks are an innovation in the design of international institutions that harnesses the benefits and minimizes the costs of delegation. By restricting itself to classic intergovernmental organizations, Hawkins et al.'s (2006) delegation framework falls short in two dimensions. First, it ignores the importance of staffing. Classic international organizations rely on bureaucratic staff that is employed on the basis of technocratic merit. Government networks in turn have little or no such bureaucracy. The second shortcoming follows from the first point. Hawkins et al. model delegation as a binary choice: agency or no agency. Government networks however exist in a spectrum between these two extremes. This is because the principals can calibrate the degree of delegation by deciding the extent to which staff consists of officials from member governments. The more an agency relies on government officials, the more its operations resemble mere interstate cooperation. As a result, states can design an institution that secures the benefits of specialization and credibility of an agency while reducing the agency slack that comes with an international bureaucracy even in the presence of consensus-based decision-making rules.

Yet even a lean government network is only useful to state principals if it has teeth. Here, analysts with a background in law and international relations have often argued that soft law instruments are not effective in changing state behavior. Raustiala (2005) provides an important analytical clarification to advance this debate. The author distinguishes between (legal) form, substance (as the degree of departure from the status quo), and structure of international agreements. IGOs rely on international public law, but often, states incorporate a generous compliance cushion or prefer vague wording in order to avoid being subjected to legal procedures in case of noncompliance. As a result, some hard law agreements are of shallow substance, barely pushing signatories to depart from the status quo.

Alternatively, substantive agreements can be reached when legal form is replaced by a strong review structure (Posner, 2015; Sabel & Zeitlin, 2008). To the extent that peer review departs from a compliance checklist exercise and comprises elements of peer learning, socialization, and joint problem solving, the procedure itself can generate momentum for compliance in the absence of the threat of legal punitive measures (Bach & Newman, 2010; Bearce & Bondanella, 2007; Bruszt & McDermott, 2012; Cao, 2012; Chayes & Chayes, 1993; DeMeritt, 2012; Elkins et al., 2008; Füglister, 2012; Meseguer & Gilardi, 2009; Simmons et al., 2008; Weyland, 2007).

Reputation arguably plays a key role in this process. IR scholars have employed game theoretical insight to understand the payoff from cooperative behavior as a function of the "shadow of the future" (Axelrod & Hamilton, 1981; Axelrod & Keohane, 1985b). States maintain commitments even in the absence of legal punishments for instrumental and normative reasons. On the instrumental side, a state that reneges on its commitments at T_0 can reasonably expect to have less influence in the negotiation stage of policymaking at T_1, and even when the consensus on future policies is in its interest, it must discount the probability that other states maintain their respective commitments. As Keohane (1997, p. 500) argues, "States cultivate reputations because of what good reputations will enable them to achieve." In addition, reputation may affect state behavior through a logic of appropriateness. Once a norm has been agreed among stakeholders in a valued institution, violating that norm can be perceived as costly even in the absence of legal repercussions. In the empirical world of global governance, such instrumental and normative incentives for cooperative behavior arguably work in tandem with each other and are analytically inseparable and mutually reinforcing. The final section of this chapter zooms in to an epistemic dispute among FSB members to show how the government network has used the peer review process to nudge or force wayward jurisdictions into compliance.

In sum, government networks offer a number of design advantages over traditional intergovernmental forms of global governance. They reduce sovereignty and negotiation cost to a point that enables policymakers to reach agreements in a flexible and iterative fashion, matching the fast-changing policy environment around them. Government networks are lean, implying a lower degree of agency slack. And the soft law instruments they employ deprive domestic players of veto power. At the same time, the substitution of legal form for a thorough review structure can galvanize interstate cooperation. Government networks can use peer reviews to leverage the power of reputation, nudging member states into compliance even in the absence of any legal repercussions. But the institutional design features of government networks empower some parts of government, not others.

Legislators – Falling Behind

Over half a century ago, Nye and Keohane (1971, p. 331) asked, "To what extent have governments suffered from a 'loss of control' as a result of transnational relations?" From today's vantage point and on the basis of the empirical material assembled in this book, it is possible to argue that transnational relations in general and transgovernmental relations in particular have implied a loss of control for some branches of the state but not for others.

Much scholarly work on the domestic determinants of international cooperation models legislative chambers as vehicles for societal interest aggregation (Milner, 1992, 1997; Milner & Rosendorff, 1997). While the executive branch is the leading actor in negotiating the terms of cross-border cooperation, the ratification or implementation of an agreement is conditional upon approval by a majority of parliamentarians who are understood as representing the interests of their respective local constituencies. Lead actors of the executive branch assess the distribution of domestic interests and anticipate the position of the "median legislator" as they negotiate at the international stage of a two-level game (Putnam, 1988). Similarly, Lavelle (2011) shows that at least in the United States, domestic interest groups seek to utilize the "indispensable legislature" of the US Congress to shape global policies in the IMF and the World Bank in line with their preferences (Broz & Hawes, 2006).

Yet by relying on soft law instruments, government networks allow their member authorities to circumvent the legislative branch of government to a significant extent. Regulators are at the center of the structural transformation in governance that gave rise to government networks, and the executive branch is increasingly involved. But legislators are lagging behind, unwilling and incapable of engaging in transnational networks themselves.

Regulators derive several benefits from engaging in government networks. First, regulatory harmonization across jurisdictional boundaries allows them to expand the de facto geographic perimeter of their authority, ideally until it is congruous with the true scope of the market they are regulating. They are thus able to regain a degree of regulatory power they only enjoyed prior to the current wave of globalization, when market barriers confined regulated subjects to individual nation-states (Culpepper & Reinke, 2014; Farrell & Newman, 2015; Newman & Posner, 2011). Second, recourse to global standards and best practices may help strengthen

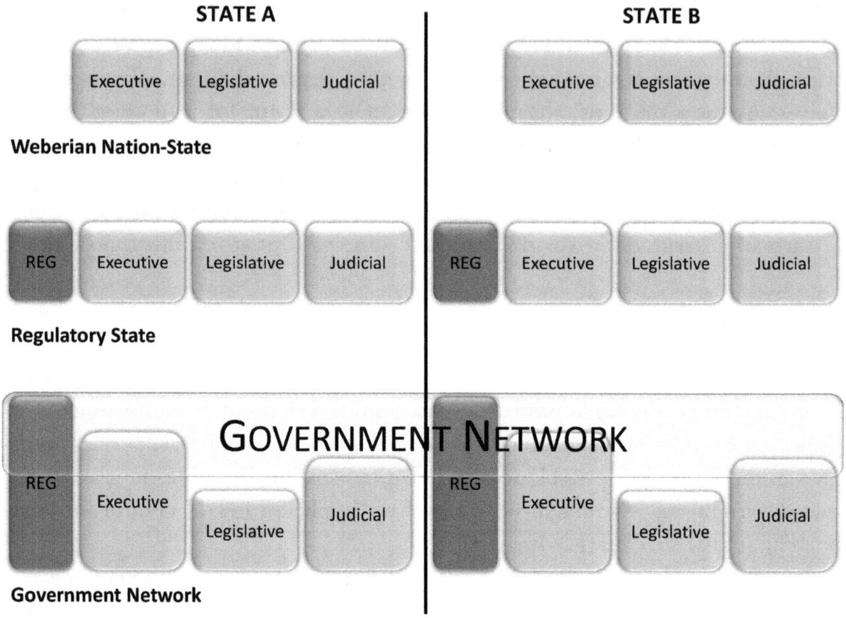

FIGURE 2.2 Evolution from State to Network

Source: Author's visualization

the position of regulators vis-à-vis domestic political actors both within and outside government (Bach & Newman, 2014; Bruszt & McDermott, 2012; Krasner, 2011). Third, government networks provide regulators with a venue for iterative interaction, an institutional environment that fosters and rewards cooperative behavior over longer time horizons (Keohane, 1984; Lipson, 1984). This mechanism may be especially pronounced in areas where government networks are in larger epistemic communities, facilitating cooperation and consensus-building. Moreover, in the financial realm at least, participation in government network allows regulators to meet their twin goals of stability and the preservation of international competitiveness for the domestic industry (D. A. Singer, 2004, 2007).

The executive branch may regard government networks as a preferential option because they minimize agency slack while facilitating cooperation and providing credibility in ways that mere interstate cooperation cannot. It also increases the degree of autonomy of the executive branch vis-à-vis the legislature (Gadinis, 2015, p. 55).

This does not mean that regulators or officials from the executive branch trade allegiance to the interest constellations of their home country for global technocratic harmony. Government networks are the site of fierce debates, and the policy areas where national interests are sufficiently overlapping for an agreement to emerge represent only a subset of all global issues that exhibit cross-border externalities. Within global finance alone, the list of issues where government networks have failed to reach consensus ranges from global taxation of financial transactions and bankers' compensation to the definition and regulation of shadow banking (FSB, 2011b; IMF, 2010a; Knaack & Gruin, 2017). Nevertheless, government networks offer venues of potential cooperation for members of the executive branch and regulators that conventional interstate channels cannot provide.

The branch of government that is challenged by the rise of government networks is the legislature. As this chapter discussed, the rise of the regulatory state has engendered an erosion of direct influence over an increasing range of policy areas for national parliaments. The reliance of government networks on soft law exacerbates this situation further. Legislators rarely had an active role in designing global policies. But because hard law agreements brokered by classic intergovernmental organizations need to be sanctioned by parliaments in order to enter into effect, legislators at least have a role as a veto player. In contrast, some institutional pathways chosen by government networks can eschew domestic sanctioning procedures, thus minimizing parliamentary involvement. The judicial branch of the state has been successful at forming government networks and engaging in transjudicial dialogue (Slaughter, 2004). An analysis of transnational involvement by the judicial branch provides an interesting avenue for research that unfortunately remains beyond the scope of this book.

In sum, delegation to international agencies of any kind involves sovereignty sharing, but sovereignty losses associated with government networks are borne unevenly by different branches of government. Legislators see their area of authority circumcised, whereas the executive and regulators are able to retain or even gain policymaking power when engaging in government networks. Existing legislation often limits the operations of government networks, however, and legislators have the power to remove these obstacles. In this respect, domestic law and domestic legislators represent the limit to the power of government networks.

Why do legislators not follow regulators and the executive branch and engage in government networks themselves? Three institutional constraints make it unfeasible and undesirable for legislators to engage in transnational cooperation.

First, legislators are elected to represent a geographically circumscribed constituency. As a consequence, legislators tend to see international issues through the prism of local interests. Showing loyalty to the local constituents and special interest groups that provide votes and campaign funds is what increases a legislator's chances of reelection. But it is hard to sell the uncertain and abstract benefits of international cooperation to local constituents, a constraint that Anderson (2005) terms "democratic parochialism." As Greenwood and Roederer-Rynning (2015) put it: "Concerning global affairs, the incentives for parties to articulate interests are likely to be low, as ordinary voters do not tend to be interested in remote issues, and consequently do not reward politicians for their engagement" (p. 327).

Second, the constituency constraints are exacerbated by the time horizon of legislators. Unlike regulators, legislators in most countries have four years in office and thus few incentives to establish long-term relationships with foreign counterparts. American political observers have argued long ago that

> a popular assembly, composed of members constantly coming and going in quick succession . . . must necessarily be inadequate to the attainment of those great objects, which require to be steadily contemplated in all their relations and circumstances, and which can only be approached and achieved by measures, which not only talents, but also exact information, and often much time, are necessary to concert and to execute.
>
> *(Jay, 1788, p. 485)*

The tension between the executive and the legislative branch has continued to attract the attention of US foreign policy analysts until today (Crabb & Holt, 1989; Destler, 1986; Hinckley, 1994; Lindsay, 1994; Nathan & Oliver, 1994; Pastor, 1982; Peterson, 1994). Martin (2000) rejects the notion of a zero-sum struggle for power, asserting that both branches of government have a common interest in making credible commitments. Game-theoretical approaches to international cooperation however have shown that the time horizon of interactions plays an important role for the emergence of credibility (Axelrod & Hamilton, 1981; Axelrod & Keohane, 1985b, Lipson, 1984).

One may nevertheless hypothesize that time is a secondary constraint for engagement in government networks. A brief glance across major global policy areas indicates that the executive branch shows interest in transgovernmental cooperation even though it also faces a short time horizon, at least in democracies. Unlike legislators however, officials of the executive represent the aggregated interests of the nation as a whole in a tightly circumscribed issue area.

Third, parliamentarians tend to deal with a wide array of policy issues. This makes it harder for them to identify their natural counterparts in other countries. Cross-border exchanges among legislators exist, but they do not foment meaningful cross-border cooperation. A European legislator recalls the following:

> There are regular trips but they are talking exercises. It's good, you get to understand a little better the power plays and the mindsets of the people that legislate elsewhere. But then again, it cannot bind your judgment when you write legislation here.
>
> *(EU Legislator 1, personal communication, November 26, 2017)*

Unlike regulators and officials from the executive branch, parliamentarians often lack specialized expertise. They thus find it difficult to identify themselves as part of a greater epistemic community at a distance from popular politics in their home country (Slaughter, 2004, p. 104ff).

Newman and Posner (2018) discuss an intriguing border case in their study of the National Association of Insurance Commissioners in the United States. Authority over insurance regulation rests at the state level, but the association was created in the late 19th century to represent the collective view of insurance regulators at the federal level, a government network within the United States of sorts. The authors note however that this association has fallen short of its goals as "roughly a quarter of its members are elected officials and thus have domestic electoral incentives that draw attention to local issues and work against the emergence of technocratic-oriented best practices" (p. 34). Thus there is some evidence that even among experts, electoral pressures may trump intellectual allegiance.

In sum, parliamentarians face a very particular set of institutional constraints. They are beholden to a tightly circumscribed constituency along the lines of geography, not substance. They must deal with a wide array of policy issues in a short period of time, with limited opportunities to develop ties to their counterparts abroad. Even legislators who understand the benefits of tackling global problems at a global level are unlikely to be rewarded in the next election because the benefits of cross-border cooperation are diffuse and may not manifest within a few years. As a consequence, they have no incentive to engage in government networks themselves.

Why would the absence of legislators in government networks lead to an unwillingness to bolster their power and support their operations? To be clear, legislative reluctance comes in several shapes, and not all can be linked to intentionality. Parliamentarians sometimes direct explicit criticism at government networks and even ask for the cessation of transgovernmental activities, as the final section of this chapter will show. Sometimes, legislators write new legal provisions that encumber the work of government networks, as in the case of derivatives data sharing (chapter 4). In many cases however, legislative reluctance is of passive nature: Parliamentarians do not remove legal obstacles to cross-border cooperation.

Bureaucratic politics provides the key insight that helps to account for both the incentive for active resistance to and lack of incentives to facilitate transgovernmental cooperation. Legislative reluctance vis-à-vis government networks becomes understandable when taking into account how the rise of the regulatory state, and the subsequent emergence of government networks has eroded the policy turf of legislators. A European legislator remarks, "I don't want democracies to be undermined. They are already undermined enough. Because the reality is that too often legislation is being written by expert bodies and just rubber stamped by parliament" (EU Legislator 1, personal communication, November 26, 2017).

Existing accounts of the IPE of financial regulation provides a plausible model of the legislature as maximizing votes and campaign contributions from the regulated industry. In the field of finance, legislators are accordingly concerned with voter confidence in financial stability and the competitiveness of domestic financial firms (Oatley & Nabors, 1998; D. A. Singer, 2004). What a bureaucratic politics perspective adds to this model is an emphasis on authority over a given policy area and the attribution of influence and responsibility. Legislators can only expect to be rewarded with votes and campaign contributions if they are perceived as being influential in shaping policy. A recent example of this relation can be seen in the insistence of the Agriculture Committees of both chambers of Congress on maintaining the Commodity Futures Trading Commission (CFTC) as the regulatory agency in charge of financial derivatives. As Chapter 4 shows in greater detail, financial special interest groups provide the majority of campaign contributions to legislators in the Agriculture Committees, and they would have been expected to direct their funds elsewhere had the CFTC been merged with the securities regulator, which is overseen by the Financial Service Committees of Congress. Regulatory agencies vary in their degree of dependence on the legislative branch, and the more independence they have or gain from their political principals, the harder it will be for legislators to attribute outcomes in a given policy area to their own work. As a result, legislators are concerned with turf as a precondition for votes and campaign contributions. When some legislators criticize government networks as unaccountable to the people, they may express a concern that they are not accountable to them.

We can expect variation in the occurrence of legislative reluctance along several dimensions. Policy areas vary in the degree to which they exhibit cross-border externalities and the degree of delegation of authority to government networks. Furthermore, there is considerable variation in the degree of political separation between the legislative and executive branch between presidential and parliamentary systems and among the latter (L. L. Martin, 2000). Finally, both jurisdictions and policy areas vary in the degree of delegation of authority to regulatory agencies and institutional fragmentation (Büthe & Mattli, 2011). To what extent such variations exhibit a systematic relation to legislative reluctance is an intriguing avenue for future research that unfortunately remains beyond the scope of this book.

Scholars have identified several phenomena of international political economy that bear a certain resemblance but deserve analytical distinction from the concept advanced here.

Newman and colleagues provide convincing accounts of legislative action that facilitates cross-border regulatory cooperation, albeit for instrumental reasons. Pre-existing soft law standards can serve as "templates-as-disruptors," allowing reformers in parliament to upset the domestic status quo and bring about legal change in line with their preferences (Newman & Posner, 2016; Newman & Bach, 2014). In such cases however, the incentive system of legislators is still confined to the domestic realm; cross-border regulatory cooperation is a by-product rather than the goal of legislative action.

Political economist have also developed a sophisticated concept of veto players. Defined as "institutional or partisan actors whose consent is needed to alter policies" (Mansfield et al., 2007, p. 403), veto players are understood to exercise decisive influence on policymaking (Tsebelis, 2002). Specifically, the probability of departure from the status quo decreases as the number of veto players increases (Mansfield et al., 2007), the policy preferences of veto players diverge, and institutional or partisan actors exhibit greater degrees of fragmentation and particularism (Henisz & Mansfield, 2006; Mukherjee et al., 2013; but see Ehrlich, 2007). However, the veto player approach fails to map onto the issue area of cross-border regulatory harmonization for two reasons. First, most scholarly work that employs the concept of veto players tends to concentrate on trade or migration, areas where winners and losers from a given policy decision are relatively easy to ascertain (Conconi et al., 2012, 2020). In the realm of financial regulation, such distinctions are less salient, especially after the rise of the regulatory state (Kastner & Rector, 2003). Second, while the veto player approach distinguishes between a policy action and the status quo, regulatory politics emphasize the difference between two kinds of policy action, that is, the development of harmonized or conflicting standards. In the area of relevance for this book, financial regulatory reform, no country has remained at the pre-crisis status quo. Instead, reform performance is determined by the ability of policymakers to agree on a harmonized standard. The veto player approach lacks inferential leverage to illuminate this phenomenon.

Scholars of international political economy have developed a rich variety of theoretical approaches that can be applied to regulatory politics in general and the track record of FSB in particular. The following section elaborates on five of them in detail.

Competing Explanations

The government network approach offers an explanation for the peculiar pattern of success and shortcomings in the global financial reform work of the FSB, but it is certainly not the only one, and it may not carry as much inferential leverage as other approaches. This section discusses key theories in international political economy, condenses them into five competing explanations, and offers a first overview regarding the extent to which their hypotheses match the empirical material at hand. A thorough systematic process analysis of regulatory reform in prudential banking (Chapter 3), OTC derivatives (Chapter 4), and ending TBTF (Chapter 5) forms the empirical core of the book. Each reform area is subjected to all competing explanations in their respective chapter. As this section merely provides an outline of the congruence analysis for each approach, it risks oversimplification and undue attention to detail in the important body of scholarship this book relies on. The concerned reader is asked to kindly move beyond this overview and dive into the empirical chapters as they provide sufficient space to engage with all competing explanations at the level of granularity they deserve.

The first approach examined here builds on the notion of market power as a source of **hegemony**. In the field of international political economy, scholars have always paid attention to the connection between market size and power (Hirschman, 1945; Kindleberger, 1973; Krasner, 1976). James and Lake (1989) famously identify market power as the "second face of hegemony." Here, the logic of hegemony operates through domestic actors in foreign countries: A large enough market alters the incentives and political power of market actors in other jurisdictions such that they advocate for their government to adopt policies that are in line with the preferences of the hegemon (Gourevitch, 1978). This notion of hegemony is a natural fit for the area of financial regulation because, unlike its equivalents in trade and monetary cooperation, global bodies of financial regulation are small, minilateral clubs restricted to a few jurisdictions with the largest financial markets (Naím, 2009; Brummer, 2014; Kaczmarek & Newman, 2011). G20 members rejected a proposal by Secretary General Ban Ki-Moon to convert a December 2008 UN Conference on Financing for Development into a summit to address the financial crisis and ignored a subsequent call by the Stiglitz Commission for the creation of a Global Economic Coordination Council under UN auspices (Cooper, 2010; Wade, 2011; Kharas & Lombardi, 2012; Knaack & Katada, 2013). And even though over 120 jurisdictions claim to adhere to prudential standards issued by the FSB and the Basel Committee, only a handful of member states were involved in their formulation (K. Alexander et al., 2006; BCBS, 2011a; E. Jones & Zeitz, 2017; E. Jones & Knaack, 2017).

Even within these small, club-like governance bodies, power is unevenly distributed (Drezner & McNamara, 2013). Simmons (2001b) and Drezner (2007), two leading thinkers of the hegemony approach, argue that the decisions of regulators in the dominant financial centers can drastically change the choices available to other countries. Effective global financial standards emerge, according to the authors, when great powers have an incentive to coordinate among themselves and when the rest faces negative externalities for nonadherence. Regulators in the dominant centers are concerned with adjustment costs of the domestic industry and the degree to which cross-border externalities can threaten financial stability at home (D. A. Singer, 2004, 2007).

The global financial crisis hit the developed economies of North America and Western Europe hardest. In line with the hegemony approach, we can thus expect low divergence of interest among the great powers and the successful promotion of club or even global standards. Indeed, policymakers on both sides of the Atlantic have become pace-setters (Quaglia & Spendzharova, 2017) and expressed unanimity in promoting the G20 reform agenda. Jörgen Holmquist, then director general of Internal Market and Services at the European Commission, put it in clear words at a Washington conference in April 2009:

> From a regulatory point of view, the G20 roadmap is mainly an EU-US intellectual product. When the process started last November, it came as a comfort to us to see how much we had a common view both on the diagnosis of the causes of the crisis and on what is needed to tackle them.
>
> *(Holmquist, 2009, p. 11)*

Even the disagreements regarding OTC derivatives rules are not the consequence of divergence in regulatory philosophy or adjustment costs, as Chapter 4 will show in detail. Moreover, developing member states of the G20 and the FSB have expressed concerns regarding the burden of higher supervisory requirements and cross-border access to capital, but there is little evidence of actual resistance to the financial regulatory reform program. Consequently, the hegemony or market-power approach predicts that the global financial crisis would lead to the emergence of a harmonized set of financial regulatory standards. Such standards are expected to be formulated in a minilateral club. But in spite of the strategic use of the G20 and FSB as club institutions, reform falls short of commitments in central areas such as OTC derivatives markets and bank resolution.

The second contender to explain the uneven progress of global financial regulatory reform revolves around **transnational bureaucracy**. It combines insight from historical institutionalism and transnational soft law with work on epistemic communities (Haas, 1989; Kapstein, 1989, 1992; J. Chwieroth, 2007; Holzinger et al., 2008; Büthe & Mattli, 2011; Pierson, 1993; Sell, 2010; Farrell & Newman, 2010). Historical institutionalists highlight the importance of institutional capacity as a source of power in global regulatory politics (Bach & Newman, 2007; Pierson, 1993; see also Krasner, 2011). Globally coherent and effective standards are likely to emerge in those areas where financial regulators have a history of deliberation, interaction, and enough time to develop a technocratic consensus and transform it into transnational soft law (Newman & Posner, 2015; Posner, 2018). Newman and Posner (2016) argue that "the pre-existence of transnational soft law is an important cause of transatlantic preference alignment; but is not the only potential cause" (p. 136).

Applied to the G20 and the global post-crisis financial regulatory agenda, the theories that comprise the transnational bureaucracy approach may expect reform to be successful in areas where epistemic communities have formed a technocratic

TABLE 2.1 Competing Explanations

	Expectation	*Critique*
1. Hegemony	Dominant countries (with convergent interests) push for global harmonization, concerned with externalities	Reform failure in some areas of convergent interests and with clear negative externalities such as OTC derivatives, TBTF
2. Transnational Bureaucracy	Technocratic consensus and soft law promote coordination (but take time to develop)	Reform success in novel prudential areas, failure in areas of decade-old transnational consensus
3. Redistributive Concerns	Concerns about adjustment costs and competitiveness impede global cooperation	Basel III full of redistributive effects but successful, failure in areas with unclear adjustment costs
4. Regulatory Capture	Industry defends status quo, race to the bottom	Global firms support harmonization because fragmentation is costly
5. Politicization	Political salience shifts authority from technocrats to politicians that favor national solutions	Advances in Basel III and TBTF loss absorbency in spite of politicization

consensus and developed soft law standards, and reform shortcomings in areas where that is not the case. Coordination failure in the area of OTC derivatives does indeed match the prediction of this approach. Transnational deliberation and soft law development was nonexistent prior to the crisis, depriving policy entrepreneurs of templates to foster regulatory harmonization. In other reform areas however, it is hard to establish a clear connection between epistemic community consensus, institutional density, and reform progress. Central pieces of the Basel III framework such as the countercyclical buffer and other macroprudential measures were at the margins of prudential regulatory debate prior to the crisis. And the most successful element of ending TBTF reform – SIFI identification based and loss absorbency requirements based on a novel definition of systemic risk – were the results of quasi-revolutionary new thinking after the crisis (Baker, 2013b). Proponents of the transnational bureaucracy approach may argue that even though the crisis triggered an upheaval in the mindset of regulators, its institutional foundations remained strong. As Chapter 5 will show in greater detail though, members of the Basel Committee had reached consensus about the need for cross-border information sharing and joint supervision of global banks at least two decades ago – yet this reform initiative falls short of G20 commitments. In other words, institutional density and epistemic consensus were neither necessary nor sufficient conditions for the emergence of effective global standards.

The third competing explanation highlights the importance of **redistributive concerns**. It is based on the recognition that global standard-setting is never a mere coordination game and that the governance of markets in general has a clear impact on the competitive position of companies in those markets (G. White, 1993; Skidmore, 1995; Fligstein, 1996; Roemer-Mahler, 2013). Thus, global standard setting entails redistributive consequences among jurisdictions. Representatives of major jurisdictions where adjustment costs threaten the competitiveness of the regulated sector are thus reluctant to agree to a global standard. Granted, Oatley and colleagues show that the great powers can build coalitions that command enough market power to coerce laggards into standards implementation, in line with the prediction of the hegemony approach (Oatley & Nabors, 1998; Oatley & Winecoff, 2012). The distinct contribution to the literature extracted here abstracts from market power and concentrates on competitiveness concerns across jurisdictions instead.

In line with this theory, global financial reform is expected to exhibit shortcomings where redistributive concerns are salient and successful where they are negligible, diffuse, or evenly distributed among jurisdictions. There is indeed plenty of evidence that negotiations in the Basel Committee and the FSB were fraught with acrimonious discussions between regulators who are worried that the new standards would negatively affect the competitiveness of the financial industry in their jurisdiction and the national economy as a whole. However, reform areas where adjustment costs were clear and vastly different across jurisdictions, such as bank capital requirements and loss absorbency for SIFIs, are among those that have reached successful implementation. Conversely, in some areas of OTC derivatives regulation such as trade reporting global financial reform is incomplete even though redistributive concerns were not salient.

Theories of **regulatory capture**, a fourth competing explanation, are as old as regulation itself. Early approaches focused on the role of special interest groups in electoral competition (Olson, 1968; Stigler, 1971; Peltzman, 1976; Grossman & Helpman, 1994, 2001). A second, more recent variety employs principal-agent theory to highlight the slack between the legislative principal and the regulatory body. Here, rent-seeking behavior occurs when the payments from the regulated sector supersede the rewards provided by the legislature for regulatory diligence (Huntington, 1952; Bernstein, 1955; Laffont & Tirole, 1991; Estache & Wren-Lewis, 2009; Djankov et al., 2002; Gordon & Hafer, 2005; D. Carpenter, 2004; D. Carpenter et al., 2010; D. Carpenter, 2013). Recent studies in financial regulatory politics have highlighted that special interest groups can mobilize human and cultural capital, taking advantage of personal networks, revolving doors, and "professional ecologies" to influence the policymaking process (Baker, 2010; Lall, 2012, 2015; Goldbach, 2015; S. Johnson & Kwak, 2010; Sell & Prakash, 2004; Pagliari & Young, 2014; Mattli & Woods, 2009). Identifying financial regulatory capture in practice is complicated by the fact that policymakers operate under conditions of Knightian uncertainty when developing a policy designed to avoid the next instance of a financial crisis, an event whose probability distribution is unknown and unknowable (Acharya et al., 2011; Aizenman, 2009; Breyer, 1993; Fernandez & Rodrik, 1991; Turner, 2012; Viñals & Fiechter, 2010). Under these circumstances, Cooley and Walter (2011) assert, "So optimum regulation is the art of balancing the immeasurable against the unknowable" (p. 35).

Regarding global financial regulatory reform, we can expect regulatory capture to operate in an area that falls short of G20 commitments if the financial services industry has communicated its opposition and deployed its resources to change regulation in that area. It is important to keep in mind, given the risk of Type I errors (false positives) of regulatory capture (K. L. Young, 2012), industry intent and action is a necessary but not a sufficient condition. Indeed, the empirical picture shows no shortage of attempts by the financial lobby to convince policymakers at the national and international level that the new regulatory standards would suffocate the financial sector, dry up credit supply to the real economy, and thus destroy economic growth for years to come. However, there is scant evidence that private sector ever lobbied against the global harmonization of financial standards. In the case of Basel III implementation in the EU, the capture of legislators by the financial lobby arguably contributed to European mock compliance, as Chapter 3 will show. In other areas however, private sector associations helped regulators in forging a derivatives-related agreement among systemically important banks where public officials failed to implement one and sued one regulator for allegedly violating G20 commitments of global harmonization.

The fifth and final competing explanation draws a causal connection between reform shortcomings and the **politicization** of financial regulation in the wake of the crisis. While regulators had relatively few constrains in the development of financial standards and their harmonized implementation in normal times (Brooks & Kurtz, 2012), they faced pressures from newly engaged political leaders and domestic activists in the wake of the financial meltdown (Helleiner & Pagliari, 2011; Helleiner, 2014a).

This approach predicts the weakening of government networks and the rise of policy divergence, albeit combined with efforts at interstate cooperation in regulatory matters. It is analytically closest to the government network approach proposed in this book, as both build on the notion that politicians tend to adopt unilateral measures, whereas regulators tend to favor cross-border coordination. In fact, in the field of OTC derivatives reform (Chapter 4), it is very difficult to make a crisp analytical distinction between the two approaches. The picture is clearer in the other two empirical chapters. Prudential banking regulation (Chapter 4) is arguably the issue area that put policymakers under the greatest political pressure, but here a globally harmonized standard (Basel III) has been implemented. In the area of ending TBTF, we witness a flurry of uncoordinated policies such as ring-fencing. But as Chapter 5 will show in greater detail, regulators and finance ministers eventually decided to roll back unilateralism and endow the FSB with the authority to develop a novel loss absorbency standard for banks.

In sum, this book shows that while the expectations from each of the five competing theoretical approaches outlined previously provide a partial explanation of the empirical evidence at hand, they do not match the full pattern of global financial reform. The government network perspective in turn provides a new explanatory framework that helps readers understand the peculiar combination of reform successes and failures that characterizes the regulatory reform project at the G20 and the FSB a decade after the global financial crisis. Each chapter provides an explanation of the regulatory reform process from a government network perspective first and engages with competing explanations of observational equivalence afterwards.

Global financial regulatory reform is the key explanandum of this book, and the FSB is at the center of the empirical investigation. But the toolbox of government networks is of relevance in other areas of global governance too. And it may be usefully applied in new issue areas where global policy coordination is lacking to date. The following section will take a look at two such issues of prime concern in the 21st century, namely, climate change and artificial intelligence. A thorough analysis of the role of government networks in both issue areas is beyond the scope of this book. Instead, the following section will share a few preliminary thoughts on the possibilities of networked governance and compare this institutional design to traditional intergovernmentalism to tease out advantages and drawbacks in tackling these two key global governance issues.

Global Governance of Climate Change and Artificial Intelligence

At first glimpse, the institutional arrangement to govern the world's fight against climate change looks like the brain child of hard law intergovernmental traditionalists. The key agreements in this area are UN conventions under international public law. The 1997 Kyoto Protocol is an international treaty that builds on the 1992 UN Framework Convention on Climate Change, and the Intergovernmental Panel on Climate Change is a UN organization. Even the 2015 Paris Agreement is an international treaty that only went into effect after the parliaments of a minimum number of states ratified it.

But look below the surface and the soft law instruments typically used by government networks start to appear. Members of the Paris Agreement issue Nationally Determined Contributions (NDC) to fight climate change, but these are unilateral pledges that are not legally binding. Using Raustiala's (2005) terminology, legal form is replaced by a deep review structure, allowing for greater substance in this international agreement. The NDCs are published and peer reviewed on a regular basis, allowing a variety of state and non-state actors to leverage the power of reputation rather than legal procedures. In the final days of negotiations of the Paris Agreement, Secretary of State John Kerry and his team insisted that the text use the word "should" rather than "shall" because the former does not imply legal obligations in UN lingo, whereas the latter does. An agreement that contained such legal obligations would have to be ratified by the US Senate, which would have killed the Paris Agreement in all likelihood (Restuccia, 2015). The Trump administration withdrew from the agreement in 2020, and the Biden administration joined again in 2021, but both decisions were made by the executive branch of the US government, without the involvement of Congress. In other words, the current institutional design of global governance to combat climate change has already moved away from intergovernmental traditions, employing soft law instruments that are commonly used by government networks.

Rallying the world to combat climate change is hard enough. Finding a way for global stakeholders to guide the development of artificial intelligence (AI) in a direction that benefits humanity and does not destroy it seems even more complicated. Yet the institutional design of government networks might be useful in this issue area too. The following paragraphs will first identify eight commonalities among AI and financial markets. Based on this analysis, the section then makes the argument that global governance is needed and that a government network might be a better institutional design for this issue area than intergovernmental alternatives.

A look at the commonalities among finance and artificial intelligence is instructive. In both areas, state-owned and private firms cooperate with and compete against each other in a context of fast-paced innovation. The markets they operate in are global (unless regulators intervene) and rife with cross-border externalities. The behavior of individual firms can be seen as merely self-motivated business (seeking profit) or as part of a national strategy (seeking prowess, self-sufficiency). Clients are widely distributed around the globe, but the leading public and private firms are multinationals that are headquartered in just a handful of jurisdictions, mainly in the United States, China, and Western Europe. Interdependence across borders can spur development and innovation, promising global welfare improvements, but it may also be weaponized by the center nodes of the network (Farrell & Newman, 2019).

Even in the absence of coercive intentions, when firms merely compete against each other for greater profits and market shares, the incentives of individual firms and the public at large are not fully aligned. Competitive advantage – at least in the short term – entails risk that is not fully internalized by firms. In finance, extending credit to risky borrowers and pushing the boundaries of innovation in derivatives can be lucrative, as the years leading up to the global financial crisis showed. In AI, companies that push the boundaries of innovation can also expect to reap immense benefits from offering cutting-edge products. But in both markets, profit-maximizing firms contribute to systemic risk, that is, the risk of a collapse that has significant negative repercussions for actors beyond those involved in the sector. In finance, the bankruptcy of a single investment bank in 2009 led not only to the collapse of the financial system but also precipitated a downturn of the real economy on a global scale. In AI, a single firm that loses control over a powerful algorithm may jeopardize not only the sector it operates in but also the digital networks that underly much of our work and life environments. In both areas, profits are internalized by individual firms, whereas losses arising from risky behavior are shouldered, at least in part, by the public.

The governance of AI poses two problems. The first is the control problem, that is, how to design the new technology to do what their designers intended it to do. The second problem, called the "political problem" by Bostrom (2017b) concerns how to make sure the institutions empowered by AI use it in ways that promote the common good. In order to find out what governance arrangements can meaningfully address both problems, scholars have often looked at the history of lethal technologies such as nuclear power.

In a recent book, Henry Kissinger and colleagues (2021) look at algorithmic failures such as the one that precipitated a massive sell-off by automated trading in the US stock market in May 2010. The authors note that "in the financial world, such errors devastate portfolios but do not take lives. In the strategic domain, however, an algorithmic failure analogous to a 'flash crash' could be catastrophic" (p. 168). In the extreme case, systemic risk in AI means existential risk for humanity (Bostrom, 2017b). Kissinger et al. (2021) provide bold and cunning insights into future trajectories of AI and their repercussions. But they are surprisingly shy about potential governance arrangements to steer the development of this technology towards the common good. The authors suggest that each advanced society should aim to convene a body at a national level to bring together AI creators, operators, government, and civil society representatives to bridge different perspectives about the technology, its uses, and the risks it entails. In their view, "At what point and in what contexts in the technology's evolution it should be subject to internationally negotiated restrictions is another essential subject of debate" (Kissinger et al., 2021, p. 216). The authors urge leaders of rival nations to speak regularly to one another about the forms of war they do not wish to fight. Thus, they seem to suggest that the design of global AI governance would be akin to nuclear arms negotiations among the two superpowers during the Cold War.

Instead, consider AI as a technology that is inherently risky but chiefly used for commercial purposes. Because incentives between individual firms and the public are not aligned, the market is beset with nontrivial externalities, and spillovers are unlikely to be confined within national borders. The need for global governance of AI is as strong as it is in finance. Bostrom (2017a) calls for a regime in which major global coordination or bargaining problems can be solved, a mechanism he calls "singleton." In Bostrom's (2017a) words,

> A world in which global coordination problems remain unsolved even as the power of technology increases towards its physical limits is a world that is hostage to the possibility that – at some level of technological development – nature too strongly favours destruction over creation.
>
> *(p. 141)*

When thinking of the design of such a singleton to address global governance challenges, the FSB in particular and government networks in prudential financial regulation in general might offer inspiration.

The case against a traditional intergovernmental design to govern AI can be made on similar grounds as that for finance. The rapid evolution of the market will likely leave regulators in constant catch-up mode, a phenomenon Caruana (2014) calls the regulatory uncertainty principle (more on this in Chapter 6). Rigid rules and even mandates of governance bodies risk becoming outdated fast. Moreover, a static rulebook is the "meat and drink of regulatory arbitrage," where firms have an incentive to find innovative ways to circumvent regulations (P. Tucker, 2014). Elected legislatures may lack the requisite technological expertise to make meaningful contributions to regulation and supervision, and courts may be reactive and too slow to influence firms' behavior (Dafoe, 2018). The task of governing AI will likely have to be delegated to regulators who operate in either an independent agency or in a specialized department of the executive branch. Extensive expertise and access to private-sector knowledge will be necessary, requiring a tightrope walk between supervisors and supervisees that is well documented in the financial sphere, with all its flaws and shortcomings (Igan & Lambert, 2019). Instead of international agreements that require ratification, effective governance arrangements would likely take the form of nonbinding pledges that can be adjusted quickly, combined with a peer review structure to ensure consistency in implementation and compliance. Moreover, because the market is likely concentrated with leading firms headquartered in just a few jurisdictions, policymakers might want to prefer a minilateral club (Naím, 2009; Brummer, 2014; Simmons, 2001b) over a multilateral organization with wide membership.

Regulatory measures to curb systemic AI risk will not receive an enthusiastic welcome by the industry. Here, as in finance, safety measures are likely to handicap performance. Take speed as an example. AI firms that outpace their competitors may reap significant commercial benefits. But the speed of AI deployment may be at odds with the common good. It can exacerbate the control problem mentioned previously. And it can lead to what Bostrom and colleagues (2020) call turbulence, that is, a situation of fast-changing and hastily implemented agreements in which the gains from coordination are hard to realize. Thus, regulators may want to devise safety breaks and subject new algorithms to tests in a safe but realistic environment, a regulatory sandbox of sorts that is already a common instrument in the world of financial technology (Jenik & Duff, 2021). Any methods to slow down the speed of AI deployment will have to be coordinated across borders, because such safety measures would imply competitive disadvantage in a global market unless implemented in consistent fashion in all major jurisdictions (Bostrom, 2017a). The Basel Accords were indeed borne out of such concerns over international competitiveness. In the 1980s, major banks in the United States and Britain pushed their respective regulators towards internationalizing the domestic safety standard they were bound by and to threaten market exclusion for banks (including fast-and-furious Japanese ones) that did not abide by it (Oatley & Nabors, 1998). A similar logic of international political economy may conceivably play out in the realm of AI in the near future. Even when regulators in the major jurisdictions agree on a global safety standard, AI firms can be expected to lobby for a domestic implementation that favors them (Quaglia, 2019). They might even portray their firms as national champions that generate domestic employment, tax revenues, and technological leadership that supports a greater national strategy against rival AI superpowers. Hence the need for regulatory consistency assessments among experts that are somewhat isolated from politics, a form of peer review that is common practice in the FSB and other government networks in global financial governance.

Complexity and reputation are two partially offsetting features of relevance for governance both in finance and AI. Even at the early stage of AI development we currently find ourselves in, algorithms have become so complex that their designers struggle with the control problem mentioned previously. When Microsoft's online chat bot Tay became a Nazi in March 2016, the engineers who created it were not able to merely make a few premeditated adjustments, they had to take the bot offline and study what went wrong (Schwartz, 2019). The situation is not dissimilar in financial markets. Financial experts needed months of work to disentangle the web of derivatives obligations surrounding Lehman Brothers in 2009 (Haldane, 2012a). But the system opacity brought about by high complexity does not necessarily undermine effective regulation. The collapse of a bank with significant cross-border exposure triggered the formation of the Basel Committee (see Chapter 3). But its members struggled for years to find a simple, unified, and effective approach to make cross-border banking safer. Only in the 1980s did financial economists develop a set of prudential indicators such as "probability of default" and "loss given default" to formulate a single, simple capital adequacy standard (Basel I) that could be applied to all relevant banks in spite of significant differences across jurisdictions and business models (Kapstein, 1989). Arguably, AI experts may develop a similar safety standard for algorithms in the future. In both areas, deep technical expertise is required, and thus few people will be able to scrutinize the work of the experts in charge of setting standards. But in the tight-knit networks of experts that form epistemic communities, reputation can play a powerful role (Haas, 1989; Keohane, 1997). Bostrom (2017a) notes that "skill signaling" is a motivating force for AI developers even in the absence of monetary rewards. AI regulators in charge of devising a global safety standard for AI can be expected to be seeking recognition as skillful experts among their peers, and dreading the reputational fallout from regulatory failure. Moreover, as civil servants they will be subject to hierarchical accountability, as Chapter 6 explains in greater detail.

In sum, this section presented eight features (summarized in Table 2.2) that characterize both finance and artificial intelligence and that suggest government networks as a fitting institutional design for their global governance. Unilateral pledges that can be adjusted quickly promise to keep up better with the fast pace of innovation in AI than legally binding agreements. High-level principles and

TABLE 2.2 Commonalities in Finance and Artificial Intelligence and Their Governance

Sector Characteristics	*Government Network Solutions*
Fast-paced innovation	Unilateral pledges instead of ratified agreements
Regulatory uncertainty and risk of arbitrage	Standards and principles rather than rules and laws
Competition among public and private companies	Market regulation that is agnostic regarding ownership
Imperfect alignment between firm-level incentives and the common good	Regulation by public authorities
Negative cross-border externalities	Cross-border regulatory coordination
Market concentration in a few jurisdictions	Minilateralism
Supervised firms with incentive to lobby for global standards and domestic implementation that favor them	Global coordination in standard setting, peer review to ensure globally consistent implementation
High complexity	Regulation and supervision by experts constrained by reputation and hierarchical accountability, not generalists

standards help address regulatory uncertainty and reduce the scope for regulatory arbitrage. Global standards can be agnostic regarding whether an AI firm is private or government owned. But because the incentives of firms are not perfectly aligned with the common good, self-regulation by the industry is likely to be insufficient. Cross-border externalities may be significant, but the market will be concentrated among a few jurisdictions, who can use a minilateral club as a forum to develop a common standard and impose it on the rest of the world. Supervised firms have an incentive to lobby their regulators, but peer review can ensure global consistency in standards implementation. The field is beset with complexity, but because AI safety experts have a reputation to lose, they can be expected to hold themselves accountable not only to their peers but also to a wider public who will be rationally ignorant of the technicalities of their work.

All the previously noted considerations may appear quaint and naïve if artificial intelligence indeed turns out to be a lethal technology that will be controlled by military commanders of rival digital superpowers. But if AI algorithms turn out to be more similar to an interest rate swap than an atomic bomb, the FSB and similar government networks may be a more fitting governance blueprint than Cold War–era antiballistic missile negotiations.

These considerations conclude the theoretical framework that guides the rest of this book. The following three chapters engage in a systematic process analysis of the main reform items on the agenda of the G20 and the FSB, exploring the inferential utility of the government network approach against competing explanations. Readers who are unenthusiastic about the nitty-gritties of financial regulation and who would like to explore questions of government network effectiveness and legitimacy instead are kindly advised to skip to Chapter 6.

3

TIMELY IMPLEMENTATION AND MOCK COMPLIANCE WITH BASEL III

Banks were at the center of the financial turmoil that shook much of the world in 2007–2009. The series of bank failures and takeovers leading up to the fateful collapse of Lehman Brothers in September 2008 highlighted the shortcomings of existing regulation, especially in the world's dominant financial centers. In recognition of this regulatory shortfall, G20 leaders pronounced their will to overhaul prudential banking standards at the Pittsburgh Summit in September 2009:

> We commit to developing by end-2010 internationally agreed rules to improve both the quantity and quality of bank capital and to discourage excessive leverage. These rules will be phased in as financial conditions improve and economic recovery is assured, with the aim of implementation by end-2012.
>
> *(G20, 2009c, paras. 13, Annex 1)*

G20 leaders committed to the intended implementation deadline again during the subsequent Toronto Summit and meetings of G20 Finance Ministers and Central Bank Governors. They authorized the Basel Committee on Banking Supervision (BCBS), a government network that is a key member of the FSB, to develop internationally consistent banking standards to meet that goal. The BCBS agreed on a new set of rules to improve capital buffers and ensure adequate leverage and liquidity for banks in September 2010 (Schneider, 2010a), ahead of the stipulated deadline. The core elements of the new agreement, Basel III, were published in December of 2010. At the same time, the phase-in of the new requirements was extended much beyond the two-year period foreseen in Pittsburgh. At the Seoul Summit in November 2010, G20 leaders stated, "The new framework will be translated into our national laws and regulations, and will be implemented starting on January 1, 2013 and fully phased in by January 1, 2019" (G20, 2010b, para. 29).

DOI: 10.4324/9781003290001-3

A closer look at the details of the phase-in agreement reveals that the implementation period stretches beyond 2019. The new global rules entail a stricter definition of capital and risk-weighted assets that are used to calculate capital, leverage, and liquidity ratios, as explained in further detail in the next example. A report on Basel III implementation states that "capital instruments that no longer qualify for non-common equity Tier 1 capital or Tier 2 capital will be phased out over 10 years beginning 1 January 2013" (FSB, 2010c, p. 4). In other words, while the original aim was to complete prudential banking reform by 2012, banks had until 2023 to fully implement the new capital requirements. More global rules under the Basel III umbrella were developed in subsequent years: Regulators reached agreement on two liquidity ratios in 2013 and 2014, respectively (BCBS, 2014f; BIS, 2014b). The BCBS published a framework on the leverage ratio (capital requirements as a percentage of non-risk weighted assets) in 2014, and implementation started in 2018. It agreed on the principles for a countercyclical buffer in 2015, with rules entering into effect in 2019. Additional loss absorbency requirements for too-big-to-fail financial institutions were developed in 2012–2014 and are analyzed in detail in Chapter 5. Between 2013 and 2016, Basel Committee members updated the requirements for large credit exposures, interest rate risk, margin and capital requirements for derivatives trading, equity investment in funds, and securitization exposures that only started taking effect after 2017 (BCBS, 2017a). Basel III negotiations finally reached completion in late 2017 when bank supervisors agreed on revised capital requirements that constrain the use of internal risk weighting models, with the final rules coming into effect in 2023 (BCBS, 2017b). The BCBS postponed the implementation and review process by a year in 2020 to help supervisors concentrate on the COVID-19 crisis. All told, the phase-in period for the finalized Basel III package stretches to 2028 (BCBS, 2020b).

Nevertheless, in comparison with all other items on the financial reform agenda, Basel III can be considered a success. The government network in charge (BCBS) managed to incorporate new elements into the global regulatory standards that represent a departure from the pre-crisis status quo. It generated consensus on prudential standards and consistency in its implementation in spite of a concurrent drastic increase in number and heterogeneity of its membership, incorporating all remaining G20 members in 2009 (Chey, 2016). Furthermore, several important jurisdictions have decided to issue rules that exceed the new global standard. Only one Basel member has failed to issue rules that are consistent with the global standard: the European Union. Why is prudential banking regulation the most successful item on the G20 post-crisis financial reform agenda, and why do policymakers fail to meet Basel standards in a core jurisdiction that has been significantly affected by imprudent banking behavior in the lead-up to the crisis? This chapter analyzes the political economy of Basel III formulation at the Basel Committee and its implementation among its members. It seeks to provide insight into the reasons for both European mock compliance and the successful implementation of the new banking standard among all other FSB members.

The chapter is organized as follows: The first section briefly presents the evolution of Basel III negotiations at the BCBS and provides an overview over the adoption of the global rules among members jurisdictions. Basel III encompasses a much larger set of new and revised rules than envisioned at the outset, and the full regulatory package was not finalized until 2017. But even though rule revisions and corresponding phase-ins mean that Basel III will only enter into full effect in the 2020s, banks adjusted to the new standard within less than a decade after the global financial crisis. The main section of the chapter traces the institutional pathway of Basel III implementation around the world, highlighting the effectiveness of the regulatory agencies that are members of the Basel Committee. But the power of this government network has clear limits: the chapter shows how and why the only jurisdiction that failed the Basel III cross-border consistency test is also the only one where parliamentarians played a role in implementation. The chapter concludes with a discussion of alternative explanations that are derived from the rich scholarly literature on the topic.

Following the call to overhaul banking standards at the Pittsburgh Summit, regulators at the Basel Committee started developing a new global standard, reaching a general agreement within less than a year. The new Basel standards were first published in September 2010 and slightly revised at the end of the year. Implementation of the new capital rules proceeded fast in some but not all member countries. By the end-2012 deadline, 11 out of 27 Basel member jurisdictions had final Basel III rules in force. Implementation lagged behind in the nine member jurisdictions that are part of the European Union and the United States, among others. In other words, many emerging economies did not wait for the great powers to implement Basel III first, a result that contrasts starkly with reform progress in OTC derivatives regulation, as Chapter 4 will show. In 2013 all remaining jurisdictions finalized the rulemaking progress and Basel III capital rules are effective in all 24 member jurisdictions since 2014 (BCBS, 2014f).

As mentioned previously, Basel III goes beyond capital adequacy standards, introducing new liquidity and leverage requirements. The development of these new regulatory tools follows a different timeline. The liquidity coverage ratio was published in 2013 and came into effect in 2015. Negotiations over the second liquidity ratio, the so-called net stable funding ratio started later, with final standards agreed in 2014 and to be implemented from 2018 onwards. The leverage ratio required several years of bank-level reporting to national supervisors before the final standard was issued in late 2017. But as Figure 3.1 shows, at that time even implementation of the newer Basel III components is advancing fast. By end-2020, the Net Stable Funding Ratio was effective in 12 countries (up from 2 in 2017), and final rules were published in all remaining jurisdictions. The leverage ratio, as agreed upon in 2014, is now binding for banks operating in all jurisdictions except Australia, where regulators have already published rules in line with the 2017 update (BCBS, 2020b).

Even though Basel III capital requirements were not fully phased in until 2019, banks adjusted their balance sheets to meet the new requirements several years

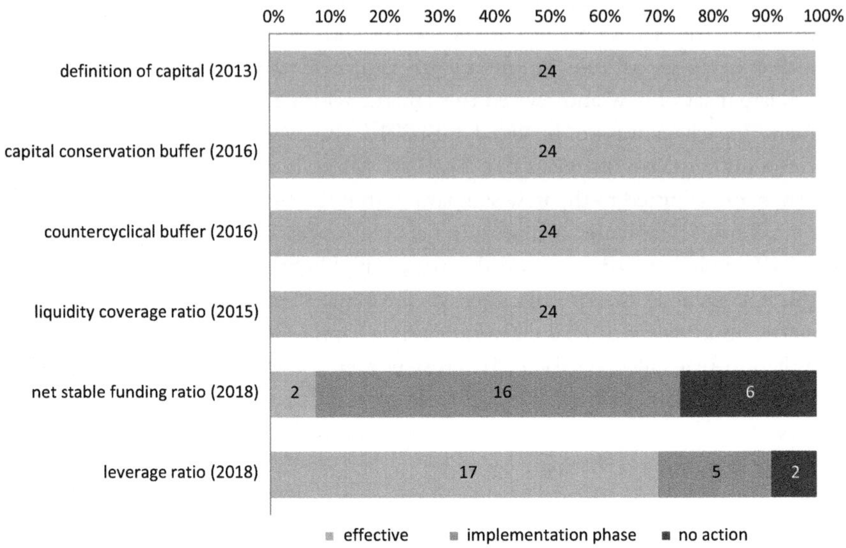

FIGURE 3.1 Basel III Implementation in 2017 (With Deadlines)

Source: (BCBS, 2016e, 2017a)

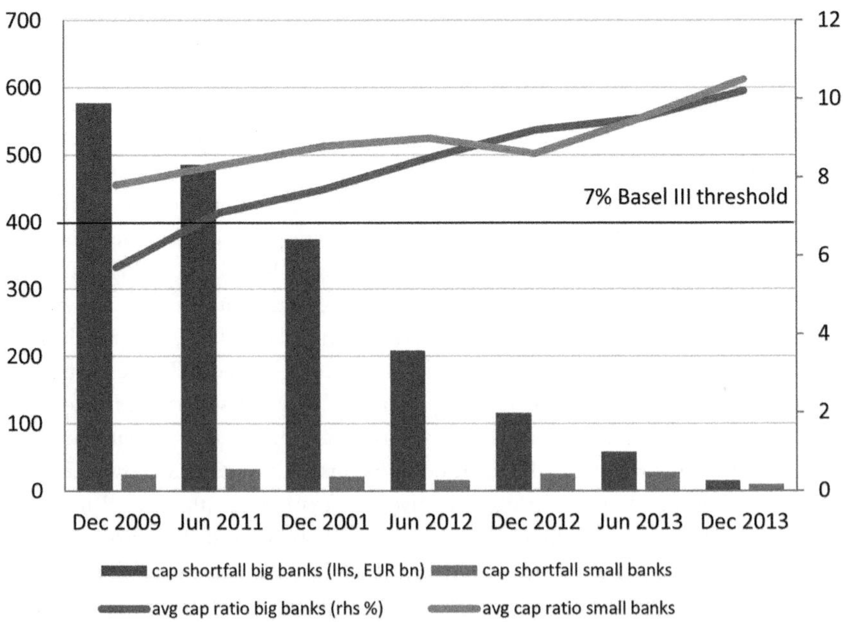

FIGURE 3.2 Basel III Capital Shortfall and Average Core Capital Ratios (CET1)

Sources: BCBS (2010c, 2012a, 2012c, 2013a, 2013e, 2014b, 2014e)

early (BCBS, 2013d). The Basel Committee uses semiannual data from a sample of over 200 banks in member jurisdiction to trace the evolution of their capital buffers. In a series of reports, it shows that the gap between actual and required capital levels for big banks in the sample decreased from €577 billion in December 2009 to €15.1 billion by end-2013. This compares to an after-tax profit of €419 billion for the same group of banks in 2013. By 2014, over 90% of the sample already reached the final 7% core capital (CET1) target. Moreover, the big and small banks in the sample reached average core capital ratios of 10.5% and 10.2%, respectively, substantially exceeding the minimum requirements (BCBS, 2014e).

What explains the rapid, widespread, and consistent adoption of Basel III standards, with the conspicuous exemptions of the European Union?

Government Network

The government network approach highlights the importance of institutional pathways of global reform. Policies that are channeled through government networks are expected to be implemented in a timely and globally consistent fashion. Delays and cross-border inconsistencies in turn are expected where policies are subject to parliamentary involvement. The case of Basel III provides rich empirical material for a plausibility test of the government network hypothesis.

The Basel Committee is a quintessential government network. It is comprised of banking regulators from member jurisdictions, and neither the agreements made in the BCBS nor the organization itself carry any weight in international public law. Member countries do not "ratify" the agreement. Instead, Basel III was published as a nonbinding declaration of intention to implement the global standard unilaterally in each jurisdiction.

The domestic implementation process eschews legislative bodies in the large majority of member jurisdiction. Basel III was implemented in administrative acts such as the issuance of regulations, communiqué, circulars, directives, directions, and guidelines by domestic organizations that have been granted the authority to regulate banks by law. Such administrative documents were issued by the central banks of Argentina, Brazil, Hong Kong, India, Russia, and Singapore (BCBS, 2013b, 2013g, 2015a, 2015c, 2016a, 2016c). They were published by banking regulatory agencies in Australia, Canada, China, Korea, and Mexico (BCBS, 2013f, 2014c, 2014d, 2015b, 2016d) and by agencies and central banks together in Indonesia and the United States (BCBS, 2014a, 2016f). Japanese regulators implemented Basel III domestically by publishing so-called "legal announcements" (*kokuji*) (Aosaki, 2013).

Basel III did require legislative changes in several jurisdictions: So-called delegated acts were required in some countries to provide regulators with supervisory powers. South Africa and Switzerland had to make amendments to the primary banking law (the Banks Act and *Bankenverordnung*, respectively) (BCBS, 2013c, 2015d; FINMA, 2018), but the substantial rules of Basel III were implemented by central banks and regulatory agencies.

The difference in Basel III implementation in the world's two biggest banking markets are instructive. In the United States, Congress was excluded from weighing in on Basel banking rules. In contrast, the European Parliament is the only legislature among BCBS members that played an important role in translating Basel standards into hard law. The following paragraphs will analyze in what ways this difference in institutional pathways led to overcompliance with Basel III in the former case and mock compliance in the latter.

In the United States, Basel III rules were published in 2012 in the form of three so-called notices of proposed rulemaking (NPR) and one final rule. NPRs were subject to a comment period in which all interested parties were free to submit feedback on the rule proposals. The regulatory authorities then finalize the rules and publish them in the Federal Register (Davis Polk, 2012; Harper, 2010). The circumvention of legislative involvement is conspicuous. While the Basel Committee was developing a new regulatory standard for banks, lawmakers in the US negotiated and finalized an encompassing law on financial regulation, the Dodd-Frank Act. However, the law mentions neither the Basel Committee nor capital adequacy standards. With the exception of the Collins amendment that stipulates that capital buffers under the advanced approach must not be lower than under the standard approach, the Dodd-Frank Act does not interfere in prudential banking regulation. Instead, it explicitly endows regulatory agencies with the powers to engage in "international policy coordination" (Dodd-Frank Wall Street Reform and Consumer Protection Act, 2010, sec. 175).

The carve-out of prudential standards from Dodd-Frank can be attributed to concerted efforts by the executive branch and regulators. The US Treasury and the Fed worked to avoid legislative intervention in order to preserve regulatory autonomy for the central bank and to prevent a watering down of regulatory stringency (Newman & Posner, 2018; K. Young, 2016; Zaring, 2015). US regulators were nevertheless subject to pressure from Congress. Following concerted lobby activity by special interest groups representing community banks (CCBA, 2012; ICBA, 2012), 50 senators sent a bipartisan letter to US agencies requesting relief from Basel III rules for small domestic banks. US regulators responded by instituting a tiered approach, subjecting small banks to simpler (but tighter) capital and leverage ratios while retaining regulatory consistency with Basel III for all other banks (Quaglia, 2019).

That Congress did not play a role in Basel III implementation does not mean however that this was an easy process. The United States features a unique system of regulatory fragmentation where supervisory authority is divided between three agencies the OCC, the FDIC, and the Fed. A fourth bank supervisor (the OTS) was dismantled in post-crisis reform, but all other agencies struggled successfully to retain or even expand their turf. The three US banking supervisors are not united in their regulatory outlook and preferred degree of regulation. Therefore Basel III implementation only came about as the result of a lengthy inter-agency negotiation. US regulators impose a leverage ratio that exceeds

Basel standards. When asked about the reasons for this decision, a US Regulator responded,

> You want to know the real reason? I don't know if it's ever been said. This was the price of getting the FDIC to agree to Basel III. The FDIC did not adopt Basel III at the same time that the OCC and the Fed did. This was the price of their adopting it. That was the cost.
>
> *(US Regulator 4, personal communication, June 30, 2014)*

Whereas domestic implementation of Basel III in the United States was achieved by way of gold-plating the global standard, the opposite was the case in the European Union.

A year after Basel III standards were published, negotiations between the European Commission, the Council, and the European Parliament opened on how the global standards should be translated into European legislation via the Capital Requirements Directive and Regulation (CRD IV). Basel III implementation in Europe is of global relevance for two reasons. First, European Union countries comprise a third of the Basel Committee (9 out of 27 jurisdictions, with EU authorities as a 28th member). Second, as the result of a decade-long process of centralization and internal market integration, the European Union today is regarded both as a powerful actor in international financial negotiations and as a "hardening agent" of international soft law (Campbell-Verduyn & Porter, 2014; Newman & Bach, 2014; Posner, 2009; Posner & Véron, 2010; Quaglia, 2014a). From a government network perspective, the European case is outstanding in that it is the only Basel member jurisdiction where implementation occurred with significant parliamentary involvement.

Although political economists often regard individual European nation-states as key actors in the history of global banking standards, the European Commission has a three-decade history of involvement. The BCBS invited the European Commission in 1987 to send observers to the negotiations of the first Basel standard. The commission began work on the coordination of banking regulation as early as the 1960s, but it made significant steps towards cross-border regulatory harmonization after the 1992 Maastricht Treaty and the gradual strengthening of the Economic and Monetary Union throughout the 1990s (Goodhart, 2011; Pauly, 2008).

Similarly, the European Parliament was involved in the implementation of all three Basel agreements because each required follow-up legislation. But it has only gained power vis-à-vis the other European institutions with recent treaty changes (Crum & Fossum, 2009; Judge & Earnshaw, 2008). The Parliament lacked the institutional authority to amend or reject the legislative proposal made by the commission when Basel I was implemented. The implementation of Basel II in the Capital Requirements Directive (CRD I) in 2006 required a co-decision by the council and the Parliament. But the technical issues of banking regulation did not acquire much political salience even though a few members of the European

Parliament (MEPs) criticized Basel II implementation as undemocratic. A banking regulator notes, "The European Parliament wasn't quite interested in its own power as it is now" (UK Regulator 3, personal communication, 2017). Greenwood and Roederer-Rynning (2015) argue that "in the last decade a new era of parliamentarization has started, where MEPs have supplemented their quest for legislative empowerment on internal matters with a will to parliamentarize the external relations of the EU" (p. 328).

In contrast to its predecessors, the implementation of Basel III in the EU was a contentious political process (Barker & Masters, 2012a, 2012b). In July 2011, the European Commission presented its legislative proposal to turn the new Basel agreement into a regulation (CRR) and a directive on capital requirements (CRD IV). For the following two years, it was debated and amended in "trilogue" negotiations with the council and the Parliament. The Economic and Monetary Affairs Committee (ECON) led negotiations on behalf of the Parliament, drawing MEPs from five party groups. The final version of CRR/CRD IV left regulators and some officials of the executive branch worried about regulatory stringency. Howarth and Quaglia (2013) quote the British finance minister George Osborne as saying, "We are not implementing the Basel agreement, as anyone who will look at this text will be able to tell you" (p. 336).

The Basel Committee confirmed Osborne's admonition in December 2014. All BCBS members are subject to a new peer review process, the Regulatory Consistency Assessment Programme (RCAP) (BCBS, 2012b). Established in 2011, the RCAP combines remote and on-site review to assess the completeness and consistency of Basel III implementation. The peer review team first compiles a list of deviations from the global standard and then uses data on a sample of domestic banks to assess whether these deviations are material.

The consistency assessment of CRR/CRD IV found that material divergences with Basel III exist in 6 out of 20 components in three main areas. First, the European law lacks stringency regarding the definition of capital and minimum capital requirements for banks. Second, banks have more leeway in Europe than elsewhere in calculating credit valuation adjustments for counterparty risk. Third, several risk weights as implemented by the EU are too lax for Basel III, including permanent exemptions for some credit exposures in the internal ratings-based approach, certain mortgage loans, and loans to small and medium enterprises (SME) (BCBS, 2014g).

The European Union is the only Basel Committee member jurisdiction that has failed the global regulatory consistency test. What explains this instance of mock compliance in one of the jurisdictions that has suffered most from imprudent banking behavior in recent years?

Scholars of financial regulatory politics have analyzed mock compliance in several East Asian cases. Walter (2008) argues that mock compliance is the result of international pressures to comply with global standards and concurrent strong domestic opposition to regulatory stringency, a definition that fits the European case. However, analysts of East Asian financial systems have identified both the executive branch and regulatory agencies as key players in regulatory forbearance but not parliamentarians. This is not surprising given the marginal relevance of legislators for financial regulatory issues in most countries. European mock compliance becomes understandable when looking at how regulatory agencies and the European Parliament differ in the range and relative power of special interest groups they interact with.

Legislative involvement is meant to provide a costly and credible signal of the viability of a global regulatory standard. Newman and Bach (2014) argue that European legislative involvement in particular can serve as a "hardening agent" for soft law, thus catalyzing the diffusion of global standards. Similarly, Martin (2000) asserts that legislatures can bolster global cooperation by giving greater credibility to a jurisdiction's global commitments. European mock compliance with Basel III appears to be the inverse of this mechanism: By watering down the global standard in the process of domestic implementation, European legislators have undermined the credibility of European commitments to global financial stability and reduced the incentives of other jurisdictions to adopt or strictly enforce the new global banking standard.

The greater permeability of parliamentarians to special interest groups might explain why the European Union became a "weakening agent" of Basel III. Young (2014, 2016) shows that global banking lobby organizations had limited success in shaping the negotiations at the Basel Committee. European financial interests however were able to win back concessions in the local implementation of Basel III (Quaglia, 2019). This phenomenon can be distinguished from transnational regulatory capture (as discussed in the next section) in that what Goldbach (2015) terms "national voice coalitions" of politicians and smaller domestic financial lobby groups played a decisive role in shaping European prudential banking rules. A European parliamentarian comments,

> The unhealthy relationships between governments and banks of different shapes and forms across the continent sets the tone. . . . The rationale is "ok maybe they're bastards, but they're our bastards." They're our national champions so whatever they do we support.
>
> *(EU Legislator 1, personal communication, November 26, 2017)*

A look at the list of European inconsistencies with Basel III lends support to this observation. The laxer definition of capital in CRR/CRD IV benefits two kinds of banks, cooperatives and mutuals on the one hand, and banks with wholly owned insurance subsidiaries on the other. The latter is a unique feature of the largest French banks, whereas community banks with a cooperatives or mutually owned corporate structure exist in Germany, France, Spain, and several other European countries. A European regulator notes,

> What the negotiators for CRD IV did was probably predominantly try to protect the existing model of the respective national market. So if you really

> want to know who's screwed up CRD IV, the best thing is to go to the Deutsche Sparkassenverein [the German savings bank lobby] and ask them if they are content with what they manage to achieve in the course of the negotiations.
>
> *(EU Regulator 3, personal communication, October 21, 2014)*

Interestingly, while the Basel peer review identified capital definitions for these community banks as deviant from the global standard, they were not deemed material and thus not relevant for the RCAP verdict (BCBS, 2014g).

In contrast, noncompliance with Basel III was material for the capital definition of large French banks with insurance subsidiaries, and large banks across Europe whose trading books are not required to incorporate sufficiently prudent credit valuation adjustments for counterparty risk. These two "victories" for large financial conglomerates are not simply attributable to parliamentary involvement, though. Permanent country representatives at the Council also played an important role in incorporating industry demands in the European law (K. Young, 2016). Quaglia (2019) provides a detailed and insightful account of how both Parliamentarians and Council members were instrumental in incorporating industry demands into CRD IV that made European rules inconsistent with Basel III.

Unlike Council representatives, European Parliamentarians are depicted by some observers as champions of wider societal interests. Greenwood and Roederer-Rynning (2015) argue that "MEPs were able to achieve policy gains that both undercut strong interests in the financial industry and, on some points, overrode the EC's longstanding preference . . . for a strict harmonization of the Basel standards" (p. 331). But an analysis of MEP involvement in the European trilogue does not lend much support to this argument. Finance Watch, Europe's foremost civil society representative in financial matters, published a list of demands for CRR/CRD IV in February 2012, including higher capital requirements and a mandatory leverage ratio (Finance Watch, 2012). Some MEPs did indeed take up some of the demands, but the large majority of these items disappeared during the negotiations for a unified parliamentary position paper. A civil society representative recalls that at the end of the European trilogue, "every single idea we had pushed for had disappeared from the text" (EU Civil Society Representative 2, personal communication, 2017).

The third area of divergence between Basel III and the European law also offers insight into the process of parliamentary involvement. MEPs advocated for a reduction in risk weights in bank loans to small and medium enterprises (SME) in order to improve financial access for this class of companies. This notion of selective regulatory laxity was not endorsed by Finance Watch but a parliamentarian with a strong procedural position in the trilogue. A European legislator recalls,

> The rapporteur Bullmann presides the SME group in the European Parliament, so he was adamant that he wants this done and we had some other priorities so we agreed with the SME factor but in order to get something else.
>
> *(EU Legislator 1, personal communication, November 26, 2017)*

The so-called SME support factor (SF) allows banks to apply the same risk weight to SME loans as they did under Basel II. While no proposal of greater prudential stringency in risk weights and capital requirements for banks survived parliamentary negotiations, this carve-out did. The Basel peer review found that the SF sets loan risk weights are about 15% below Basel III, representing a material deviation from the global standard. The same legislator states, "There I tend to side with the Basel Committee: Prudential regulation is about risk management and risk management should not be tweaked this or that way for political purposes" (EU Legislator 1, personal communication, November 26, 2017). Two years after the support factor came into effect, the European Banking Authority conducted a study on its effectiveness using bank data and a survey among European SMEs. The report concludes that "there is no evidence that the SME SF has provided additional stimulus for lending to SMEs compared the large corporates" (EBA, 2016, p. 10).

In sum, the involvement of European parliamentarians played a key role in making the European Union the only jurisdiction whose prudential banking rules do not live up to Basel III standards. Some MEPs did take up civil society calls for more stringent regulation, but rather than adopting a principled position as some observers assert, they traded regulatory rigor for industry benefits and non-prudential features such as a bonus cap for bankers. What emerged at the end of legislative involvement in domestic standard implementation were carve-outs for large financial firms and special provisions for SMEs that are both imprudent and ineffective in stimulating the real economy. European legislators were not receptive to the results of the Basel peer review, stating that

> a large majority of Members of the European Parliament cannot accept that the Basel Committee puts into question the tools to finance the economy (especially SMEs and corporate). . . . The opinion of a body that is working without legitimacy and without any transparency cannot modify the decisions taken democratically by the European institutions.
>
> *(ECON committee of the European Parliament, 2014)*

To conclude, the trajectory of prudential banking reform supports the government network hypothesis. Global standards were successfully negotiated in a government network that relies extensively on soft law instruments. Domestic implementation avoided parliamentary interference to a large extent in almost all member jurisdictions. The exception is the European Union, where the partial unraveling and renegotiation of Basel III in the European Parliament, the council, and the commission resulted in mock compliance. But even though not all legislators are satisfied with the substantive outcome of domestic implementation, they defend parliamentary involvement on procedural grounds. An MEP sums up his position as follows:

> Sometimes I have a feeling that these people at Basel or the OECD is always reacting angrily when national or regional legislatures are doing more than

> what they recommend. It's not for them to decide. . . . I do resent the fact that the majority of elected people tend to do the will of big systemic banks, because that is the case in the end. But then again it's for the people to choose their representatives. That's the only way to fix it.
>
> *(EU Legislator 1, personal communication, November 26, 2017)*

While the European failure to implement Basel III in a consistent manner might best be explained by the government network approach, the successful diffusion of the global standard elsewhere is congruent with the predictions of several other competing explanations.

Alternative Explanations

The rapid and coherent implementation of Basel III among almost all Basel Committee members is expected from the vantage point of the great power theories of regulatory politics. In line with Simmons' (2001b) theory of regulatory hegemony, prudential banking regulation is an area where market incentives for emulation operate. In a market characterized by fundamental information asymmetries, investors find it difficult to obtain a full assessment of a bank's risk exposure. Meeting and even exceeding capital requirements as mandated by the BCBS can serve as a signal of financial soundness to markets. Not all analysts agree on this conjecture however. Hardy (2012) looks at the hasty pace at which US banks repaid government-sponsored assistance under the TARP program. He argues that under-capitalization signals to the market that a bank has little risk exposure and thus no need to build up capital buffers. The eagerness to pay back TARP assistance however may reflect bank management's intention to steer free of government dependency as fast as possible in order to obtain a better negotiation position in post-crisis regulatory debates. Indeed, major banks have made clear attempts to reach and exceed Basel III capital requirements much before the 2019 implementation deadline.

Hegemony theories of both the Simmons and the Drezner (2007) variety focus on the degree of divergence in the interests between the great powers and the rest of the world. When the dominant regulatory innovators are concerned that other countries will not adhere to their new global standards and that such nonadherence will entail negative externalities, they will work through club-like international institutions to ensure consistent implementation and compliance. In line with this prediction, the G20 authorized the Basel Committee to overhaul the prudential banking regulatory system. BCBS membership was extended in 2009 to include all G20 members, but it remains a club-like governance body with only 27 member jurisdictions. Assessments of the degree of interest divergence between the great powers and the rest vary. On the one hand, the FSB has published a series of reports voicing concern that stricter capital requirements curb credit availability in emerging market economies (FSB, 2012c, 2013e, 2014c). On the other hand, developing countries are not lagging behind in Basel III implementation, and 89 countries that are not Basel members have declared their willingness to adhere to the new standards (FSI, 2014). In sum, G20-mandated reform of prudential banking standards has evolved in ways that are congruent with the expectations of great power theories of global financial governance. At the same time, they lack inferential leverage to explain why one of the core jurisdictions would engage in mock compliance.

Kapstein's (1989) analysis of the 1988 Basel Accord provides the first theoretical explanation of global financial regulatory cooperation that highlights the work of **transnational bureaucrats** and their embeddedness in epistemic communities. The author argues that Basel I is the product of the successful development of consensual knowledge regarding risk in the banking system and Anglo-American leadership. It is the same community of financial economists and banking regulators that developed the new Basel III standards. Because this transnational community of experts had more than two decades to develop and refine its consensus regarding stability in the international banking systems and the optimal regulatory tools to achieve it, the epistemic community approach expects reform success in prudential banking regulation (Newman & Posner, 2016).

These expectations rely on the important assumption that consensual knowledge develops gradually over time. Regulatory consensus is built on a large number of academic studies regarding market operations, policy modeling, and impact assessments. In new areas of regulation global cooperation is unlikely until a corresponding body of knowledge is developed to facilitate consensus in the regulatory community. This approach thus produces a more specific hypothesis: Regulatory reform is successful where existing regulatory tools are further refined, and reform progress lags behind where new tools and measures have to be developed.

From the transnational bureaucracy perspective, it is thus not surprising that the Basel Committee rapidly reached consensus on higher capital requirements as a portion of a bank's risk-weighted assets. Changes in risk weights for certain asset classes can also be understood as the result of gradual change and adaptation, along with the plethora of revisions to existing Basel rules agreed on in 2017. However, this approach struggles to explain why reform was fast and successful even though there are substantive discontinuities between Basel II and Basel III. The new global standard does not only contain novel regulatory tools, it also engenders a fundamental shift from a micro- to a macroprudential perspective on global banking as the following paragraphs will show.

Basel I and II approach the banking system from a microprudential perspective. Hanson et al. (2011) explain the shortcomings of this approach in simple terms:

> When a microprudentially oriented regulator pushes a troubled bank to restore its capital ratio, the regulator does not care whether the bank adjusts via the numerator or via the denominator – that is, by raising new capital or by shrinking assets.
>
> *(p. 5)*

From a macroprudential perspective however, concurrent asset shrinkage of several financial institutions may lead to a credit crunch as banks engage in early termination of loan contracts and cease to offer new ones. Furthermore, fire sales of assets reinforce this credit crunch because other financial intermediaries may prefer to spend available capital on purchasing these cheap but distressed securities with high-risk-adjusted rates of return rather than extending (less profitable) loans on their own. This cycle of fire sales and liquidity shortages was the main reason why the fall of Lehman Brothers in September 2008 had such wide repercussions (FCIC, 2011).

The global financial crisis thus taught regulators that resilience to shocks cannot be successfully achieved for each bank in isolation but rather at the systemic level. As a consequence, the Basel Committee introduced several systemic safeguards, including a capital conservation buffer, a countercyclical buffer, and two new liquidity requirements. It also strengthens capital requirements for counterparty credit exposures arising from derivatives, repo, and securities financing transactions. The additional surcharge to large, interconnected global banks (so-called global systemically important banks, or G-SIB) is another regulatory innovation that will be discussed in Chapter 5 (BCBS, 2011a).

The capital conservation buffer allows banks to refrain from hasty asset sales under duress but forces the institution to curb bonus and dividend payments in order to prevent further capital reduction. The higher capital requirements for counterparty credit exposures in turn deals with a potential downward spiral in capital markets that regulators call "wrong-way risk." Since the amount of regulatory capital that banks have to put aside depends on the credit rating of a counterparty, capital requirements would increase in times of crisis when its credit quality deteriorates. Basel III therefore calculates capital requirements for exposures to counterparties as if under duress (BCBS, 2009).

Basel Committee members had not developed anything like consensual knowledge regarding liquidity requirements prior to the crisis, and experience with this kind of regulatory tool was confined to one member jurisdiction, the United Kingdom. A UK regulator recalls the onerous process of deliberation inside the epistemic community of banking regulators:

> The experience I've had of fairly simple, high-level liquidity rules and how when you try to apply them at the national level, every country just has this exception that doesn't quite fit the rule and wants special treatment and how much tension there is between the ways different countries regulate their system and how they're integrated into the political system. You only have to look at the UK and France who are 20 miles from each other and then our whole theology and fundamental approach to how we regulate our banks is so different. We come into conflict on every single issue because we just have different views.
>
> *(UK Regulator 1, personal communication, 2014)*

The preceding measures increase the capacity of financial institutions to absorb external shocks without producing knock-on systemic effects such as fire sales and credit freezes. But along with measures that seek to improve the alignment of managerial incentives with those of depositors and investors and new liquidity requirements, they merely address specific market imperfections (Rajan, 2006; Stanton, 2012). According to former FSA Chairman Adair Turner (2012), these measures represent the perspective of a "micro-structuralist school" that assumes that global financial markets operate in an efficient and stable manner when certain identifiable glitches in the system are repaired by regulatory action. In contrast, the "macro-Minsky" school proposes a more radical approach to financial regulation. It assumes that financial markets are inherently prone to boom-bust cycles with negative spillovers for the real economy.

The countercyclical buffer, a new addition to the Basel Agreement, reflects the concerns of the latter school. The buffer is built on the insight that financial crises throughout the world in modern times tend to be preceded by large credit expansion (Reinhart & Rogoff, 2009). Basel III provides the regulators with the power to raise the capital requirement up to an additional 2.5% in order to curb credit expansion by banks during a boom phase. Because credit cycles vary among countries, prudential regulators in each jurisdiction have the authority to use the countercyclical buffer at discretion. It is important to note that unlike other regulatory tools, this measure does not hinge on any specific market imperfection but rather on the recognition that financial markets in general exhibit certain undesired tendencies.

In sum, some elements of the Basel III package represent gradual developments from a regulatory consensus that developed in the Basel Committee over the last two decades. Cooley and Walter (2011) for example regard the new rules merely as a modification of pre-crisis laissez-faire policies. Others contend that even the shift to a macroprudential perspective does not represent a fundamental departure from the pro-market bias of financial regulation (Bair, 2012; Engelen et al., 2011). In a similar vein, Helleiner (2014a) states,

> The containment of systemic risk became the rallying call for policymakers and regulators rather than values that might have led to stronger controls on markets, such as distributive concerns relating to wealth and power of the financial sector vis-à-vis public authorities and other societal interests.
>
> *(p. 128)*

On the other hand, scholars argue that the innovative features of Basel III represent nothing short of a Polanyian shift in thinking about financial regulation. Baker (2013b, 2013a) shows how until 2008, the global consensus among regulators was firmly based on the efficient market hypothesis. At the height of the global financial crisis however, the few economists and policymakers that espoused a view of financial markets as prone to network externalities, pro-cyclicality, herding phenomena, and other market failures gained protagonism. They acted as norm entrepreneurs in promoting a macro-Minskian diagnosis on the causes of the crisis and corresponding policy advice, changing the nature of the debate on prudential regulation in a rather short six-month period. Baker (2013a) asserts, "Consequently, the macroprudential ideational shift had the characteristics of 'an insider's coup d'état,' instigated by existing technocratic elites" (p. 424). However, while the ideational change was revolutionary, the process of devising and applying policy measures in line with a macroprudential approach is inherently slow and incremental, subject to extensive experimentation phases and political resistance by existing veto players.

With the benefit of hindsight, more scholars start to appreciate the discontinuities in financial regulation that are incorporated in Basel III as an instance of policy layering (Mahoney & Thelen, 2010). Tsingou (2010) for example explains the "milimetric" change in regulatory reform in the following words: "The coherence has given way to a more adversarial debate but much of the agenda continues to be formulated by the same policy community of experts and focuses on tweaking rather than reforming the system" (p. 22). Three years later, the author revisits regulatory reform and argues that incremental changes do not preclude radical transformations. Moschella and Tsingou (2013) reject the argument that reform can only be the product of a large exogenous shock and argue that "in finance . . . paradigm-change is instead associated with incremental, endogenously driven dynamics" (p. 4). In other words, minor "tweaks" in a given regulatory repertoire might not only be no obstacle to radical reform, they may indeed be the modus operandi of revolutionary change in the world of financial regulation.

By end-2020, both the gradualist and the "revolutionary" elements of the Basel III package exhibit considerable reform progress. The evolution of post-crisis prudential banking reform thus lends support to an approach that highlights the power of transnational bureaucracies in global financial governance. At the same time, it challenges the hypothesis that regulatory cooperation is unlikely in new areas of regulation where consensual knowledge has not been developed yet. Moreover, mock compliance in a jurisdiction that has been at the heart of the global banking regulator's network for years is difficult to explain from the transnational bureaucracy perspective.

Oatley and Nabors (1998) challenge the idea that global financial regulation arises from the successful operations of epistemic communities, arguing that **redistributive concerns** play a major role. They squarely take on Kapstein's account of the Basel Accord and show that rather than consensual knowledge, the global agreement was driven by domestic tension in the United States. In the wake of the Latin American debt crisis, many American banks faced serious liquidity and solvency problems that threatened to have systemic repercussions. Investors and depositors thus called for a more stringent regulatory framework that safeguards the stability of the US banking system. However, any regulatory approach entails costs for the private sector, and any regulation that only applies to domestic corporations affects their competitiveness in the international marketplace. By developing the Basel Accord and threatening to exclude foreign banks from doing business in the financial centers unless they adhered to it, the Anglo-American coalition behind

Basel I was able to increase financial stability while shifting adjustment costs to competitors in foreign jurisdictions (D. A. Singer, 2004, 2007).

The redistributive theory of global financial regulation is successful at highlighting the link between certain constellations in the domestic political economy with outcomes in the international realm. It combines the domestic political and interstate approach to regulation in rather parsimonious ways that remain productive for hypothesis generation and testing. However, several shortcomings merit attention. First, the theory described in the previous section assumes that once international standards are in place, domestic tensions regarding financial regulation are resolved. In particular, the private sector in the dominant center should be appeased by the net income transfer from foreign competitors that results from global regulation. Yet the empirical evolution of regulatory politics calls this prediction into question. Second, the theory models a tightening of regulatory standards, while the reverse tendency is not contemplated. This might be one of the reasons why this approach has been of little help in explaining agreements that bring about a relaxation of regulatory standards. Third, banks are assumed to employ lobby power only domestically in order to gain advantage vis-à-vis their foreign competitors. However, financial institutions today cooperate across borders, dedicating considerable resources to transnational lobby organizations.

The theory of redistributive cooperation is nevertheless very useful in that it highlights the importance of difference in adjustment costs to new global standards. Furthermore, it portrays Basel Committee members not as footloose members of a transnational community of experts but rather as representatives of their respective countries (Thiemann, 2014). Much of the current IPE literature has indeed examined Basel III as a process of negotiation among nation-states. A group of economists at the Brookings Institution comments,

> Negotiations came up against the familiar tension between the role of banking supervisors as guardians of financial stability and their role as champions of domestic banking sector interests. In the latter role, supervisors take on the role akin to trade negotiators, their objective to secure the 'best deal' for domestic interests.
>
> *(Brunnermeier et al., 2012, p. 24)*

In their analysis, many scholars highlight the fact that the final agreement sets lower standards for prudential banking regulation than the initial draft documents. In their assessment, Basel Committee members started with high ambitions but managed to only find a low common denominator in the end. Unlike Basel II, this result is attributed to individual jurisdictions, not transnational regulatory capture (Hall & Soskice, 2001; E. Jones & Knaack, 2019; Pagliari, 2013a; Quaglia, 2012; Quaglia & Spendzharova, 2017). According to journalistic and academic accounts, an Anglo-American coalition pushed for tougher prudential standards against Continental European and, to a lesser extent, Japanese resistance (Barker & Masters, 2012a; T. Braithwaite, 2010; Guerrera & Pimlott, 2010; Lall, 2012; Quaglia,

2014a, 2014b). Admati and Hellwig (2013, p. 193) bluntly states, "The watering down of regulatory reform was largely due to the efforts of France, Germany, and Japan."

This alignment of jurisdictions is reminiscent of the negotiations that led to the first Basel agreement in 1988. Oatley and Winecoff (2012) for example see a return of the dynamics of redistributive cooperation. The comparison is problematic, however.

Without a doubt there are significant historical parallels to the first Basel Accord. The main stakeholders of the new Basel Agreement, just like its predecessors, are the major advanced countries. Even though China, India, and other emerging market economies have evolved into major powers in the realm of trade, their protagonism in global finance has mostly focused on governance reform of the international financial institutions (Wade, 2011). In contrast, emerging markets took the backstage in the negotiations on financial regulatory reform, again (J. Hawkins & Turner, 2001; Knaack, 2017; Mügge, 2014; Persaud, 2010; Reddy, 2012; Walter, 2016; E. Jones & Knaack, 2019).

However, unlike in the 1980s, US banks have not lost market share to European or Asian competitors in recent years (A. D. Singer, 2010). Even though foreign branches and foreign-owned subsidiaries chartered in the United States increased their relative presence in the subprime bubble years of 2004–2007, they performed even worse than domestic competitors during the crisis. Consequently, the market share of foreign banks in the US dropped since mid-2007, that is, three years before the finalization of Basel III (Goulding & Nolle, 2012).

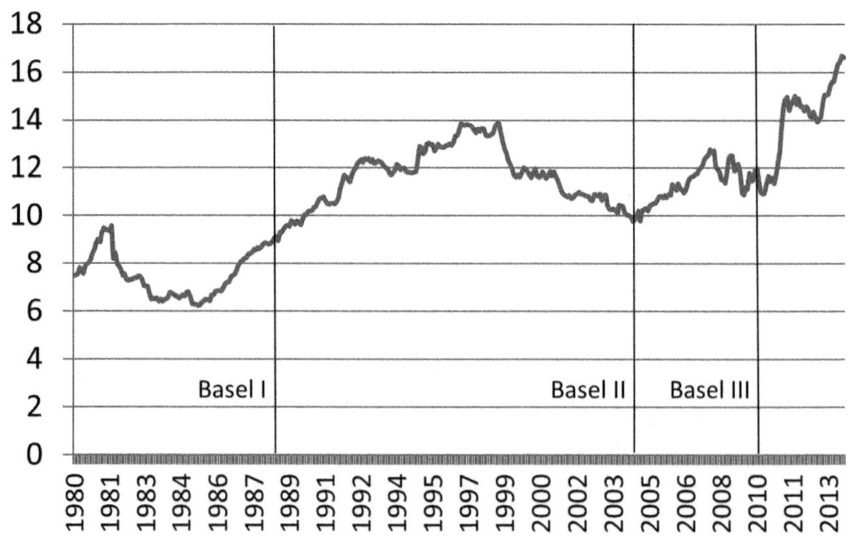

FIGURE 3.3 Share of Foreign-Related Institutions in US Banking Market, Percentage of Total Assets

Source: Federal Reserve of New York

In sum, Basel III can be understood to balance the competing interests of financial stability and international competitiveness much like its predecessors. Adjustment costs to the new standard were unevenly distributed across jurisdictions, and regulators were aware of it. Redistributive concerns clearly played an important role in Basel III negotiations. But the push by Anglo-American regulators for stricter regulatory standards cannot be linked to a loss of competitiveness by banks headquartered in the US and the UK. Neither did these two jurisdictions threaten market exclusion in order to obtain adherence to Basel III.

In the absence of threats of market exclusion, significant differences in adjustment costs can be expected to undermine global cooperation. But while Basel Committee members had access to quantitative data on adjustment costs and were thus acutely aware of it, they still reached consensus on a global standard in record time and proceeded with implementation in a timely manner. The redistributive concern approach to global financial governance thus cannot fully account for the success of this item on the G20 reform agenda.

The **regulatory capture** approach has a strong intellectual history in analyzing the work of the Basel Committee. As this section will show, scholarly work on Basel II emphasized the mechanisms of capture that resulted in the gradual weakening of regulatory standards. Basel III is portrayed by this camp as another instance of capture because the new capital requirements are not stringent enough and because they carry over important elements of the discredited old standard. Furthermore, the increased complexity of the new Basel agreement is seen to reduce public scrutiny and open additional channels of influence by special interest groups. This section reviews both of these arguments, taking into account previous work on regulatory capture of Basel II.

Five years after the implementation of the original Basel Accord, the BCBS presented a proposal for extending regulation to cover market risks. The banking industry, led by the Working Group on Capital Adequacy of the Institute of International Finance (IIF), criticized the proposal from the beginning and argued that the BCBS should provide incentives for firms to adopt more sophisticated risk management systems. It promoted the use of banks' internal risk models to compute risk weights and corresponding capital adequacy levels (Barth et al., 2012; Bayoumi, 2017; BCBS, 2004; Dewatripont et al., 2010; Howarth & Quaglia, 2016; Underhill & Zhang, 2008).

In 1996, the Basel Committee agreed on an amendment to the Capital Accord to Incorporate Market Risks that lets banks choose between a standardized approach and an advanced approach that relies on the internal risk model of the regulated institution (BCBS, 1996). This regulatory design became a centerpiece of Basel II, and notably so, one that has carried on to Basel III (Hellwig, 2010). As Rochet (2010) points out:

> To an outside observer the succession of reforms that created Basel II out of Basel I look rather like a series of pragmatic contingent adjustments in which the committee sought to protect itself as far as possible from criticisms originating in the banking industry, finally ending up allowing the major

> international banks to determine for themselves the manner in which they would be supervised.
>
> *(p. 81)*

But the changes to the original Accord were not restricted to the risk weights of assets, that is, the denominator of the capital adequacy ratio. The numerator, that is, the measure of capital that banks have to provide to absorb losses on the asset side of the balance sheet, was watered down too. The original Basel Accord restricted Tier 1 capital to equity and retained earnings. As Herring (2011) states,

> However, over time, pressures from banks and creative investment bankers led to the acceptance of a number of hybrid instruments that appeared to be sufficiently like equity to placate the regulators and sufficiently like debt to convince the tax authorities that payments on such instruments could be counted as interest payments and deducted in computing taxable income.
>
> *(footnote 4)*

Thus, banks were able to reduce the common equity share of the capital requirement to a mere 2%. The drive towards greater flexibility on both sides of the capital adequacy ratio was clearly in line with industry preferences.

The banking lobby used a powerful combination of strategic information provision and exit threats to push for relaxed banking standards. A British regulator argues that prudential authorities actually aimed for tougher regulatory requirements even before the crisis, but their efforts were thwarted:

> It isn't the case that before 2007 we just always believed that light touch regulations it's the right way to go. There's a huge amount of political interference pushing the head, the top of FSA towards that. So there's a lot of

TABLE 3.1 Basel Capital Requirements

Requirements	*Basel I*	*Basel II*	*Basel III*	
			minimum	incl. capital conservation buffer
Common Equity Tier 1		2%	4.5%	7%
Tier 1	4%	4%	6%	8.5%
Total Capital	8%	8%	8%	10.5%
G-SIFI Surcharge				0–2.5%
Countercyclical Buffer				0–2.5%

Source: BCBS

> anecdotal evidence that whenever they tried to be strict on banks they were called off by politicians. . . . The line from them to politicians was "You don't want to kill us. You don't want us to go elsewhere."
>
> *(UK Regulator 1, personal communication, 2014)*

Not everybody regards Basel II as an exemplary case of regulatory capture, however. Young (2012) raises the bar of causal inference by stating that "it is spurious to simply assume that policy changes which benefit a group are made at the behest of that group" (p. 7, see also Carpenter, 2013). He shows that regulators at the US Fed, the Bank of England, and the BCBS produced somewhat critical reports on the validity of banks' internal risk modeling systems and that Basel II requirements are systematically above those suggested by the IIF. That the financial industry did not get everything it bargained for is barely a counterargument to regulatory capture, but Young's point about inference standards is well taken.

If regulators were not captured by private sector interests, what else could have motivated them to water down prudential standards during the 1990s and early 2000s? An alternative explanation can be found in Aizenman's (2009) Paradox of Under-Regulation. The author's theory is based on a fundamental asymmetry of information: The benefits of a crisis avoided by strict prudential regulation are unknown, whereas the costs of regulation are evident. The agents that set the optimal level of regulation update their expectations of crisis probability repeatedly, applying Bayesian inference. Thus, a prolonged period of success in avoiding a financial crisis actually generates complacency, eroding the demand for prudential regulation. This is arguably what happened during the so-called Great Moderation period of 1985–2005 (Engelen et al., 2011). Even though the late 1990s were shaken by a series of financial crises, they occurred in the periphery of the global financial system, allowing Western policymakers to attribute their occurrence to cronyism and sloppy implementation of the high-quality prudential standards that supposedly kept financial markets in developed countries safe.

The combination of constant industry pressure and growing complacency among the public and regulators in a period of calm can be regarded as a plausible explanation for increasingly lax regulation in the lead-up to the global financial crisis. In the transition from Basel I to Basel II, prudential standards were relaxed to a point that they were unable to prevent the fall of an individual institution, let alone the entire banking system. Just before its collapse, British bank Northern Rock featured a capital ratio that over-complied with Basel II standards by 146% (Friedman, 2011; Rochet, 2010).

Basel III has come under similar criticism by analysts who assert that the new standard represents gradual change rather than a significant departure from Basel II (Lall, 2012, 2014; Lockwood, 2015; Rixen, 2013). One of the reasons why Basel III has been depicted as an instrument of minuscule rather than dramatic change is that scholars perceived the new capital requirements as insufficiently high (Vickers, 2017). In one of the most critical assessments to date, Admati and Hellwig (2013) state,

> There is no legitimate reason for the proposed Basel III requirements to be so outrageously low. These requirements reflect the political impact that the banks have had on the policy debate and the flawed and misleading claims that are made in discussions about banking regulation – the bankers' new clothes.
>
> *(p. 180)*

The main claim that Admati and Hellwig set out to debunk is that equity financing is costly for banks. The authors argue that the expected return on equity decreases as the equity ratio increases. This is because downward risk is distributed among more shareholders, who consequently demand a lower risk premium. At the same time, a bank with a higher share of equity financing is likely to make more prudent decisions because shareholders as a whole have more "skin in the game," that is, they are more exposed to losses in the case of insolvency than bondholders and depositors (Admati et al., 2011). Admati and Hellwig (2013, p. 191) conclude that "increasing equity requirements from 3 percent to 25 percent of banks' total assets would involve only a reshuffling of financial claims in the economy to create a better and safer financial system. There would be no cost to society whatsoever."

The preceding arguments are met with criticism by fellow economists (Cline, 2017). Charles Calomiris (2013, p. 14) writes, "In their well-intentioned zeal to make the case for how beneficial, simple, and costless it would be to mandate dramatic increases in bank equity ratios, they overstate the benefits and understate the costs associated with their proposed reforms." Calomiris cites several reasons why the costs that banks are facing are usually greater and only indirectly related to the returns expected and received by investors. Admati and Hellwig's work acknowledges two of these reasons. First, the current tax system subsidizes debt, and much of the literature on the optimal capital structure of a firm takes these "skewed incentives" for granted. Second, equity issuance occurs in a market that is subject to a fundamental information asymmetry between management and (potential) shareholders. Investors may perceive a firm's decision to issue equity as a signal that management has adverse private information about the state of the company, which leads it to believe that the market is overvaluing the stock of the company at a given point (Myers & Majluf, 1984; Myerson, 2013). One way of overcoming this adverse selection effect is for public authorities to make equity issuance an obligation. This is what occurred in May 2009 when the Fed published nominal requirements of capital that had to be raised by banks that failed its Supervisory Capital Assessment Program. Hanson et al. (2011, p. 10) reviewed the process and concluded, "Here is a case where a strong regulatory hand appears to have had highly beneficial effects. Indeed, by being tough and giving banks no choice, regulators probably made it easier for banks to do the capital raising."

A central stone of contention is the Modigliani-Miller theorem (Modigliani & Miller, 1958). It states that the cost of capital is independent of a firm's capital structure. A larger equity base reduces cash flow per share, but at the same time, it reduces the volatility of earnings and the likelihood of bankruptcy. As a consequence, investors require a lower risk premium. However, the theorem is based on two central assumptions: exogenous total cash flow (no taxes, no bankruptcy cost, perfect contracts) and perfect markets (Titman, 2002). The case for the cost neutrality of a high equity ratio rests on the argument that these assumptions hold in reality.

The private sector (unsurprisingly) also disagrees with Admati and Hellwig's argument. A report by the most important bank lobby organization (Institute of International Finance, 2011, p. 45) states, "Most Industry practitioners question the validity and applicability of the M-M theorem. This may reflect a huge collective failing of insight and understanding by the Industry, but it seems more likely to reflect the outcome of experience." Years before the outbreak of the global financial crisis, Titman (2002) offered his intuition on why the relative cost of debt versus equity financing differs. The author notes that capital markets are not fully integrated. Investors are constrained by institutions (pension funds have restrictions regarding the equity share of their portfolio, for example) and lack of experience. As a consequence of this market segmentation, risk is priced differently in bond and equity markets.

This structural argument is compounded by concerns over capital market cycles. In this regard, Calomiris coincides with some of the concerns expressed by the banking lobby (Protard, 2010). He points out that equity markets fluctuate and that during periods of depressed equity prices, high funding costs force banks to raise the price of lending or reduce assets. Furthermore, bankers argue that the cost of equity financing is high due to (1) investor perception of risk in the banking sector as a whole, (2) limited near-term supply of capital, and (3) perceived "regulatory risk," that is, uncertainty about future regulation (Calomiris, 2013).

The empirical picture confirms that these considerations are not irrelevant. A variety of studies have estimated the increased financing costs that come with Basel III capital requirements and how banks would pass on them on to customers. The transmission channel of macroeconomic relevance is that increased lending rates would raise the price and decrease the availability of bank credit, with negative repercussions for investment, growth, and employment.

The bank lobby presented the study with the most dramatic result: According to its predictions, banks will raise loan rates by 364 basis points (bp) on average, thus reducing economic expansion by 0.7% per year and employment by 7.5 million people by 2015 (IIF, 2011).

The large majority of studies undertaken by academics estimates a much lower, albeit nontrivial impact on lending rates, credit, and growth (Allen et al., 2012; BIS, 2013; Cline, 2017; Elliott, 2009; Kashyap et al., 2010). In an IMF review of the field, Oliveira and Elliott (2012, p. 6) state, "The Institute of International Finance is an association representing over 400 financial institutions across the world. Its study, although admirably comprehensive and detailed, shows a far larger cost to financial reform measures than seems plausible." The estimates of an impact study undertaken by the Basel Committee predict a 66bp increase in lending rates and a slowdown of economic growth by merely 0.08%. According to the study, the economic benefits of reducing the likelihood of another global financial crisis significantly outweigh these costs (BCBS, 2010a).

Facing the apocalyptic projections of the banking lobby and growth concerns among politicians, regulators suggested an extension of the phase-in period of Basel III. In a letter to G20 leaders in 2010, then FSB chair Mario Draghi (2010) states, "We should provide transition arrangements that enable movement to robust new standards without putting the recovery at risk, rather than allow concerns over the transition to weaken the standards" (p. 2). Subsequently, full implementation of Basel III was extended to 2019, and financial lobby organizations welcomed the adjustments (Schneider, 2010b).

Four years after the start of Basel III implementation, an empirical study finds that banks increased their capital ratios mainly through the accumulation of retained earnings rather than equity issuance. Lending rates remained stable or even decreased, and a tightening of qualitative lending standards was only observed in the eurozone in the wake of the Greek sovereign debt crisis. According to the authors, the negative credit growth of the early years of Basel III implementation thus cannot be attributed to a shortage in loan supply but rather to lackluster demand, especially in the crisis-stricken European Union (Cohen & Scatigna, 2014).

In sum, the discussion over the optimal level of capital requirements in Basel III reveals a wide spectrum of opinions. It helps clarify the assumptions of traditional theories of corporate financing and the conditions under which they hold. Empirical research to date has shed further light on the real adjustment costs to banks, undermining the claims of the bank lobby that Basel III imposes unbearable costs on the banking system.

Another take on Basel III from a regulatory capture perspective focuses on the increasing degree of complexity of prudential standards. What Haldane (2012a) calls the "Tower of Basel" has grown from 30 pages (Basel I) to 300 (Basel II) and now to over 600 pages (Basel III). Undoubtedly, the regulatory design of the original Basel Accord was rather crude, and subsequent upgrades have improved the alignment of risk exposures and capital requirements.

But the finer granularity in prudential regulation is tied to greater complexity and thus lower transparency in two crucial relationships. First is the one between regulators and the regulated (S. Johnson & Kwak, 2010). Tsingou (2010) argues, "It has been amply documented that as finance became more complex, public officials found it more difficult to keep up and compensation structures contributed to a shortage of competency in the official sector" (p. 32). There is no evidence that this dynamic has changed in the wake of the crisis. In fact, the suspicion that complexity helps the financial sector escape supervisory scrutiny lead regulators to call for the introduction of simpler, more transparent regulatory tools, such as the leverage ratio (Haldane, 2012a; Hoenig, 2013).

Second, complexity contributes to slack between principal and agent. Detailed information about the operations of a given sector is a prerequisite for effective regulation, but obtaining this information is costly. Legislators endow specialized agencies with the responsibility of supervision because they lack the time, resources, and expertise required for this task. However, the information asymmetry between the agency and the principal provides the former with leeway to pursue its own agenda (Laffont & Tirole, 1991). Increasing complexity compounds this problem of information asymmetry, reducing the principal's power to subject the agency to scrutiny. For example, Fed Governor Daniel Tarullo (2008) expresses his concern that rather than increasing risk sensitivity, the complexity of Basel II might just make the regulatory process more impenetrable for outsiders. In a similar vein, Rochet (2010) reviews the internal ratings-based approach of Basel II and concludes, "The above regulatory formula is far too complex to permit anyone external to the relationship between bank and supervisor to judge whether the supervisor has done its work properly" (p. 84). Thus, regulatory complexity raises concerns of an erosion of democratic accountability. Major (2012) goes one step further to claim that Basel represents the deliberate technocratic obfuscation and insularity from democratic political pressure that is a hallmark of neoliberal depoliticized re-regulation (see also Dorn, 2012).

In sum, criticism of Basel III from a regulatory capture perspective has focused on two arguments, the lack of departure from lax Basel II standards and the increase in complexity. The debate between the financial sector and regulators regarding adjustment costs and the repercussion of new requirements for credit, growth, and employment shows that private lobby organizations made efforts to water down the global standard. This book however focuses on the gap between G20 commitments and their implementation; it does not assess the difference between the final Basel standard and a hypothetical tougher one. Once the final Basel standards with a longer phase-in period were published, the industry did not seek to undermine implementation across all major jurisdictions. But as this chapter shows, it succeeded in derailing the consistent implementation of Basel III in the one jurisdiction where Parliament played a key role, that is, the EU. In this respect, the regulatory capture hypothesis finds conditional support.

Because banks were at the center of the financial turmoil, it is not surprising that prudential banking regulation received much public attention in the wake of the crisis. Social movement organizations and politicians in G20 countries and beyond called for stricter regulatory standards to reign in reckless bank behavior. From a **politicization perspective**, we can thus expect transnational regulatory networks such as the Basel Committee to be sidelined by politicians who respond to public pressures with unilateral initiatives.

Policymakers in some jurisdictions have indeed imposed requirements on banks that exceed the globally agreed standard without consulting their peers abroad. It is important to note however that all such instances of "super-equivalence" insert themselves into the Basel III framework. Basel standards are designed to be minimum requirements, and all agreements in the history of the Basel Committee have provided regulators with leeway to set higher standards in their jurisdiction.

The only case where overcompliance with Basel III can be regarded as a unilateral measure that undermines the global standard is the United States. The Federal Reserve Board in its new role as banking supervisor obliges large foreign banking organizations to establish intermediate holding companies in the US and subjects these to super-equivalent capital and leverage requirements. The so-called FBO rule was debated in end-2012, proposed in 2013 and finalized in February 2014 (Comizio, 2013; Federal Reserve Board, 2012, 2014; "US Banks Must Boost Capital under Leverage Rule," 2014). And even though the FBO rule can be understood as one among several unilateral structural measures that undermine efforts of globally harmonized bank resolution (as discussed in Chapter 5), it subjects banks to prudential rules that are fully compatible with the Basel III framework. Responding to complaints by foreign banks, the Basel Committee itself declared its support for the US initiative (International Regulator 5, personal communication, December 18, 2014).

In sum, widespread politicization of banking regulation in the wake of the crisis did not undermine the efforts of regulators to develop a global standard. Politicians in member jurisdictions avoided unilateral measures that would have undermined Basel III, waiting instead for the Basel Committee to find a regulatory consensus and implementing it in a consistent way.

In conclusion, reform progress in the area of prudential banking regulation is congruent with the expectations of four of the six theoretical approaches to global financial governance discussed here. Both the politicization and the redistributive concerns approaches highlight the importance of adjustment costs and inter-jurisdictional differences in the optimal degree of regulatory stringency. Even though both struggle to explain the success of Basel III, they provide an interesting and useful perspective on global regulatory negotiations. Great power theories correctly predict the protagonism of the leading financial centers and their strategic use of club standards to promote consistent implementation, as does the transnational bureaucracy perspective. Regulatory capture can account for failed implementation in the European Union but is challenged by the consistent adoption of Basel III standards elsewhere. The government network approach is both able to explain the fast and consistent implementation of transnationally developed standards in jurisdictions that circumvented domestic legislative bodies and their failure to do so in the European Union. It relies on regulatory capture theories to make sense of the EU debacle, however. The government network perspective conceives of European mock compliance as one way in which parliamentary involvement can obstruct global financial regulatory reform. Shortcomings in other areas of the G20 global reform agenda are difficult to attribute to regulatory capture, but they have legislative involvement as a common denominator. The relationship between parliamentary initiative and inconsistent standard development in the field of OTC derivatives will be explored in the following chapter.

4

OTC DERIVATIVES

Prior to the crisis, derivatives contracts that are traded not on exchanges but over the counter (OTC) received scant attention by policymakers and academics, let alone the general public. This changed drastically when the role of derivatives in the fall of investment banks such as Bear Stearns and Lehman Brothers became clear.

In 2009, G20 leaders pledged to bring OTC derivatives under regulatory control. Reform progress over the subsequent decade shows however that this was one of the most daunting tasks for the FSB. G20 members have missed all original deadlines in implementing their commitments, and even today OTC derivatives reform is far from complete. In the first half of the 2010s, the major jurisdictions devised domestic rules without consulting their counterparts abroad. Moreover, they tried to exert extraterritorial authority over market actors and transaction outside of their home jurisdiction, a decision that triggered a half-decade of trans-Atlantic bickering, as this chapter will document. But in the second half of the 2010s, the FSB was able to address many cross-border inconsistencies by creating and orchestrating institutions to issue globally harmonized rules for the OTC derivatives market, harnessing the power of transnational networks.

The government network approach highlights both the power of the FSB in governing this vast market and its limits. It provides three arguments to explain the gap between G20 commitments and their implementation.

First, existing government networks in this area of financial supervision were weak and ill designed to coordinate the G20 reform process. In their absence, legislators on both sides of the Atlantic took the initiative, developing domestic rules with extraterritorial authority and, importantly, without considering parallel regulatory efforts abroad. The result was a patchwork of rules that are similar in substance but inconsistent in technical details. Some regulators have resorted to

DOI: 10.4324/9781003290001-4

negotiating bilateral mutual recognition agreements, while reform efforts in other jurisdictions have slowed down significantly.

Second, in the United States, regulatory cross-border cooperation was further encumbered by domestic institutional fragmentation. Rather than nominating a single regulator for the OTC derivatives market, Congress waged a turf war to split regulatory purview among two agencies. The agency with the larger share of regulatory responsibility lacked the transnational involvement and budgetary resources necessary for meaningful cooperation across borders in the wake of the crisis. Over the course of the 2010s however, informal coordination among several standard setters under the FSB umbrella was instrumental in forging compromises across authorities within jurisdictions and across borders that led to the eventual issuance of globally coherent rules regarding the governance of key market infrastructures.

Third, even in areas where domestic implementation has reached completion, it took years to remove legal obstacles to global cooperation, and fragmentation along jurisdictional lines persists today. The chapter zooms in on the area of trade reporting to show that in spite of major efforts by the FSB to provide a global data standard, such fragmentation prevents financial supervisors from obtaining coherent aggregate data on OTC derivatives trades even today. Thus, a decade after the G20 commitments were made, regulators still lack the means to observe the potential accumulation of systemic risk in derivatives markets on a global scale.

The next section of the chapter identifies the puzzle of shortcomings on the OTC derivatives reform agenda. It is followed by an analysis of the global regulatory process from a government network perspective that highlights the power of the FSB in galvanizing global regulatory efforts and its limits. The chapter ends by discussing hypotheses from competing explanations and testing them against the empirical material.

The Puzzle

Recognizing the need to bring OTC derivatives markets under supervisory control, G20 leaders at the Pittsburgh Summit in September 2009 made the following pledge:

> All standardized OTC derivative contracts should be traded on exchanges or electronic trading platforms, where appropriate, and cleared through central counterparties by end-2012 at the latest. OTC derivative contracts should be reported to trade repositories. Non-centrally cleared contracts should be subject to higher capital requirements.
>
> *(G20, 2009c, p. Annex 1 pt. 13)*

Yet a decade after that statement was made and more than eight years after the deadline passed, reform progress is partial at best. The considerable gap between policy goals and implementation is well documented in the series of progress reports that the FSB has submitted to the G20 to date. Concerns started surfacing as early as 2010. The progress report to G20 Finance Ministers and Central Bank Governors in October 2010 recognizes, "Much work and considerable coordination lie ahead in this area" (FSB, 2010b, p. 2).

The lack of progress in OTC derivatives reform prompted the FSB to blow the whistle in a progress report one year later. To make sure that no stakeholder oversees the message, the executive summary of the document starts with the following lines:

> As of now, with only just over one year until the end-2012 deadline for implementing the G-20 commitments, few FSB members have the legislation or regulations in place to provide the framework for operationalising the commitments. . . . This report concludes that jurisdictions should aggressively push forward to meet the end-2012 deadline in as many reform areas as possible.
>
> *(FSB, 2011a, p. 1)*

By the time the deadline passed, not a single G20 member was close to implementing the commitments made at the Pittsburgh Summit. According to the September 2013 progress report, less than half of interest rate and credit derivatives were cleared by central counterparties. And even though almost all trades in these two asset classes have been reported to trade repositories, commodity, equity, and FX derivatives were neither centrally cleared nor reported with high frequency. Very few jurisdictions expected to have mandatory clearing obligations in effect "in the near future," and regulation regarding margin requirements for non-centrally cleared trades was not even in the consultation stage outside the European Union and the United States. The report highlights the holes in the global regulatory patchwork of OTC derivatives markets: "Reforms to legislative frameworks and implementing rules are still underway in many jurisdictions, with few having frameworks in place that will support implementation of all of the G20 reform commitments" (FSB, 2013d, p. 4).

The progress report of November 2020 shows that even today, OTC derivatives reform progress is far from complete (see Figure 4.1). The 24 FSB member jurisdictions are at different stages of implementation, with some having rules in place to meet their regulatory commitments for over 90% of OTC derivatives transactions in their jurisdiction, while others barely count on a legal framework that would permit them to issue such rules in the future. The following paragraphs will take a look at the state of affairs in (1) trade reporting, (2) central clearing, (3) platform trading, (4) margin requirements for derivatives that are not traded on platforms, and (5) capital requirements for banks trading OTC derivatives.

The reporting of derivatives trades is among the most successful items on the G20 reform agenda in this area, with rules in place for all 23 FSB member jurisdictions that have a trade repository. But as this chapter will show, the trade reporting system is encumbered by legal obstacles to cross-border sharing of

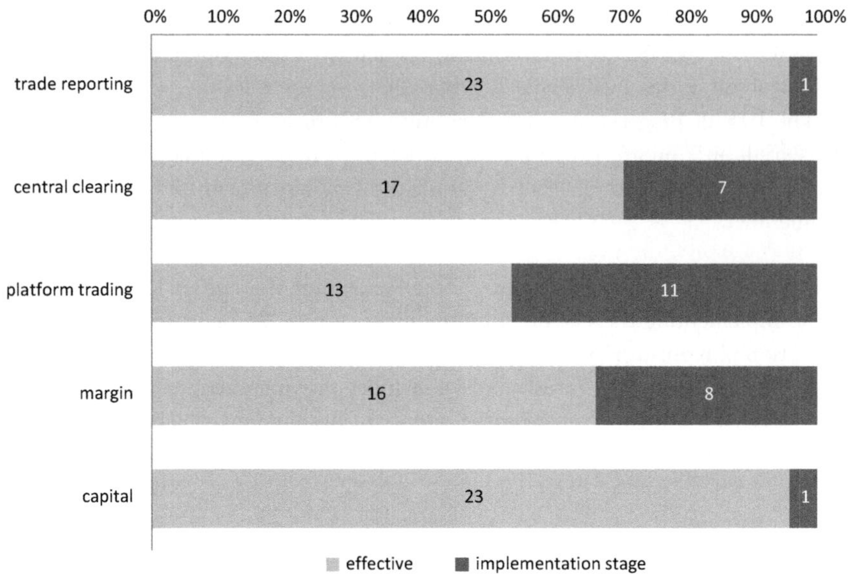

FIGURE 4.1 Reform Progress in OTC Derivatives Regulation, November 2020

Source: FSB (2020c)

information to an extent that makes it very hard if not impossible for regulators to obtain a global picture of systemic risk in the OTC derivatives market (FSB, 2018d, 2020c).

A majority of FSB members now require eligible trades to be cleared through central counterparties (CCP). The FSB has made major efforts in coordination with other standard setters to issue global standards that govern the operations of CCP in recent years (Quaglia, 2021; Quaglia & Spendzharova, 2021b). Yet reform progress has slowed down, and the number of jurisdictions that have central clearing rules in effect has not changed since 2017. Moreover, the actual rate at which derivatives are cleared at CCPs varies widely among the five derivative asset classes. By 2020, only seven jurisdictions report that at least 80% of all new interest rate swaps eligible for central clearing are actually cleared at CCPs. Only India meets the 80% threshold for foreign exchange derivatives, only Brazil for equity derivatives, only the US for credit, and only Indonesia and China for commodity derivatives (FSB, 2020c, p. 14).

Roughly over half of FSB members have effective rules to require trading on platforms and higher margin requirements for trading elsewhere. The progress reports of the FSB show that a large number of jurisdictions are currently "implementing" reform commitments, but this notion flatters reality as countries can remain in the implementation stage indefinitely. A look at country-specific policy actions from 2017 reveals that only a portion of FSB members actually report planned implementation steps in the near future (FSB, 2017c). By 2020, two additional jurisdictions made progress in implementing margin rules, and only one made platform trading rules effective (FSB, 2020c).

Curiously, the most advanced item on the G20 reform agenda in OTC derivatives regulation concerns capital requirements for banks to incentivize them to clear derivatives trades at a central counterparty. This success can be attributed to the Basel Committee, which included higher requirements for bank exposures to derivatives trades in its Basel III standard (see Chapter 3).

Beyond formal implementation of individual reform commitments, the more fundamental issue concerns cross-border cooperation. The new rules of OTC derivatives regulation lead to a degree of fragmentation along jurisdictional lines that undermines the G20 reform goals. For example, central clearinghouses are established in several countries, but most are not authorized to offer direct or indirect clearing services to clients from other jurisdictions. There is no global standard that would subject a given derivatives product to identical clearing or platform trading requirements independent of location (Lockwood, 2018). National margin rules for derivatives trades differ in scope and detail, leading to overlapping and inconsistent requirements for traders that operate across jurisdictions. FSB members with relatively small shares of the global OTC derivatives market such as India, Turkey, and even Singapore voice concerns that such cross-border inconsistencies disincentivize market participants from using platforms or clearinghouses in their jurisdictions (FSB, 2017c, p. 26).

At the same time, the FSB has succeeded in fostering cross-border cooperation regarding the governance of CCP. After years of coordination efforts between the FSB and the global standard setters for market infrastructures (CPMI) and securities markets (IOSCO), globally consistent rules for CCP resilience and resolution are published and likely to become effective in coming years (Quaglia & Spendzharova, 2021b).

While the coordinated development of global standards in the field of OTC derivatives regulation (with the conspicuous exception of capital requirements) experienced long delays, market participants witnessed the emergence of a spaghetti bowl of bilateral recognition agreements, so-called deference or equivalence decisions. When regulators deem the regulatory framework of a foreign jurisdiction strict enough, they allow companies registered abroad to abide by the foreign rules rather than imposing their own. But in practice, such equivalence decisions are based both on prudential and political considerations and sometimes apply to certain derivatives dealers or asset classes only. As a legal analysis for derivatives dealers clarifies,

> Equivalence decisions can be unilaterally withdrawn at any time. In particular, if third country frameworks diverge and the conditions for equivalence are no longer fulfilled. Equivalence is, therefore, an unharmonised, discretionary, highly technical and potentially unstable basis for facilitating comprehensive market access.
>
> *(Allen & Overy LLP, 2020, p. 9)*

By 2022, only 14 clearinghouses in 10 of out the FSB's 24 jurisdictions were covered by bilateral equivalence agreements with either the EU or the US (Kiff et al., 2022, p. 7). And only Australian and Canadian authorities had signed agreements to obtain derivatives data stored in trade repositories abroad by 2020.

Why is the gap between G20 commitments regarding OTC derivatives regulation and the reality of their implementation so large? This chapter shows that even though the FSB has made major efforts in coordinating global standard setters across jurisdictional lines and sectoral siloes, legal impediments to the power of this government network explain the slow progress of regulatory reform in this area.

In the first half decade of reform efforts at the FSB, the failure of the two dominant centers of global finance, the United States and Europe, to engage in regulatory harmonization was a major impediment to progress. Because the vast majority of OTC derivatives transactions take place within or between these two jurisdictions, other countries have an incentive to wait (Li, 2018). In the language of international regulatory diplomacy, they are "continuing to monitor their markets and are seeking to align their regimes with those of other jurisdictions when considering whether and which requirements to adopt in this commitment area," as the FSB (2014d, p. 7) reports. De facto progress has stalled, and the number of FSB members that have implemented clearing mandates has not changed between 2018 and 2022 (Kiff et al., 2022). Today, even in policy areas where implementation has already advanced significantly, cross-border cooperation is encumbered by a variety of legal and nonlegal barriers. The chapter will trace policy evolution in derivatives clearing requirements and trade reporting to illustrate these points.

Government Network

From a government network perspective, OTC derivatives reform falls short of G20 commitments because it developed along institutional pathways that did not harness the strengths of transnational networks. In the first half decade, the government network in charge of coordinating regulatory efforts in this area was formed ad hoc and proved to be weak and inconsequential. At the same time, legislators in the United States and the European Union took the lead by unilaterally writing new rules (Title VII of the Dodd-Frank Act and EMIR, respectively), marginalizing the coordination potential of the FSB. They did not endow domestic regulators with the requisite incentives and power to coordinate with their peers abroad. The Dodd-Frank Act also enshrined regulatory fragmentation, which further exacerbated this issue, as the regulator in charge lacked experience and the requisite budget for meaningful cross-border coordination. In recent years, the FSB has caught up, strengthening its coordination efforts across standard-setting bodies, including IOSCO, CPMI, and the Basel Committee. But preexisting and new legislation represents an additional obstacle to cross-border harmonization. This section will analyze the development of inconsistent rules on both sides of the Atlantic first. A subsequent section traces regulatory fragmentation among two agencies with authority over the derivatives market in the US back to turf concerns among legislators in Congress. It also shows how informal coordination under the umbrella of the FSB eventually succeeded in overcoming fragmentation among domestic regulatory agencies and across borders. The final section zooms in on the area of trade reporting, where a sprawling network of data warehouses gathers domestic data, with no avenue cross-border data aggregation or global risk assessment on a timely basis in place today.

Trans-Atlantic Coordination Failure

Following the previously mentioned G20 commitments at the Pittsburgh Summit in September 2009, the FSB was put in charge of coordinating the formulation and implementation of OTC derivatives reform. In April 2010, the board set up the OTC derivatives working group (ODWG), comprised of regulators from nine member jurisdictions, officials of several international financial institutions and representatives of the standard-setting bodies for banks (the Basel Committee), securities markets (IOSCO), and settlement systems (CPSS). By bringing together only a handful of the most involved jurisdictions and only financial market regulators and central bankers, the composition of the ODWG makes it a quintessential government network. This innovative institutional design gave rise to the optimism that is manifest in Helleiner's (2014b) words: "Both consensus formation and the development of specific new international regulatory standards for OTC derivatives were greatly facilitated by the density of transgovernmental networks among technocratic officials" (p. 11).

Yet by relying on technocratic consensus among regulators, the group was oblivious of the political obstacles to its functioning. A US regulator recalls that the absence of high-enough-level representatives encumbered the coordination process from the beginning:

> The European Commission was basically out there saying, whatever you guys do, if it doesn't include us, forget about it. . . . Frankly we couldn't come to an agreement because every arrangement that we came up with, it was basically . . . the market regulators at least in the US had the biggest clout and the European Commission again, Brussels has the biggest clout but they're not a member of Basel or CPSS or IOSCO per se. So we ultimately came up with the kind of a fudge solution which wasn't particularly appealing.
>
> *(US Regulator 1, personal communication, July 23, 2012)*

In 2011, when the lack of progress in the ODWG became evident, FSB chairman Mark Carney decided to establish the so-called OTC Derivatives Coordination Group, a more high-profile group that brought together the chairs of the standard-setting bodies and Carney himself in order to coordinate "the international work to achieve the progress on the safeguards that is needed by mid-2012" (Carney, 2012b, p. 3). But even though this group had more authority in the regulatory world, it ignored the political realities on the ground. A US regulator explains,

> They've got basically four central bankers or one bank supervisor and three central bankers. And the SEC, the CFTC and the European Commission which are frankly the major players in the OTC Derivatives Regulation are not there. . . . So there still is a question as to who's going to have the big stick come December 31st.
>
> *(US Regulator 1, personal communication, July 23, 2012)*

The failure of any jurisdiction to deliver on the G20 commitments regarding OTC derivatives by the 2012 deadline serves as an indicator that the stick of Carney's Coordination Group was not big enough. The group itself never appeared again in subsequent progress reports. In its stead, a new group, the so-called OTC Derivatives Regulator's Group, gained importance. It largely overlaps with the ODWG but is comprised solely of officials with direct supervisory authority over the ten major derivatives markets. The Regulator's Group deals specifically with all the cross-border conflicts, inconsistencies, gaps, and duplicative requirements that have arisen in OTC derivatives regulation over the last years.

In addition to the absence of a proper government network, global OTC derivatives reform is hampered by the existence of legislative and legal barriers to cross-border harmonization. In successful areas of financial regulatory reform such as Basel III, new global standards are developed by a government network before they are implemented domestically. In contrast, OTC derivatives markets regulation was driven by domestic legislation: Dodd-Frank in the United States and EMIR/MiFID 2 in the European Union.

Proposed in June 2009 and signed into law by President Obama in 2010, the Dodd-Frank Act significantly increases the perimeter of financial regulation, including the OTC derivatives market in particular. It is important to note, however, that this initiative was driven by the US Congress, not by the G20. Persaud recognized as much in 2010:

> The US bill on financial regulation currently before the Senate makes no acknowledgement at all of what the EU, China, India, Brazil and Russia are up to. Across a wide set of issues, from financial regulation, bankers' pay and bank taxes to competition policy, national regulators are going down different avenues from their G20 colleagues.
>
> *(Persaud, 2010, p. 638)*

The global nature of derivatives markets exacerbates the inconsistencies of current and past lawmaking. Unlike the banking sector where regulators attach regulatory requirements to licenses and charters in a given jurisdiction, derivatives markets represent an infrastructure that defies a territorial approach to regulation (K. N. Johnson, 2011). Market participants cannot easily be excluded, and even though the main participants in the OTC derivatives markets are big financial firms, their broker-dealer operations can change location rather easily, at least on paper. Riles (2011) provides the example of a derivatives transaction between a Japanese and a British bank, posted to their subsidiaries in the Cayman Islands and involving a swap between Chinese Yuan and Singaporean dollars. In which jurisdiction does this trade take place, the author asks, and what law should apply?

Lawmakers both in Europe and the United States have found an answer to this question: theirs and only theirs. Both Title VII of the Dodd-Frank Act and Article 23 of the European Market Infrastructure Regulation (EMIR) stipulate that entity- and transaction-level requirements apply to counterparties irrespective of location when the trade has a 'direct, substantial and foreseeable effect' on the jurisdiction (Dodd-Frank Wall Street Reform and Consumer Protection Act, 2010; Coffee, 2014; Regulation (EU) No 648/2012 of the European Parliament and of the Council on OTC Derivatives, Central Counterparties and Trade Repositories, 2012). This assertion of extraterritorial authority has been the main source of friction between regulators on both sides of the Atlantic for over six years (Knaack, 2015; Gravelle & Pagliari, 2018).

In early 2012, proposed rules that envision the extraterritorial application of the Volcker Rule irritated political leaders in Europe. EU officials had previously voiced their concern that Dodd-Frank did not even grant the European Central Bank exemption from its rules (Shipkevich, 2011). The British Finance Minister George Osborne wrote a letter of concern to Fed Chairman Bernanke in January, and the EU Commissioner for financial services Michel Barnier argued a month later that it was "not acceptable that U.S. rules have such a wide effect on other nations" (Onaran, 2012; Standish, 2012). In diplomatic fashion, Treasury Secretary Geithner responded that "because in some areas U.S. reforms are tougher or just different from the rules forthcoming in other markets, we need to figure out a sensible way to apply those rules to the foreign operations of U.S. firms and the U.S. operations of foreign firms" (H. Jones, 2012).

The biggest move into extraterritoriality however did not concern the Volcker Rule but OTC derivatives regulation. This was not initially the case. EU Commissioner Barnier and CFTC Chairman Gensler appeared to work closely together in the early days of OTC derivatives reform. After one of many meetings in September 2010, Gensler and Barnier (2010) even stated,

> We have proven on OTC derivatives regulation that close transatlantic cooperation can work." Furthermore, a joint paper by the SEC and CFTC in February 2012 that highlighted the need for further cross-border cooperation to identify gaps and inconsistencies in OTC derivatives regulation was welcomed by foreign regulators.
>
> *(CFTC & SEC, 2012; Greene & Potiha, 2012; Helleiner, 2014c)*

In July 2012 however, the CFTC issued a policy statement regarding "Cross-border Application of Swaps Provisions" that extends the reach of US rules to a wide array of transactions and market participants. The rules proposed by the CFTC apply to every trade executed in the US (no matter by what kind of firm) and every trade that involves a US counterparty (no matter where it is executed). For example, a London-based affiliate of JPMorgan engaging in a swap with a Norwegian counterparty would be covered by US rules. Even a swap between a French bank and a French pension fund is subject to CFTC authority if the trade takes place in the bank's New York affiliate. In fact, only transactions between two firms that have no significant connections to the US market are exempted from the CFTC rules (CFTC, 2012a; Coffee, 2014).

European officials were dismayed by such a wide extraterritorial application of US rules. In a comment in August 2012, the European Commission expressed concern that the proposed guidance

> will maximize the potential for overlap and duplication of US regulatory requirements with those of other jurisdictions, including the EU. An EU and a US firm that conclude an OTC derivatives contract will be simultaneously subject to EU and US requirements. This will lead to duplication of laws and to potentially irreconcilable conflicts of laws for market operators.
>
> *(European Commission, 2012, p. 2)*

The CFTC released an update on its proposed guidance in December 2012, insisting on the majority of its extraterritorial provisions. The European response this time was not restricted to a mere comment letter. Instead, European Commissioner Michel Barnier brought this issue to a higher level by drafting a letter to Treasury Secretary Lew. The letter, signed in April 2013 by Barnier and the Finance Ministers of Brazil, France, Germany, Italy, Japan, Russia, South Africa, Switzerland, and the United Kingdom, openly criticized "the lack of progress in developing workable cross-border rules as part of reforms of the OTC derivatives market." The undersigned clearly took aim at the CFTC's extraterritorial provisions by stating that "we hold the view that as a principle, local regulations should not be extended beyond national borders" (Barnier, 2013). The change not only of tone but also of stakeholders deserves attention. While the 2012 comment letter was signed by a European bureaucrat and sent to the CFTC, essentially a bilateral exchange among regulators, the 2013 letter was a highly visible altercation among G20 politicians. The regulatory agencies that were targeted with the comments were "copied," but so were the legislative commissions that oversee the CFTC's operation in the United States, the Agriculture Committees in the House and the Senate. The letter highlights the political influence that these Committees exert on the CFTC. Again, what had started as a technocratic exchange of opinions within a government network of regulators had acquired significant political salience. Secretary Lew dismissed both content and form of the letter, calling it "ill-informed" and "not a helpful way to promote conversations with two independent regulatory agencies" (Stephenson & Lynch, 2013).

The CFTC finalized its guidance in July 2013 with provisions that, while less extraterritorial than the initial guidance, would still bring a large portion of European derivatives markets under American regulatory control (CFTC, 2013b). In September 2013, the head of the UK Financial Conduct Authority published a piece of unusually candid criticism in the Financial Times:

> Does it make hard-nosed, practical sense for any one national regulator to attempt to regulate all derivatives activity with any link to its jurisdiction? . . . The clear risk is that a patchwork quilt of national and regional rules runs the risk of becoming unworkable. A mess.
>
> *(T. Braithwaite & Mackenzie, 2013)*

The hoped-for solution to sort out this patchwork quilt is "substituted compliance," a legal concept that stipulates deference to the rules of another jurisdiction whenever they are deemed "functionally equivalent." Substituted compliance is a relatively new concept and one that has not received widespread acceptance among regulators. Coffee (2014) remarks that "the attitude of U.S. financial regulators towards 'substituted compliance' has approached the schizophrenic. Unlike securities and derivatives regulators, banking regulators have largely ignored or disdained substituted compliance, preferring to rely on a more traditional territorial approach" (p. 13).

Nevertheless, both in earlier comment letters and in the April 2013 letter, regulators and politicians outside the United States have expressed support for substituted compliance as a solution to cross-border regulatory duplication problems in OTC derivatives markets. In principle, this is also the approach envisioned by the CFTC. In its proposed guidance, the agency clearly stipulates which transactions are strictly subject to US rules and which ones are eligible for determination of functional equivalence as a prerequisite for substituted compliance. This common ground among regulators on both sides of the Atlantic formed the basis for the so-called "Path Forward" initiative. Made public in July 2013, the agreement between CFTC Chairman Gensler, European Commissioner Michel Barnier, and the European Securities Market Authority (ESMA) envisioned a joint approach in determining equivalence in regulatory regimes in order to pursue substituted compliance and mutual recognition (CFTC, 2013a). The FSB's OTC Derivatives Regulators' Group in its commitment to "avoid, to the extent possible, the application of conflicting rules to the same entities and transactions" and to "eliminate the application of inconsistent and duplicative requirements" explicitly endorsed the initiative (ODRG, 2013).

But what started as a promising attempt at regulatory coordination ran out of steam only half a year later. Whereas the European authorities support an outcomes-based approach that assesses equivalence in rather broad terms of contribution to systemic risk, the CFTC employs a much more meticulous rule-by-rule approach that is designed to identify loopholes and prevent regulatory arbitrage. As the end-2013 deadline for determination of equivalence passed, the CFTC had only cleared a few rules for substituted compliance. In a statement of dissent, CFTC Commissioner O'Malia expressed his disappointment: "If the Commission's objective for substituted compliance is to develop a narrow rule-by-rule approach that leaves unanswered major regulatory gaps between our regulatory framework and foreign jurisdictions, then I believe that the Commission has successfully achieved its goal today" (CFTC, 2013c). The last in a series of setbacks, the CFTC issued new guidance in November 2013 that again asserts extraterritorial authority over cross-border swaps. The European Commission responded with "surprise" regarding the new rules "which seem to us to go against both the letter and spirit of the path forward agreement" (Brunsden, 2013). Even by the mid-2010s, no comprehensive equivalence decision regarding OTC derivatives was reached, although regulators on both sides of the Atlantic made progress in mutually recognizing margin rules for some derivatives and some trading platforms (Dempsey, 2017; European Commission, 2017b, 2017c).

In sum, legislators took lead in creating OTC derivatives rules in the wake of the crisis where government networks were ineffectual. The two leading jurisdictions failed to consult with each other or anyone else when devising their domestic rules, leading to cross-border inconsistencies and a half-decade of trans-Atlantic acrimony over who holds regulatory authority over a highly interconnected, global market. A European regulator comes to a revealing conclusion: "Lots of these inconsistencies would be avoided if we had spoken. I mean once you publish the rule, it is very difficult then to render it coherent" (EU Regulator 6, personal communication, November 14, 2014).

Regulatory Fragmentation in the United States

It might not come as a surprise that parliamentarians across the Atlantic did not talk to each other when developing the post-crisis regulatory framework for OTC derivatives. But why did regulators not reach out to their counterparts abroad? One key reason is that the US Congress split regulatory authority over the derivatives market among two agencies. According to the Dodd-Frank Act, the Commodity Futures Trading Commission (CFTC) is required to regulate swaps, whereas the Securities Exchange Commission (SEC) regulates "derivatives defined as security-based swaps" (CFTC & SEC, 2012). Due to this odd separation of regulatory powers and the limited international experience of the CFTC, regulators in other G20 countries struggled to identify their American counterpart when trying to implement the OTC derivatives reform agenda.

Why was regulatory authority over this financial market not assigned to a single agency? A look at the bureaucratic politics of congressional purview over this sector provides an answer to this question. Created in 1934, the SEC was a lesson learned from the 1929 stock crash and the Great Depression. Its mandate is to exercise regulatory control over brokers and companies that trade their securities at the stock exchange. The CFTC in contrast was established in 1975 to regulate derivatives markets of commodities. Farmers have used futures for decades as an insurance against price volatility of their crops. It was thus an obvious choice to place the CFTC under the oversight of bipartisan Agriculture (Ag) Committees in the House of Representatives and the Senate.

Over the last ten years, the overall market for OTC derivatives has grown 665% in notional value. The commodity-based contracts that farmers rely on, however, have hardly increased in that period, and today they represent less than 1% of all OTC derivatives (Engelen et al., 2011, p. 42f.; Helleiner et al., 2018). When the Obama administration considered bringing all OTC derivatives under regulatory control with the Dodd-Frank Act, it would have been a commonsense solution to subsume the activities of the CFTC under the authority of a strengthened SEC. However, the Ag Committees in both chambers of Congress started a fierce turf battle to ensure not only that the CFTC continued to exist but that it would have wide regulatory authority over the OTC derivatives market. The Obama administration finally recognized that without the goodwill of Ag Committee members, the Dodd-Frank Act would never be passed. For the committee members, propping up the CFTC has significant benefits because it attracts campaign contributions from the financial sector (US Legislature Aide, personal communication, July 27, 2012). In the 2008 and 2010 election cycles, Senate committee members received $41.6 million from Wall Street, whereas agribusiness only made $17.6 million in campaign contributions. The situation is similar for House committee members (Puzzanghera, 2009). This means that there was a multi-million-dollar incentive for certain US legislators to maintain a bifurcated domestic regulatory regime in the derivatives market.

The two agencies differ significantly with respect to their budget and degree of integration into government networks. The SEC has been actively involved in transgovernmental exchanges with securities regulators in Europe, Japan, and elsewhere. It is a founding member of and protagonist in the securities standard-setting body (IOSCO) since 1983. The CFTC in contrast only holds the status of an associate member. Furthermore, the SEC has been the American regulator at the table of the FSF since its inception in 1999. It also holds one of the seats in the FSB Plenary today, with the other two reserved for the Treasury and the Fed. The CFTC in turn has only occasionally participated in the FSF. The situation changed to some extent with the creation of the FSB. The agency obtained a seat at both the OTC derivatives working and regulator's groups in 2010, but its then-chairman Gary Gensler has not been in extensive contact with this crucial government network. A US regulator recalls, "Gensler has been invited from time to time to the steering committee meetings where they've been talking about OTC derivatives in particular" (US Regulator 1, personal communication, June 16, 2014). Arguably, if CFTC regulators had established the long-term professional ties that lubricate transgovernmental interaction, some of the early post-crisis coordination failures could have been avoided.

In addition, the CFTC had a much smaller budget ($208 million in 2013 as compared to the SEC's $1.35 billion), and thus much fewer resources to engage in regulatory cooperation with its counterparts abroad. A US regulator explains,

> It's kind of an interesting state of affair as where, I mean [the CFTC] got 90% of the market, mas o menos, [the SEC got] 10% but [the latter] got nine people to work on things for every one person that [the former] have. So [the SEC] can afford to throw more resources at it.
>
> *(US Regulator 1, personal communication, June 16, 2014)*

A CFTC Commissioner admitted in 2014, "Our staff is on its knees, some reaching for the exit doors and others already having bailed" (Abrams, 2014). This dire situation threatened the independence of the agency. A civil society representative points out, "The House Republicans have proposed to cut the CFTC budget. They hold them up before Congress, and wag their fingers up, and they write letters, they use various points of leverage to try to get them to dilute their rules" (US Civil Society Representative 2, personal communication, July 26, 2012). With a scant history of cross-border engagement, facing significant pressure from the legislature and burdened with formulating the rules for the largest share of the derivatives market on a meager budget, CFTC officials understandably dedicated few resources to coordination with their counterparts abroad.

Fortunately, this has changed since the mid 2010s. By 2017, CFTC officials were at the helm of seven international standard-setting committees, and the agency had taken a lead role in the arduous task of reducing cross-border inconsistencies in OTC derivatives regulation (Rubin, 2018).

As Quaglia (2021) and Quaglia and Spendzharova (2021a, 2021b) document in illuminating detail, the FSB has played the role of an orchestrator, providing venues for coordination both among regulatory authorities within the same jurisdiction and across borders. The power and adaptability of government networks is particularly visible in the collaboration between two of the standard setters that are FSB members, namely, the Committee on Payment and Settlement Systems (CPSS) and the International Organization of Securities Commissions (IOSCO). While CPSS brings together central bankers from G20 member jurisdictions, IOSCO is the forum for 224 securities market supervisors from around the world. The two standard-setting bodies differ not only in breadth of membership and regulatory remit but also in mandate and philosophy. CPSS collaborated with IOSCO in developing what was initially a complex, wide-ranging, and imprecise set of principles for financial market infrastructures (CPSS & IOSCO, 2012a). But the standard setter, renamed Committee on Payments and Market Infrastructures (CPMI) in 2014, continued working with IOSCO under FSB coordination, issuing subsequent guidance that set the foundation for globally consistent standards regarding CCPs.

The CPMI-IOSCO joint working group exemplifies the power of informal coordination that government networks are capable of. It was instrumental in overcoming domestic fragmentation in the key jurisdictions, namely, the EU and the

US. Quaglia and Spendzharova (2021b, p. 9) quote an interview partner stating that "the only policy location in which domestic regulators from the same jurisdiction talked to each other was in international standard-setting bodies." On the US side, the working group included representatives from the CFTC, the SEC, the New York Fed, and Board of Governors of the Federal Reserve. Similarly on the European side, it provided a joint forum for representatives from the European Commission, ESMA, eight EU member states, and the European Central Bank.

Over the last decade, the CPMI-IOSCO working group provided a key venue for its members to identify regulatory differences based on jurisdiction (EU vs. US, Anglo-American vs. Continental traditions) and philosophy (central bankers vs. securities regulators). It was able to forge compromises and delineate the regulatory perimeter that distinguishes between CCP resilience/recovery and resolution (Quaglia & Spendzharova, 2021b). CMPI and IOSCO issued further guidance on the recovery of market infrastructures in general (CPMI & IOSCO, 2014), and CCPs in particular (CPMI & IOSCO, 2017, 2018). Together with FSB work on resolution of CCPs (FSB, 2017f), these new standards provide the foundation for globally consistent rules that govern a key aspect of the global derivatives market, meeting the G20 commitment.

As Quaglia and Spendzharova (2021b) point out, the main coordination mechanisms between regulatory authorities under the FSB umbrella were informal. Representatives of one standard-setting body would meet informally or engage in regular phone calls with those of another one. They would exchange draft documents before they were made public and invite each other to participate in meetings of topics of joint relevance. Such measures were complemented by more formal ones, such as cross-membership in different committees and cross-referencing of published documents. In other words, regulators were able to harness the informal powers of government networks to address the manifold cross-border inconsistencies in OTC derivatives regulation that had manifested in the early years of the post-crisis reform process.

Fragmentation in Trade Reporting

The reporting of OTC derivatives trades to so-called trade repositories (TR) exhibits a similar dynamic where government networks seek to overcome legal barriers and fragmentation along jurisdictional lines that hampered early efforts in this issue area. Trade reporting appears at first glance like an early success on the G20 derivatives reform agenda. Yet as this section will show, legislators passively and actively posed obstacles to cross-border coordination for much of the 2010s. Only in recent years, government networks coordinated under the FSB umbrella have gained protagonism, developing a globally consistent language to record derivative trades, and removing legal barriers to cross-border cooperation in data sharing.

In principle, the trade reporting commitment faces relatively few obstacles to its successful implementation. Unlike higher capital and margin requirements, it does not impose significantly higher costs on OTC derivatives dealers, and unlike the commitment to trade derivatives on platforms, it does not undermine the informational advantage that is an essential source of competitiveness for the major dealer banks. To the extent that dealers can use a standardized reporting infrastructure to feed their internal risk management systems with high-quality market data, it even provides tangible benefits to the industry.

Yet over a decade after the Pittsburgh Summit, prudential regulators are still far away from achieving the G20 goal of increasing global OTC derivative market transparency. At first sight, trade reporting seems to be on track to full implementation. As shown in the previous section, 23 out of 24 FSB members have reporting requirements in place that cover 90% or more of OTC derivatives transactions in their respective jurisdiction. However, trade reporting is fragmented along jurisdictional lines. Currently there are 36 trade repositories (TR) in operation across the globe, but only a small fraction of them share data across borders (FSB, 2020c). The first post-crisis years witnessed an industry-led effort to establish a small group of TR that were specialized along OTC derivatives asset classes but global in scope. Legislative barriers in member jurisdiction however obstructed the sharing of OTC trade-related information across borders until very recently. A survey of TRs undertaken by the FSB in 2018 revealed that "only a minority of these TRs noted that direct data access had been provided to foreign authorities, with some TRs indicating that no foreign authority had initiated the related process to obtain access" (FSB, 2018d, p. 14). The resulting fragmentation along national lines prevents regulators from obtaining a global picture of the OTC derivatives market.

The G20 Pittsburgh Declaration mandates reporting to trade repositories (in the plural), but neither the FSB nor individual regulators specified how many TRs should be established. The FSB did however endorse the idea of centralized data storage from the beginning, stating that "one beneficial solution would be to establish a single global data source to aggregate the information from TRs" (FSB, 2010b, p. 47). Industry interests and best practice pointed to the creation of one TR for each of the five asset classes (i.e. interest rate, credit, commodity, FX, and equity derivatives) (Thompson, 2015). The credit derivatives market was leading the way in terms of standardization and trade reporting due to "targeted supervisory encouragement" (FSB, 2010b, p. 15). Two years before the outbreak of the global financial crisis, credit derivatives dealers started reporting their trades to the New York–based Trade Information Warehouse, the first and only TR until 2010. Operated by a subsidiary of DTCC, a private provider of securities settlement and reporting services, it claimed to register 98% of all credit derivative transactions worldwide.

In the wake of the Pittsburgh Summit, the International Swaps and Derivatives Association (ISDA) played a key role trying to establish a trade repository for each remaining asset class. The business association issued public Requests for Proposals and an ISDA Steering Committee that represented both dealers and buy-side firms selected among the applying service providers. In mid-2011, ISDA announced the winner for the creation of a commodity derivatives TR, following the establishment of two repositories for interest rate and equity derivatives, respectively (ISDA,

2011a, 2011b). The division of labor along functional lines would facilitate the centralized aggregation of trading data for each asset class, allowing regulators to gather crucial information on the accumulation of systemic risk on a global scale (CPSS & IOSCO, 2013; FSB, 2010b; Helleiner, 2011, 2014c).

But even before the system of specialized and global TRs was fully developed, it fell apart in the face of legal obstacles. In 2010, most if not all planned and established TRs were located in the United States. The Dodd-Frank Act requires TRs to make data available to all relevant domestic regulators, but it provides the CFTC with the authority to reject data requests from foreign regulators and ministries (Dodd-Frank Wall Street Reform and Consumer Protection Act, 2010, sec. 728).

The CFTC conditions for data release became a stone of contention during the 2010 episode of the Greek crisis when European policymakers were seeking detailed information about the credit derivatives market from DTCC (Helleiner, 2014c). A congressional staffer recalls,

> The CFTC got a provision put in Dodd Frank that said, "If we're regulating a clearing house, or a swap data repository, no one else can have that information unless they indemnify the repository and us in case there's any problem." This has caused massive international havoc, because the Europeans look at this and they say, "Well if you're going to make it so hard for us to get information from your repositories, we're going to set up our own repositories here and see if you can get the information from our repositories."
>
> *(US Legislature Aide, personal communication, July 27, 2012)*

US Regulators (both from the CFTC and SEC) spoke out against the indemnification requirement in mid-2012, that is two years after the transatlantic row over Greek derivatives. The US Congress eliminated the requirement from the Dodd-Frank Act in December 2015, at a time when trade repository fragmentation along jurisdictional lines was already well advanced.

Business pressures also contributed to the demise of the ISDA-envisioned TR system. While granting a monopoly for a TR in each asset class would be the most efficient solution for data aggregation, it was not in the interest of all industry stakeholders. Securities exchanges in particular were eager to create proprietary TRs in order to provide customers with a one-stop-shop for the trading, clearing, and reporting of OTC derivatives. European legislators also voiced monopoly concerns (DTCC had won ISDA approval for TR in all five asset classes). However, coordinated action by regulatory agencies in cooperation with ISDA could have trumped these concerns. The establishment of a singular TR for each asset class, either as a public utility (housed under the BIS for instance) or as a private firm subject to public interest utility regulation, would have delivered, as the Brazilian example shows, "a single, correct trade report" (FSB, 2015a, p. 34).

Following the breakdown of the system of specialized but global TR, regulators witnessed a dizzying proliferation of trade repositories. Accounts of their number and location varied. The 2014 FSB progress report on OTC derivatives stated that

23 TR are operational in 13 member jurisdictions (FSB, 2014d). An FSB study in the same year counts 25 TR in 11 jurisdictions (FSB, 2014a). Most repositories only store trade information for certain OTC derivatives, few cover all asset classes. This patchwork of firms with overlapping services would still be able to collectively provide useful information to regulators if a global system of data recording and aggregation were in place. Yet this is not the case. IOSCO Chair David Wright summarized the situation in 2014 by stating that "there are 22 trade repositories that don't talk to each other" (H. Jones, 2014).

The 2020 OTC derivatives progress report distinguishes between 22 TRs authorized and operating in 15 jurisdictions (counting the UK and the rest of the EU as separate) and an additional 14 TR-like entities, such as central banks and stock exchanges that perform trade reporting functions, bringing the total to 36 data warehouses in 17 jurisdictions (FSB, 2020c). Figure 4.2 shows the fragmentation of this network. The nodes represent FSB members, and ties indicate that TR in one jurisdiction are recognized or under consideration for recognition in another jurisdiction. The sparsity of the network is obvious. Australia and Canada, two countries without domestic TR, have signed cooperation agreements that allow foreign TR to register domestic trades and share information with regulatory agencies. In 2016, Swiss regulators issued an equivalence decision that allows for data sharing with the European Union, and UK data depositories have reached out to their counterparts in Switzerland. The European Commission has made 30 equivalence decision regarding specific subsets of the derivatives market since 2014. Some of them concern data sharing, allowing regulators to request access to derivatives trade data from their counterparts (rather than automatic or direct access to TRs) (European Commission, 2021). As the consequence of Brexit, the EU has refused to grant equivalence to the UK in the area of trade reporting. That means that at the beginning of 2021, TRs on the island and on the continent have stopped sharing derivatives data, creating a new fault line in a key area of the global derivatives market where there was none before (Allen & Overy LLP, 2020; ESMA, 2020). On a global level, the FSB reports that in principle, foreign authorities have access to TR information in 9 out of 24 jurisdictions (FSB, 2018d, p. 18). Other than that, the TRs around the world still do not cooperate.

From the beginning, the FSB was aware of legal barriers as a potential obstacle to implementation of the G20 trade reporting commitment (FSB, 2010b). The magnitude of these barriers became clear by the mid-2010s. The OTC Derivatives Regulators Group observed in a letter to FSB Chair Carney in mid-2014: "We have concerns that since April 2013 little has been done in many G20 and FSB jurisdictions to address the barriers that prevent reporting of the information necessary to improve transparency in the derivatives markets"(ODRG, 2014, p. 3). The group encourages the FSB Chair to impose a clear deadline for member jurisdictions to make necessary legislative changes. A year later, the FSB thematic peer review on trade reporting tries indeed to tighten the screws by recommending that member countries establish the necessary legal framework for "direct, . . .

FIGURE 4.2 The Global TR Network in 2020

Source: Data from FSB (2020c), base map from www.mapchart.net/ (CC BY-SA 4.0)

continuous and un-intermediated access to relevant TR-held data" across borders by June 2018 (FSB, 2015a, p. 8).

Recognizing that the FSB lacks authority to fully implement the trade reporting requirement, FSB Chair Carney addressed G20 leaders before the 2014 Summit in Brisbane with the following words: "G20 support is required to remove legal barriers that exist in some jurisdictions that block the reporting and sharing of counterparty information" (Carney, 2014a, p. 3). He repeated the same statement one year later, this time mentioning the mid-2018 deadline. But while both G20 heads of state and finance ministers at 2015 meetings in Antalya and Ankara declared their willingness to "expedite our efforts" (G20, 2015, para. 14), they only committed to the deadline at the G20 Hamburg summit two years later (G20, 2017).

Pressure via the G20 and the FSB resulted in the removal of the most egregious legal obstacles in the United States and the European Union in recent years. As mentioned previously, the indemnification provisions for information sharing in the Dodd-Frank Act were removed by end-2015. European legislation encumbered transnational regulatory cooperation in similar ways. The European Market Infrastructure Regulation (EMIR) of 2012 was a major part of EU efforts to transpose G20 commitments into domestic legislation. According to EMIR, regulators in countries that do not have a TR are allowed to contact the European Securities Market Authority (ESMA) directly to establish a transnational cooperation agreement for information exchange in the form of a MoU (Art. 75). Regulators with TR in their own jurisdiction however did not have that privilege. EMIR (Art. 76) required them to seek an international agreement for data access, a process that involves the European Commission, the Council, the foreign government, and parliamentary approval in both countries (Regulation (EU) No 648/2012 of the European Parliament and of the Council on OTC Derivatives, Central Counterparties and Trade Repositories, 2012). Given the sprawling network of TRs, the European Union would need to negotiate, sign, and ratify over a dozen international treaties in order to make cross-border sharing of OTC derivatives data globally a reality. No foreign authority tried to initiate that process (FSB, 2018d). In an implicit recognition of this quagmire and following an FSB peer review on legal obstacles to data sharing, the European Commission (an FSB member) instituted a regulatory fitness and performance program (called REFIT) in 2016, including EMIR in its revisions. As a consequence, the international treaty requirement of Article 76 was removed in 2019 (Regulation (EU) 2019/834 of the European Parliament and of the Council of 20 May 2019 Amending Regulation (EU) No 648/2012, 2019). Instead, a foreign regulator can now reach out to ESMA if the regulatory framework of their jurisdiction is deemed to be equivalent by the European Commission. Such equivalence decisions can be understood as mechanism to replace simple regulatory cooperation with a sophisticated bargaining process if something is to be gained from the partner country – unfettered access to trade information for example. European authorities have used such negotiation techniques successfully with foreign counterparts before, especially with the United States (Posner, 2009).

However, being able – in principle – to obtain derivatives trade data from supervisors abroad is very different from making sense of it to assess global risk in a timely fashion. In order for the authorities to understand and address risk accumulation and vulnerabilities in the global derivatives market, they would need to combine and match data stored in TRs in different jurisdictions. Here, again, the FSB has tried to harness the power of government networks in the face of fragmentation along jurisdictional lines (Knaack, 2018).

The FSB's first OTC derivatives progress report of November 2010 still talks about OTC derivatives "transaction data" in rather vague terms. At the same time, the newly created Office for Financial Research (OFR) in the United States took the lead by publishing a policy statement to promote the establishment of a Legal Entity Identifier (LEI) for financial contracts that it envisioned to be in place by mid-2011 (OFR, 2010). The G14 and other industry stakeholders endorsed the initiative (G14 et al., 2011). Trade associations published a joint paper with specific recommendations for the information contained in an LEI and its operational terms as early as May 2011 (AFME et al., 2011). A year earlier, the derivatives trade reporting firm DTCC had already purchased entity reference data management technology. It created a so-called global market entity identifier utility in 2012 in order to become a leader in the future LEI registration market (Flanagan, 2014).

In parallel, securities market regulators in several jurisdictions published consultation papers, and CPSS and IOSCO created a task force on counterparty identification standards (CPSS & IOSCO, 2012b; Haldane et al., 2012). The FSB convened regulators and industry representatives to a workshop in September 2011 in order to facilitate the convergence of private and public standardization efforts.

Even though industry representatives and regulators agreed on the principles of this trade identification system, implementation of the LEI initiative slowed down subsequently. Almost year after the LEI workshop, the FSB published its proposal for a "uniform global system for legal entity identification" in the OTC derivatives market, and G20 leaders endorsed it at the Los Cabos Summit in June 2012.

The LEI assigns a unique identity number to each counterparty engaged in a financial transaction, while an additional product identifier would carry information about the financial product traded and its attributes. From a network perspective, LEI represents the nodes, while the product identifier characterizes the ties between the nodes in the OTC trade network. Both elements combined would produce a unique trade identifier for each OTC derivatives transaction.

The FSB then helped establish the Global LEI Foundation (GLEIF) as a government network: Run by industry participants and supervised by regulatory agencies, it is merely a Swiss foundation in legal terms, with no existence under the terms of international public law. GLEIF consists of two bodies: The Central Operating Unit is responsible for maintaining the virtual global LEI database and ensuring cross-border consistency and compatibility of the LEI code assignment to firms by a network of local operating units. The Regulatory Oversight Committee brings together regulatory agencies from over 40 jurisdictions to oversee the Central Operating Units. GLEIF became operational in mid-2014.

The delayed creation of the Central Operating Unit encumbered the creation of a global trade identification system. The CFTC (2012b) published regulation that made trade reporting of OTC derivatives mandatory in 2012, earlier than the European Union (ESMA, 2014). In order to comply with the CFTC reporting requirement, derivatives parties had to register with a CFTC-sponsored local operating unit and obtain a so-called unique swap identifier that contains a ten-digit identification number for the trading firm. This system was established before LEI stakeholders agreed on a 20-digit firm identifier. Subsequent efforts to achieve cross-border compatibility stumbled initially when industry participants discovered that different local operating units may have assigned the same identifier to different firms. The confusion extends beyond the firm ID to the product code of the unique trade identifier. An industry representative asserts, "These transactions are neither able to be ingested by [trade repositories] nor aggregated for risk analysis. Industry members are shoveling them out the door, but swaps regulators can't use them" (Grody, 2014).

Due to two-sided reporting without trade reconciliation, duplicate reporting requirements in different jurisdictions, and uncertainty regarding which party has the obligation to report, double-counting of OTC derivatives trades became rampant (FSB, 2015a, p. 49). Because OTC trade data is only useful for prudential purposes when duplicates and omissions are identified and eliminated, such cross-border inconsistencies further complicate the work of supervisors (Knaack, 2018).

Several regulators shared the private sector frustration about the LEI initiative. A US Regulator asserts, "I mean it's just Babel. And in the last year and a half, I've been working on the LEI. So I am trying to help solve that Babel but there is a lot of Babel" (US Regulator 1, personal communication, June 16, 2014). In the European Union, OTC trade reporting requirements are elements of the European Market Infrastructure Regulation (EMIR) and the Markets in Financial Instruments Directive (MiFID II). But even though the EU thus has a unified regulatory system for OTC derivatives markets, the lack of a consensus on the details of a reporting standard poses difficulties even for intra-EU data aggregation. A British regulator reports,

> Never underestimate the technology problems in the gathering of data. It's actually tremendously difficult. We spend a huge amount of time just trying to understand that data from the trade repositories. . . . It was done by directive, MiFID, every country implements it slightly differently. And every country just has a bunch of guys who take the reports but they never really look at them. So a lot of what has been reported is complete rubbish.
>
> *(UK Regulator 1, personal communication, 2014)*

After a critical peer review, the FSB took action again. It tasked the CPMI and IOSCO with developing global standards for unique product and trade identifiers by 2017. It also developed rules for these data formats in house and designated

GLEIF to be responsible for their governance (Quaglia & Spendzharova, 2021a). Data quality issues remain a concern to date, however. In its first report on derivatives data quality, ESMA notes that pairing and matching rates remain low, at 53% and 29% of reported trades in Europe (Angelini, 2021). Nevertheless, due to the rule-setting work by the FSB in cooperation with CPMI, IOSCO, and a host of other government networks, a globally consistent data template is in place a decade after the global financial crisis.

In sum, the government network approach shows how the FSB has tried to address three issues that complicate cross-border harmonization of OTC derivatives regulation. First, the government network that was set up to coordinate OTC derivatives regulation initially did not have the right composition and authority to do its job properly. Legislators in Europe and the United States took the lead, devising a mutually incompatible set of derivatives rules with extraterritorial authority that triggered a half-decade of trans-Atlantic acrimony. Second, turf wars among legislators in the United States led to domestic institutional fragmentation that made cross-border harmonization among regulatory agencies more difficult. Third, legislators created legal obstacles to cross-border cooperation. A decade later, the FSB has forged a community that is able to coordinate OTC derivatives policies among relevant regulatory authorities within and across borders. But its power to address existing fragmentation in the trade reporting network along jurisdictional lines is limited, and regulators still are not able to monitor the evolution of risk in the global OTC derivatives market in a timely fashion. The following paragraphs look at the FSB reform trajectory from alternative perspectives.

Alternative Explanations

Hegemony theories of both the Simmons and Drezner variety concentrate on the interests of the great powers (see Chapter 1). In her approach to the politics of financial harmonization, Simmons (2001b) distinguishes between the dominant center where market power is concentrated, such as the United States and Great Britain, and the rest. The global governance arrangement in a given issue area is a two-dimensional function of (1) externalities of nonadherence to the center's standards and (2) market incentives for emulation. If the externalities of nonadherence are low, multilateral institutions play a marginal role, and market incentives decide whether harmonization occurs or not. Conversely, in areas where negative externalities of nonadherence are high, the dominant centers use multilateral institutional arrangements for a variety of task that range from information exchange and technical assistance to outright political pressure for harmonization.

The global financial crisis represents a fortuitous occasion to revisit the assumptions and conclusions of this theory. The crisis revealed the high degree of cross-border interconnectedness of the contemporary financial system. It can thus be argued that one of Simmons' dimensions has contracted, turning all sectors of financial activity into areas with significant cross-border externalities. This becomes clear when looking at the two sectors where Simmons previously regarded non-adherence as innocuous for financial stability at the core: accounting standards and securities regulation.

Generally not considered one of the most thrilling areas of global finance, accounting standards have gained unprecedented salience in the wake of the crisis. The inconsistencies between accounting standards applied in the United States (GAAP) and elsewhere (IFRS) have been the subject of debate among regulators for over a decade. The standard-setting bodies on both sides of the Atlantic signed the Norwalk Agreement in 2002 in order to institutionalize a convergence process between the two standards (Posner, 2009; Posner & Véron, 2010). State leaders however started paying attention to this issue area only in the wake of the global financial crisis (Friedman, 2011; Stiglitz, 2010; Tirole, 2010; Mügge & Stellinga, 2015). Since then, the Financial Stability Board (FSB) has included accounting standards in every progress report to date. Gadinis (2013, p. 171) notes with surprise, "That accounting inspires this level of detail in a report to government leaders is, on its own, a fascinating development."

The emergence of political pressure for international regulatory harmonization is even clearer in securities markets. Largely uncoordinated and even unregulated before the crisis, derivatives markets in particular have risen to the top of the G20 global financial reform agenda.

Thus, it can be argued that the 2 × 2 taxonomy of Simmons' theory of regulatory harmonization collapsed into a 2 × 1 roster after the crisis (see Figure 4.3). This implies that independent of the degree of market incentives for emulation,

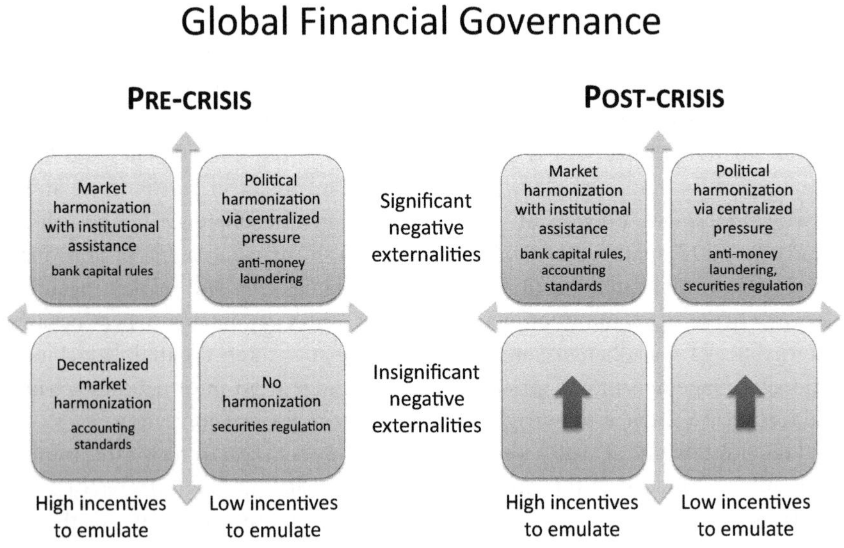

FIGURE 4.3 Global Financial Governance

Source: Author's visualization

the dominant center is likely to employ multilateral institutions to ensure global harmonization of regulatory standards and the elimination of free riding.

The idea that great powers remain the primary rule-makers of the global economy is further developed by Daniel Drezner (2007). The author distinguishes between the degree of interest divergence among great powers on the one hand and that between great powers and other international actors on the other hand. Drezner contends that in the realm of financial regulation, great powers exhibit a low degree of conflict whereas their interests significantly diverge from that of the periphery. Given this constellation of interests and power, the dominant players are likely to establish what Drezner calls "club standards."

The 2007–2009 financial crisis has only reinforced this alignment of costs and benefits. Developed countries, especially the United States and Europe, were hardest hit by the crisis, whereas most developing countries survived the crisis relatively unscathed. Consequently, the dominant powers are driving post-crisis reform efforts because they are willing to incur the costs of a regulatory overhaul that is designed to protect themselves from another financial breakdown. Developing countries on the other hand are voicing concerns not only about the burden of higher supervisory requirements but also the negative impact that regulatory reform would have on their access to capital abroad (FSB, 2012c, 2013e, 2014c).

In sum, both Simmons' and Drezner's approaches lead to the prediction that the global financial crisis will lead to the emergence of a harmonized set financial regulatory standards. The great financial powers are expected to drive the development of global rules in a minilateral club such as the G20 and the FSB and to push for subsequent global harmonization, making sure that all relevant jurisdictions adhere to the dominant standards and that none resorts to free riding. Yet this prediction does not match the empirical material at hand.

In contrast, the **transnational bureaucracy** approach to global financial governance provides a possible explanation for the empirical evidence. Before the crisis, OTC derivatives markets were only regulated in peripheral emerging economies such as Brazil (Yazbek, 2009; Lima de Carvalho, 2011). In the United States in contrast, OTC derivatives were explicitly exempted from regulation. There was political momentum to bring this asset class under regulatory purview following the turmoil with highly leveraged institutions in the 1990s, and then-CFTC Chairman Born was proposing concrete measures to do so until the now-famous 13 Bankers and Assistant Treasury Secretary Lawrence Summers spoke out against her advances (S. Johnson & Kwak, 2010; Roig-Franzia, 2009). The industry was successful at lobbying Congress to exempt OTC derivatives from regulatory supervision with the 2000 Commodity Futures Modernization Act (Spagna, 2018). Thus, before the crisis, regulatory experts had dedicated relatively little time and energy to finding out how to best regulate this market.

That does not mean however that regulatory proposals were nonexistent. Roughly half a year before the collapse of Lehman Brothers, the FSF and external financial experts recommended the establishment of central clearing and reporting requirements for OTC derivatives (FSF, 2008a; L. Alexander, 2008). OTC derivatives reform in the G20 and the FSB can be understood as the intellectual heir of these early recommendations. Nevertheless, the transnational community of derivatives market experts had not developed a consensual knowledge base that could compare to that of banking regulators (Newman & Posner, 2018; Posner, 2018). Therefore, the lack of reform progress can be attributed to the scant development of an epistemic community and the absence of transnational soft law in the field of OTC derivatives prior to the crisis.

At first sight, the **redistributive concern** approach seems to provide great inferential leverage to explain the complicated performance of OTC derivatives reform. It can be argued that concerns about competitiveness play a major role in the current spat between the United States and Europe. Unlike the field of banking regulation, it is not firms but trading infrastructures that compete in the OTC derivatives markets. London and New York in particular are major competitors as trading hubs of derivatives today. London's Canary Wharf emerged as the main hub for these trades in the late 1990s because the regulatory environment of the United Kingdom provided a lucrative arbitrage opportunity for American firms.

These concerns are compounded by differences in the timetables of OTC derivatives rulemaking and implementation. While US regulators took the lead in the implementation of Dodd-Frank, the European Union lagged about a year behind (CFTC & SEC, 2012). As shown in the previous section, other G20 countries deliberately delayed OTC derivatives reform until finalization of the rules in the two main markets. This in turn generated problems for the United States. In a 2012 testimony to the US Senate Banking Committee, a high-level US regulator stated the following:

> Given our commitment to convergence with international standards, our primary concern with the ongoing efforts to reform OTC derivatives markets is one of timing. If the U.S. is unable to implement market reforms in a coordinated and contemporaneous fashion with all significant derivatives market jurisdictions, we face the risk that trades will move to an unregulated market.
>
> *(Walsh, 2012, p. 19)*

US officials like Treasury Secretary Geithner (cited previously) and civil society organizations believed that the post-crisis derivatives regulation contains more loopholes in Europe than in the United States. A hasty, "outcomes-based" assessment of functional equivalence would thus have entailed a competitive disadvantage for the US. In line with this idea, Coffee (2014) draws the conclusion that "for the United States, substituted compliance will mean a loss of market share, revenues, and jobs as trading moves overseas to marginally less regulated markets" (p. 45).

A closer look at cross-border inconsistencies in OTC derivatives regulation however does not provide a clear picture of such a tilted playing field. For example, Dodd-Frank requirements cover a smaller product range of the derivatives market, and minimum risk management standards for central clearing counterparties are weaker than those in Europe (Eurofi, 2014). Other regulatory differences do not seem to provide any jurisdiction with a competitive advantage. A US lobbyist explains,

> Let's take reporting, for instance. In the US at CFTC there is one counterparty that's responsible for reporting to SDR [Swap Data Repositories] and that's in the regulation. In Europe both parties report. Okay, is it better or worse? I don't know. It's different. But what that causes is great confusion.
>
> *(US Lobbyist 2, personal communication, June 18, 2014)*

In sum, there is evidence that the authorities were concerned with the redistributive implications of derivatives rulemaking and substituted compliance in some areas. It would be difficult though to attribute the continued existence of legal obstacles to cross-border cooperation to competitiveness concerns. Therefore, it is hard to argue that redistributive concerns themselves are a significant obstacle to a successful completion of the G20 OTC derivatives reform.

It is not easy to analytically separate the **politicization** approach from the government network approach discussed at the beginning of this chapter. OTC derivatives regulation certainly evolved from a marginal topic to a highly politicized issue in the wake of the crisis.

Prior to the crisis AIG, a US government-sponsored enterprise had issued $500 billion worth of credit default swaps (CDS) without having to post any collateral (BIS, 2014a; FCIC, 2011; Public Citizen, 2012).

After the collapse of Lehman Brothers, the Fed found itself obliged to guarantee AIG's derivatives obligations to counterparties, a bailout worth $182 billion of taxpayer's money. This AIG debacle has chiefly contributed to the politicization of derivatives regulation, arguably motivating legislators in the United States to take action (Helleiner, 2011). In fact, Helleiner (2014b) cites derivatives regulation as a salient case of what he terms cooperative decentralization.

The evolution of regulatory bickering across the Atlantic in the field of OTC derivatives regulation can thus be read both as a confirmation of the government network and the politicization approaches.

From a **regulatory capture** perspective, we can expect OTC derivatives reform to be derailed by the lobby efforts of the private sector. Large derivatives dealers were expected to see net income reduced by $2–3 billion in Europe and Japan, according to an IMF study (Oliveira Santos & Elliott, 2012). The BIS conducted a macroeconomic impact assessment in 2013, estimating the annual cost of OTC derivatives reform at a higher range of between 15 and 32 billion euros (BIS, 2013). Nevertheless, even though special interest groups in the OTC field lobbied for exemptions to the rules (Pagliari, 2018; Helleiner, 2018), they did not engage in full-out opposition against regulatory reform such as evidenced by the IIF study on Basel III (chapter 3). Even more surprisingly, they have been a staunch supporter of the global harmonization of derivatives rules.

Even faster than European and other foreign regulators, the financial sector was the first to voice opposition to extraterritoriality. In a letter to Commissioner Barnier and Secretary Geithner from July 2011, eight financial trade associations expressed concern that rules proposed in Europe and the United States would "leave the global derivatives business with ambiguity and problematic extra-territorial challenges and issues of legal uncertainty and misunderstanding which might give rise to material risk." In the same letter, the lobby firms remind the officials that the "G-20's goal of addressing key systemic risk issues cannot be met without international coordination on market infrastructure, regulatory transparency, and counterparty credit risk" (ISDA et al., 2011).

In December 2013, the finance lobby became more aggressive in reminding regulators of the G20 reform agenda. Three trade associations filed a lawsuit against the CFTC, contending that its proposed guidance on cross-border swaps was unlawful. The plaintiffs challenged not only the agency's use of guidance and staff advisories instead of a formal rulemaking process but claimed that the CFTC "imposed a series of rules that are contrary to the spirit and the letter of international cooperation and may harm global markets." In order to substantiate this claim, the lobby organizations made ample reference to the Path Forward initiative and the statements of European regulatory authorities (SIFMA et al., 2013; Chon, 2013).

Thus, four years after G20 leaders gathered in Pittsburgh to declare their joint political will to stand up against the interests of the financial sector and bring OTC derivatives markets under coordinated supervisory control, the financial sector itself was able to exploit statements of the G20 and those made by regulators of one jurisdiction to challenge the regulatory authorities of another.

Is the financial sector's expressed preference for regulatory coordination merely hypocrisy? Regulatory arbitrage has been an important element of "financial innovation" in the run-up to the global financial crisis, and regulatory coordination under the aegis of the FSB is designed to minimize arbitrage opportunities. However, uniformly strict requirements are considered less of a burden than duplicative requirements or even market fragmentation along jurisdictional lines. A US regulator explains,

> From one perspective where they make their money is arbitrage, but in another perspective where they make their money is volume. So they trade off volume versus arbitrage and compliance costs add to that. So all things being equal, you'd rather have a bigger pool with less rules.
>
> *(US Regulator 1, personal communication, June 16, 2014)*

On the other side, civil society organizations have supported the actions of the CFTC. In a response to the previously mentioned letter by Barnier and his colleagues, 25 organizations from around the world defend extraterritoriality. The letter states, "If, as you suggest, the reach of national regulation cannot extend beyond national borders, then national regulators will be helpless when faced with the global reach of financial institutions" (Action Aid International, 2013, p. 2). The organizations regard coordination around a "shared high level of financial oversight" as a goal and the CFTC's actions as a step towards this goal. Members of the same coalition have identified loopholes in EU regulation regarding derivatives (WEED, 2013).

With these alignments in the field of OTC derivatives regulation, it would be mistaken to claim that the financial sector has undermined global reform progress. Therefore, the regulatory capture hypothesis is not supported by the empirical record in this area of the G20 reform agenda.

Conclusion

OTC derivatives regulation is probably the biggest headache for FSB officials tasked with meeting G20 regulatory reform commitments. It took years for the right government networks and working groups to be created under the FSB umbrella. Member states have missed all original deadlines in the implementation of domestic rules, and even over a decade after the Pittsburgh summit, the G20 reform process in this area is far from complete. Nevertheless, the FSB has provided leadership in designing globally coherent rules and institutions where none existed before, and it has made progress in addressing some of the manifold legal obstacles and cross-border inconsistencies that manifested in the first half of the 2010s. The next and final empirical chapter will provide an analysis of the third main item on the G20 reform agenda: ending too-big-to-fail.

5

THE NEVER-ENDING TOO-BIG-TO-FAIL STORY

Large banks with extensive cross-border operations were at the epicenter of the global financial earthquake of 2007–2009. Their failure sent shockwaves through financial markets, threatening to cause global economic contraction of a magnitude not witnessed since the 1930s. In the wake of the crisis, G20 leaders became increasingly vocal about reducing the expectation that failing banks can count on public support. They authorized the FSB to devise a set of policies in order to make sure that no financial institution in the future is too big to fail (TBTF).

The FSB devised a framework to deal with systemically important financial institutions (SIFI), harnessing the efficiency of a government network. However, policy efforts bifurcate in 2013, about three years after initiation of the ending TBTF reform package. Some policies successfully entered the implementation stage along the agreed timeline. while others stalled in the negotiation stage. The division between the former and the latter was not random. It corresponded to the two sides of the FSB's "bookends' strategy" to increase bank resilience on the one hand and make them resolvable without taxpayer support on the other. While the resilience "bookend" of ending TBTF that comprises policies to identify systemically important financial institutions and increase their going-concern loss absorbency was implemented coherently and on time, FSB members missed all deadlines on the resolution "bookend" of banking reform.

This chapter argues that the different degrees of government network involvement in the two bookends explain the difference in reform progress. The successful elements of the ending TBTF reform package were developed by the Basel Committee, highlighting the effectiveness of government networks. In contrast, policies that have required the involvement of legislators fell short of G20 commitments throughout the mid-2010s. Facing a slowdown of TBTF reform and the proliferation of uncoordinated unilateral structural measures, the FSB took innovative action. Its initiative to increase the loss absorbency requirement (LAC) of global

DOI: 10.4324/9781003290001-5

banks emulates the institutional pathway of the Basel process, thus circumventing national legislators and legal obstacles to a large extent. It also galvanized renewed cross-border cooperation among regulators who seek to plan for the recovery and resolution of large banks. This chapter argues that this is the result of an institutional learning process: FSB leadership drew on the intellectual tool kit of the Basel Committee to harness the power of government networks in implementing TBTF reform.

This chapter first identifies the puzzle of uneven progress in the FSB work plan on ending TBTF. It then seeks to explain the policy process until the mid-2010s from a government network perspective, highlighting the power of the FSB and its limits. The government network argument is then subjected to scrutiny by a series of competing explanations. The subsequent section traces the institutional learning process of the FSB in the second half of the 2010s. It argues that the FSB harnessed the power of government networks to avoid (and roll back) jurisdictional fragmentation and circumvent legal obstacles to a significant degree, advancing the global implementation of ending TBTF policies. A concluding section examines caveats to the TBTF policy package and draws lessons for the relationship between government networks and nation states.

The Puzzle

While the US Fed was able to arrange and guarantee the sale of Bear Stearns in March, Countrywide in July, and Merrill Lynch in September 2008, the inability to repeat this kind of arrangement with another troubled bank, Lehman Brothers, sent financial markets into shock and triggered the most substantial state intervention program of modern times, including bailouts, forced mergers, and fire sales of failing financial institutions. G20 leaders were initially cautious in their statements, however. The declarations of the Washington and London Summits (G20, 2008, 2009a, 2009b) mentions neither moral hazard nor too-big-to-fail (TBTF) financial institutions. At the Pittsburgh Summit in September 2009, G20 leaders stated, "We should develop resolution tools and frameworks for the effective resolution of financial groups to help mitigate the disruption of financial institution failures and reduce moral hazard in the future" (G20, 2009c, para. 13 Annex 1).

The language of G20 documents regarding too-big-to-fail became gradually starker, with the June 2010 Toronto declaration asserting, "We are committed to design and implement a system where we have the powers and tools to restructure or resolve all types of financial institutions in crisis, without taxpayers ultimately bearing the burden, and adopted principles that will guide implementation" (G20, 2010a, para. 21). Finally, at the Seoul Summit five months later, G20 leaders made their commitment to end too-big-to-fail explicit: "We reaffirmed our view that no firm should be too big or too complicated to fail and that taxpayers should not bear the costs of resolution" (G20, 2010b, para. 30). This commitment has appeared in every G20 declaration since. While the G20 heads of state appeared to be ever more vocal about ending too-big-to-fail, a considerable gap opened between this commitment and the reality of regulatory reform in this issue area in the mid-2010s.

The development of a policy response to the TBTF problem took shape in several transnational government networks that have a track record in dealing with global financial firms. Figure 5.1 ranks the relevant policy proposals according to how much cross-border cooperation they would entail.

Shortly after the fall of Northern Rock in February and Bear Stearns in March 2008, the FSF submitted a report on Enhancing Market and Institutional Resilience to G7 Finance Ministers and Central Bank Governors. The report reflected the optimism at the time that the subprime crisis can be dealt with by merely fixing certain aspects of the financial system: "During the recent turmoil, cross-border cooperation has worked satisfactorily overall between authorities, and arrangements for dealing with problems at a cross-border institution have not been tested" (FSF, 2008a, p. 49). Nevertheless, the FSF recommended that national authorities should strengthen legal bank resolution powers. It further encouraged regulators to increase cross-border information sharing and to form supervisory colleges for "significant cross-border firms," most of which were indeed established by the end of 2008. The recommendations regarding cross-border information sharing in supervisory colleges were repeated in follow-up reports (FSF, 2008b, 2009a) and formed part of a set of high-level principles for cross-border cooperation on crisis management that the FSF (2009b) published in time for the G20 London Summit in April 2009. It is noteworthy that unlike earlier FSF documents, the 2009 FSF principles eschew the question of legal authority altogether. They also stop short of requiring resolution plans for cross-border firms and merely

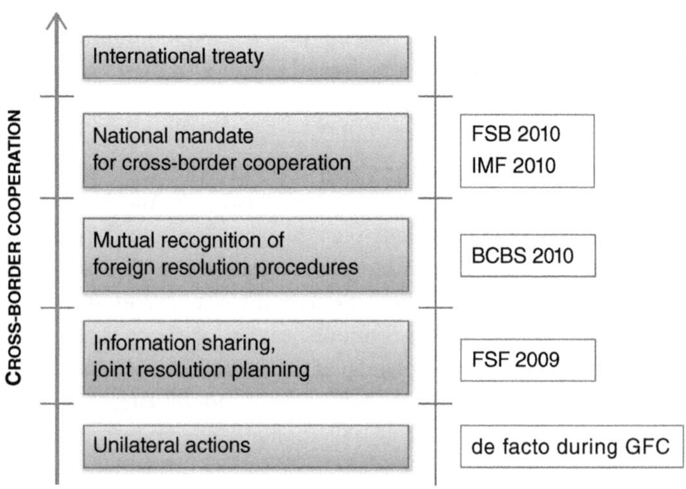

FIGURE 5.1 Degrees of Cross-Border Cooperation

Source: Author's visualization

"encourage firms to maintain contingency plans and procedures for use in a wind-down situation" (para. 8).

A slightly bolder proposal was published by the Basel Committee. It had established a Cross-border Bank Resolution Group in 2007, and its March 2010 report highlights legal obstacles to cross-border cooperation. The Basel Group points out that an international insolvency framework for financial firms is nonexistent at present and unlikely to be established in the future. Thus, as a prerequisite for cross-border cooperation, national resolution authorities should be endowed with the legal powers to wind down financial institutions fast and efficiently without recourse to domestic courts (BCBS, 2010b).

Building on earlier efforts of cross-border coordination by the G10 Joint Task force and the European Union (EU, 2008), the Basel Committee explored the idea to apply a quintessential instrument of transnational government networks: a memorandum of understanding for cross-border banking crises. However, Basel Committee members were not able to support this option: "Without more convergence and binding agreements – and in the absence of aligned incentives – coordination between national authorities has proved challenging" (BCBS, 2010b, p. 7). In the end, the Basel Committee merely recommends national authorities to "develop procedures to facilitate the mutual recognition of crisis management and resolution proceedings" (p. 1).

Arguably the most ambitious proposal for dealing with cross-border bank failure comes from the IMF (2010b). The fund does not merely encourage regulatory cooperation or mutual recognition of domestic regimes but calls for countries to "ensure that their domestic legislation *requires* national authorities to coordinate their resolution efforts with their counterparts in other jurisdictions to the maximum extent consistent with the interests of creditors and domestic financial stability" (IMF, 2010b, p. 18, emphasis added). Furthermore, the IMF calls for the development of "core-coordination standards" that would facilitate resolution coordination among those jurisdictions that comply with these standards.

The FSB followed up with a policy proposal that builds and extends upon the IMF approach. In October 2010, ahead of the G20 Seoul Summit, the FSB (2010a) published the framework for ending TBTF that would guide all efforts in this policy area to date. The so-called "SIFI framework" covers a wide range of policy initiatives that address three major issues: identification of SIFIs, loss absorbency, and resolution (see Figure 5.2). First, the FSB authorizes the Basel Committee to develop a methodology for assessing systemic importance in order to identify SIFIs. Second, financial institutions that qualify as global SIFIs should be subject to higher loss absorbency requirements as developed, again, by the Basel Committee. At this early stage of the policymaking process, loss absorbency referred to instruments that could be drawn on while the bank was still operational (going-concern). The third item on the SIFI agenda concerns the resolution of failing SIFIs.

It repeats FSF, BCBS, and IMF recommendations to make changes in legislation that give national authorities the power to resolve a failing financial institutions and bail in creditors (Draghi, 2010). However, it goes beyond earlier proposals in

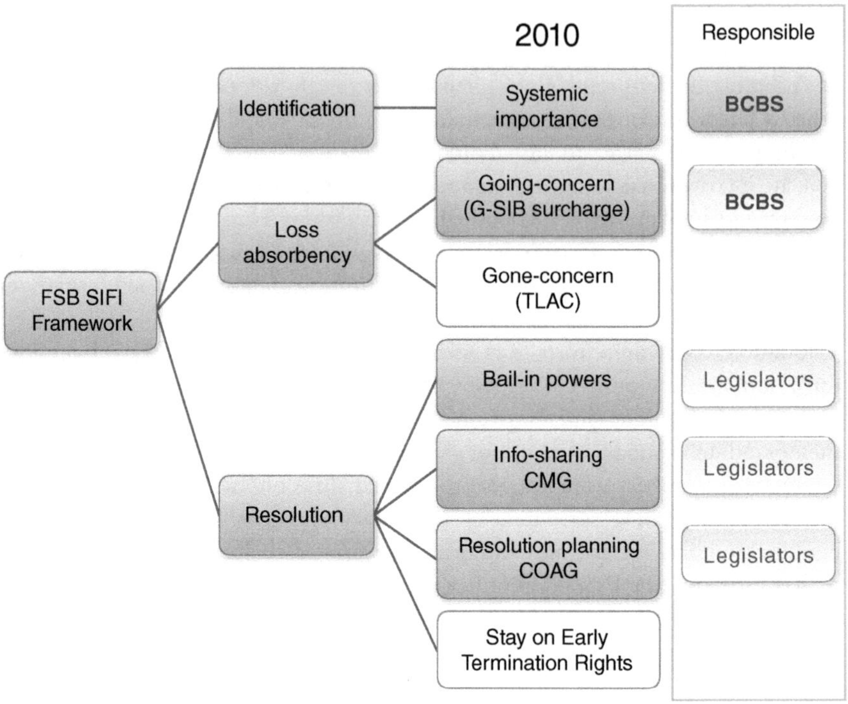

FIGURE 5.2 SIFI Framework and Progress, 2010

Source: Author's visualization

recommending that authorities should have the powers to require a bank to change its legal and operational structure in order to facilitate recovery and resolution. Regarding cross-border cooperation, the FSB also adopts a strong position, making the following recommendation: "The mandates of resolution authorities should be framed so that they are *fully obliged* to seek cooperation with foreign resolution authorities" (FSB, 2010a, p. 4, emphasis added). FSB members are recommended to establish cross-border crisis-management groups (CMG) for each global SIFI, make resolvability assessments, share information, develop a recovery and resolution plan (RRP), and sign a cooperation agreement (COAG) for the institution under supervision. At the G20 Summit in Cannes the following year, the FSB presented the so-called Key Attributes for Effective Resolution Regimes, a new global standard to end TBTF that codifies the FSB SIFI framework (FSB, 2011a).

A final element of resolution policies concerns the entanglement of SIFIs in derivatives markets and the recognition that resolution would only be feasible with a so-called stay on early termination rights. At the time however, research into the link between derivatives exposure and ending TBTF was not advanced enough to make specific recommendations, and the FSB merely refers to work undertaken by the OTC Derivatives Working Group (see Chapter 4) regarding central clearing of derivatives. The FSB also set timelines, expecting the majority of policy work on these issue areas to be accomplished by end-2011.

A decade after this deadline passed, the ending-TBTF story is far from over. Some areas have seen the rapid development of globally coherent standards and its implementation among most or all the 24 FSB member jurisdictions. Other policy initiatives of the FSB SIFI framework however have been plagued by delays and patchy implementation, as Figure 5.3 shows.

The identification and loss absorbency elements of the SIFI policy framework have seen rapid progress. In contrast, FSB members missed all deadlines in implementing the necessary legislative changes to make cross-border bank resolution without taxpayer support credible. Only in the late 2010s did FSB members make progress in resolution planning at home and in cooperation with their counterparts abroad.

Nevertheless, the TBTF problem continues to plague the global financial system. In the United States, the top five banks control 44% of all industry assets, up from less than 10% in 1990 (Menkin, 2014). The world's largest banks continue to enjoy more favorable funding conditions in capital markets because investors believe that public authorities will bail them out in case of insolvency. Credit rating agencies differentiate between "standalone" and "support" ratings for bonds issued by banks, and the resulting differences in bond spreads provides large banks with a funding advantage that amounted to the equivalent of annual profit for British

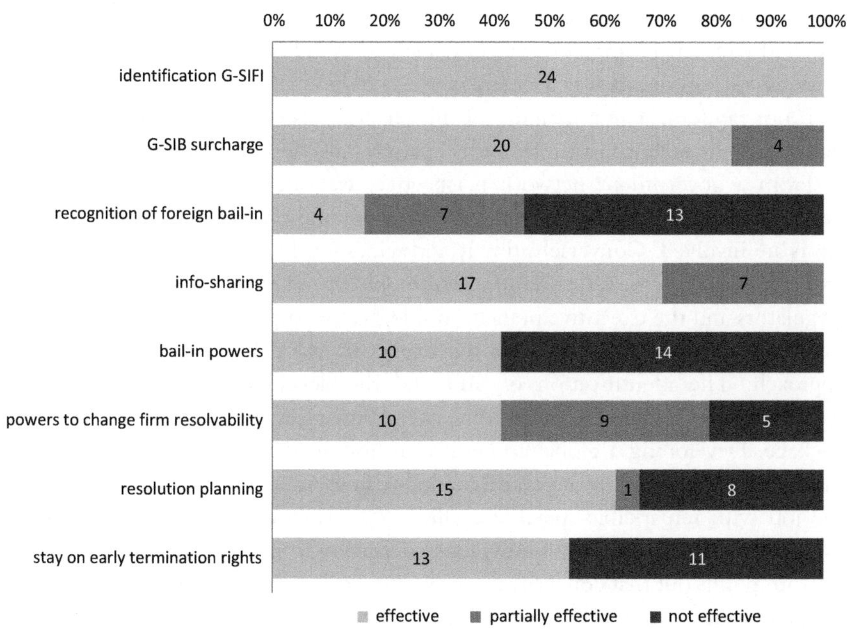

FIGURE 5.3 Implementation of FSB SIFI Framework in 2018

Sources: FSB (2018c, 2021)

banks in 2010, according to one study (Haldane, 2010). The Bank of International Settlements (BIS, 2012) reported that this TBTF subsidy has increased significantly after the crisis:

> A comparison of all-in and stand-alone ratings reveals that rating agencies deem the official support for banks to have increased substantially between 2007 and 2011. At end-2011, such support lowered the spreads that banks had to pay for long-term bonds by an estimated 1–2 percentage points, or by 10 times more than prior to the crisis.
>
> *(p. 76)*

Even today, the world's biggest banks continue to enjoy a significant funding advantage in capital markets vis-à-vis their smaller competitors because creditors still have good reasons to believe that governments will bail them out if they fail (Afonso et al., 2014; Brewer III & Jagtiani, 2013; Carney, 2014b; IMF, 2014; Santos, 2014; Siegert & Willison, 2015). A recent literature review by the FSB (2021) confirms that while the funding cost advantage of TBTF banks (measured by CDS spreads, bank debt spreads, and credit ratings) has decreased since 2012, it still remains at least as high as before the global financial crisis.

Government Network

Why did some policy initiatives designed to end TBTF experience rapid, coherent, and widespread implementation while others did not? The pattern of uneven financial reform progress that emerges over a decade after the global financial crisis is not random. The remainder of this chapter sets out to test the government network approach against the empirical pattern and five competing explanations.

From a government network perspective, we can expect shortcomings and delays of the ending-TBTF reform package to manifest in policy areas where legislators are involved. Conversely, timely and widespread implementation is expected to occur in reform areas that require action only by government network members (regulators and the executive branch), not legislative approval.

The empirical record matches the expectations of the government network approach: The identification of SIFI and the development of commensurate loss-absorbency requirements are the success stories of the ending TBTF reform package. Developing a global consensus on how to define and measure systemic importance was by no means an easy task, but government networks accomplished the job with remarkable speed and efficiency. Tsingou (2015) argues that ideational blockages prevented a more radical departure from the status quo, but Baker (2013b) points out that concerns about systemic risk remained at the margins of the regulatory discourse until the global financial crisis.

By November 2009 however, global regulators proposed three key criteria for measuring systemic importance: size, substitutability, and interconnectedness (FSB et al., 2009). The Basel Committee followed up with a more sophisticated

TABLE 5.1 2020 List of G-SIB

Bucket (G-SIB Surcharge)	*Name*
5 (3.5%)	*[deliberately left empty in order to discourage further growth]*
4 (2.5%)	*[empty after some banks reduced their systemic importance]*
3 (2.0%)	Citigroup, HSBC, JP Morgan Chase
2 (1.5%)	Bank of America, Bank of China, Barclays, BNP Paribas, China Construction Bank, Deutsche Bank, ICBC, Mitsubishi UFJ FG
1 (1.0%)	Agricultural Bank of China, Bank of New York Mellon, Credit Suisse, Goldman Sachs, Groupe BPCE, Crédit Agricole, ING Bank, Mizuho FG, Morgan Stanley, Royal Bank of Canada, Santander, Société Générale, Standard Chartered, State Street, Sumitomo Mitsui FG, Toronto Dominion, UBS, Unicredit, Wells Fargo

Source: FSB (2020a)

definition of systemic importance specifically for banks, adding two more criteria (global activity and complexity) and developing 12 indicators to measure it. In time for the G20 Cannes Summit and ahead of the end-2011 deadline, the FSB and the Basel Committee had reached consensus on a methodology for the designation of global systemically important banks (G-SIB) (BCBS, 2011c; FSB, 2011d; FSB & BCBS, 2011; Ötker-Robe et al., 2010). They compiled a list of initially 29 G-SIBs (see Figure 5.1 for the 2020 update), proposed a staggered system of capital surcharges that would increase the resilience of these banks, and estimated the macroeconomic impact of this policy.

Two elements of the G-SIB surcharge are remarkable. First, banking regulators from very different financial systems reached a cross-border consensus on what systemic risk is and how to measure it, in a matter of months. Second, they agreed to depart from the previously widespread notion that size, interconnectedness, and complexity of banks represent a valuable contribution to the stability of the financial system.

The fall of Lehman Brothers shattered conventional wisdom about the relationship between the size and resilience of a bank. Because the operations of large banks cover a wider geographic area and spectrum of business lines, they have a greater ability than small banks to diversify risk, at least in principle (Dicken, 2007; Hughes & Mester, 2013; Navaretti & Venables, 2006). That this potential for risk diversification does not necessarily lead to a greater resilience vis-à-vis exogenous shocks became painfully clear during the crisis, attracting the attention of economists and regulators alike (Arner, 2011).

Andrew Haldane, chief economist at the Bank of England, was among the first economists to conceive of bank size as a negative externality. He argues that "the banking industry is also a pollutant. Systemic risk is a noxious by-product" (Haldane, 2010). Insofar as higher capital requirements are costly for banks (an issue discussed in the next section), the G-SIB surcharge represents a "Pigouvian tax" that matches a bank's contribution to this negative externality (Acharya et al., 2011; Pigou, 1920). The debate about the adequacy of the G-SIB surcharge is not settled (Passmore & von Hafften, 2017). But the recognition and "pricing" of systemic risk represents a major departure from Basel II and the pre-crisis consensus among financial regulators. Haldane (2012b) remarks pointedly: "We are all Pigouvians now, even if most of us cannot spell it" (p. 5).

The advance of global policymaking to end TBTF until this point can be regarded as a success story for the operation of government networks. In an extremely short time span of less than three years, regulators in the major economies identified systemic risk as a negative externality in global financial markets, drawing lessons from the crisis, and developed a consensus on how this externality can be defined, measured, and addressed with a set of globally coordinated policies that impose costs on the biggest industry players. This is a remarkable feat, especially when taking into consideration the opposition from legislators.

In May 2014, leading members of the House Financial Committee sent a letter to the US agencies that are FSB members. The authors assert that the FSB designation process of a systemically important financial institution is nontransparent and "not accountable to the American people." Pointedly, the committee members state, "The last thing we should to do [sic] is surrender U.S. sovereignty on financial regulatory matters to an international 'old boy's club' that deliberates in secret" (US House Committee on Financial Services, 2014a, p. 2f). One of the signatories of the letter, Jeb Hensarling, condensed the opinion of many parliamentarians in the following words:

> Neither the Treasury, the Fed, nor the SEC has ever reported to Congress about its participation, nor have they ever asked for Congress' approval to participate in the global organization. . . . Great risks . . . lurk to U.S. financial stability and competitiveness in a shadow regulatory system in which Treasury and the Federal Reserve may have ceded U.S. sovereignty over financial regulatory matters to a secretive, unaccountable coalition of European bureaucrats.
>
> *(US House Committee on Financial Services, 2014b, p. 2)*

Congress leveled another attack against FSB work on ending TBTF in April 2015, when Richard Shelby, chairman of the Senate Banking Committee, asserted that "the FSB is not a U.S. regulator, and it is not accountable to Congress or the American people" (Jopson & Binham, 2015). More recently, House Finance Committee vice chairman Patrick McHenry addressed Janet Yellen, the Fed's chair, with a letter that is worth quoting at length:

> I am writing regarding the Federal Reserve's continued participation in international forums on financial regulation. Despite the clear message delivered by President Donald Trump in prioritizing America's interest in international

> negotiations, it appears that the Federal Reserve continues negotiating international regulatory standards for financial institutions among global bureaucrats in foreign lands without transparency, accountability, or the authority to do so. This is unacceptable.
>
> *(McHenry, 2017)*

Members of Congress did not limit themselves to words. Legislative proposals that reassert congressional authority over financial regulators have been introduced both in the House of Representatives and the Senate. The Regulations from the Executive in Need of Scrutiny (REINS) Act, introduced by several legislators throughout the 2010s and still under debate today, would make all material new rules subject to Congressional approval (*Text – S.68–117th Congress (2021–2022)*, 2021), Moreover, the Regulatory Accountability Act and the Financial CHOICE Act would repeal the parts of the Dodd-Frank Act that enable cross-border regulatory coordination (*H.R.26–115th Congress (2017–2018)*, 2017; *H.R.5–115th Congress (2017–2018)*, 2017; *H.R.5983–114th Congress (2015–2016)*, 2016; Zaring, 2016).

While Republicans in Congress have been more vocal in criticizing the FSB, this issue crosses party lines. In April 2015, Senators Heller and Tester introduced a bipartisan bill to increase Congressional oversight over the interaction of US representatives with global standard-setting bodies (*Text – S.1086–114th Congress (2015–2016)*, 2015). As mentioned in the following section, the Democrat-driven 2010 Dodd-Frank Act itself falls short of the FSB recommendation to provide resolution authorities with a mandate to cooperate across jurisdictional lines.

In spite of such congressional resistance, the identification and loss absorbency parts of the ending TBTF reform package successfully entered the implementation stage along the agreed timeline. In contrast, progress in policy initiatives related to bank resolution was disappointing. In 2013, the year that probably marks the low point in the never-ending TBTF story, a peer review commissioned by the FSB candidly acknowledges that "progress has been relatively slow both because the issue is complex and because in many jurisdictions the powers necessary for implementing a preferred resolution strategy have not yet been provided" (FSB, 2013b, p. 3). Figure 5.4 summarizes policy progress in that year. The situation had not changed significantly by the mid-2010s (FSB, 2016c). Implementation gaps were evident in three areas: bail-in resolution powers, the operation of crisis management groups, and powers to impose a stay on early termination rights.

Bail-in

The first problem area of TBTF reform concerns the statutory power of resolution authorities to bail-in creditors when a financial institution fails. All FSB members have insolvency laws for the orderly wind down of companies, but as Huertas (2011) asserts, "Bankruptcy is not for banks." This is because banks rely on "runnable financial liabilities" that are likely to be impaired or liquidated during a drawn-out insolvency process led by courts (McAndrews et al., 2014). The two alternatives are a bailout using public funds and the intervention of a resolution authority that has the power to restructure the liabilities of a distressed financial institution by writing down its unsecured debt or converting it to equity (bail-in) (IMF, 2012). Eliminating the former alternative is the purpose of ending TBTF reform, but the bail-in alternative is facing obstacles in domestic banking, insolvency, and company law (BCBS, 2010b). The FSB recognized this issue in 2013: "Very few authorities have the statutory power both to write down and to convert liabilities of a failing institution" (FSB, 2013a, p. 9).

These problems are compounded when dealing with the complex and large financial institutions that all SIFIs are. As Paul Tucker (2013), chair of the FSB's Resolution Steering Group, points out, "Even once the statutory resolution regime is in place in all key jurisdictions, many financial groups are going to need to restructure themselves in order to achieve resolvability – financially, legally, organizationally" (p. 12). Some members of the regulatory establishment argued for a size cap, breakup, and simplification of financial institutions and activities, but their suggestions were not heeded (Engelen et al., 2011; Haldane, 2010; Quaglia & Spendzharova, 2017). The lack of a legal mandate prevents resolution authorities in many jurisdictions from requiring firms to make changes to their organizational structures in order to improve resolvability (FSB, 2013a, 2019b). To make things worse, global banks have become bigger and even more complex in the wake of the financial crisis (Carmassi & Herring, 2014; Cetorelli et al., 2014; Ötker Robe et al., 2011). In its latest peer review, the FSB (2019b) reports that "authorities indicate that substantial work remains to be done to ensure bail-in strategies can be credibly executed" (p. 22).

Another obstacle to a credible resolution regime is that legal provisions in key jurisdictions disregard the need for cross-border coordination among resolution authorities (BCBS, 2011b). In a progress report from 2012, the FSB warns, "The absence of a clear mandate of resolution authorities to seek cooperation with their foreign counterparts and the lack of legal capacity to give effect to foreign resolution measures may pose significant impediments to cross-border resolutions, if not addressed" (FSB, 2012d, p. 7). Seven years later, only 3 FSB member jurisdictions report that they would rely on statutory frameworks for the cross-border enforceability of a bail-in (FSB, 2019b, p. 29). For example, Title II of the Dodd-Frank Act endows the new Orderly Liquidation Authority (OLA) with bail-in powers but does not mandate it to consult with resolution authorities in other jurisdictions. Similarly, the European Bank Recovery and Resolution Directive (BRRD) gives statutory force to bail-in regimes (Art. 50) and allows for cross-border cooperation but enables the resolution authority to act unilaterally (Art. 87) in the resolution of the subsidiaries and even branches of non-EU banks if necessary (DIRECTIVE 2014/59/EU OF THE EUROPEAN PARLIAMENT AND OF THE COUNCIL, 2014; Goodhart & Avgouleas, 2014; Wishart, 2014). Thus, even after legislative reforms in key jurisdictions, legal frameworks of FSB members to date fall short of the provisions of Key Attribute 7 to *empower and strongly encourage*

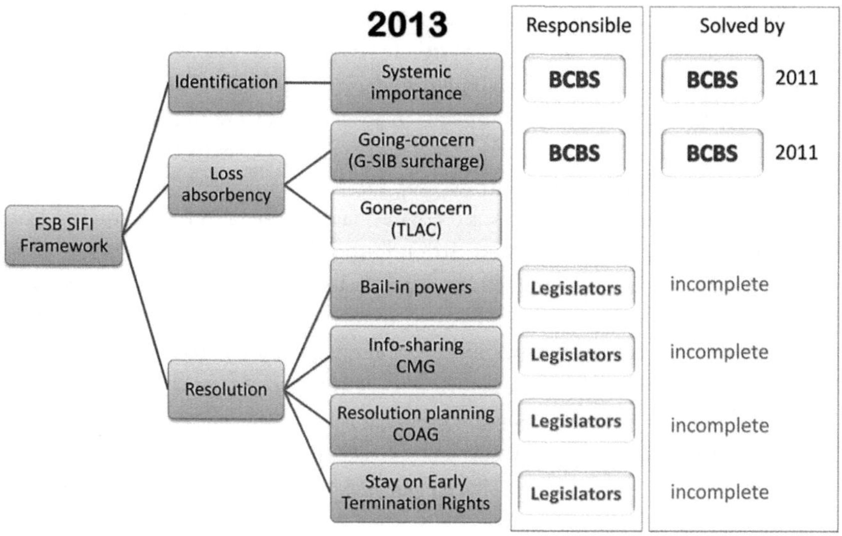

FIGURE 5.4 SIFI Framework and Progress, 2013

Source: Author's visualization

cross-border cooperation. In the most recent peer review to date, the FSB (2019b) notes that "the limited progress in recent years reflects the largely unchanged legal and institutional framework for resolution across FSB jurisdictions" (p. 8).

Crisis-Management Groups and Cooperation Agreements

The second policy with significant implementation gaps concerns the operation of crisis-management groups (CMG). FSB members committed to establishing supervisory colleges for each G-SIFI where home and key host authorities share firm-specific prudential information. Even though CMGs for all G-SIFIs have been established by 2012, it is hard to assert that they are operational. When asked about the status of CMGs in 2014, a US Regulator responds,

> You checked, yes, we've got a college, okay, but one of the guys here talks about having our annual quarterly meeting of the college, because it's just a waste of time. And you talk about, we're doing a review, scheduled review next month and we've done a review last month and that's about as much information as you share.
>
> *(US Regulator 1, personal communication, June 16, 2014)*

In addition, supervisory agencies of G-SIFI were expected to sign cross-border cooperation agreements (COAG) on resolution planning by end-2011. The first cooperation agreement was signed only in 2014. However, after the FSB facilitated cross-border coordination around loss absorbency requirements (TLAC, see the next section) and the European Systemic Resolution Board started exerting authority over all large banks headquartered in the eurozone, the pace of cross-border cooperation picked up. Cooperation agreements were in place for 19 banks by 2017 (FSB, 2017e), 25 banks by 2019, and for all 30 G-SIBs by 2021, a decade after the original deadline passed (FSB, 2019b).

The main obstacles that prevent CMGs and cooperation agreements from becoming a meaningful instrument in ending TBTF are of legal nature. CMG members often do not have the statutory authority to share firm-specific data with their foreign counterparts. This is because much of the information that is necessary to make meaningful resolvability assessments are protected by privacy laws, and legal reform in many FSB member jurisdictions failed to include provisions to override these laws for prudential purposes.

In its first peer review report, the FSB (2013a, p. 10) points out that

> few FSB jurisdictions have clear and dedicated statutory provisions for domestic authorities to share confidential information with foreign resolution authorities. . . . Unless home and host authorities have the capacity to share such information, it is unrealistic to expect them to meaningfully discuss cross-border resolution strategies and plans or to cooperate effectively in a crisis.

Tellingly, the second peer review report three years later states that "progress in reforming the legal frameworks for bank resolution in FSB jurisdictions has slowed since the 2013 Thematic Review – indeed, many of the shortcomings identified in this review are similar to the ones of the previous peer review" (FSB, 2016a, p. 6).

In a congressional hearing in the United States, the director of the Fed's Division of Banking Supervision and Regulation on Cross-Border Resolution described "completing firm-specific cooperation agreements with foreign regulators that provide credible assurances to those host-country regulators to forestall disruptive ring-fencing" as one of the "key challenges" for the authorities (Gibson, 2013). Asked about the current state of COAGs in 2014, a US Regulator admits: "It is a disappointment they aren't farther along. I just don't know. I think it's a matter of priority" (US Regulator 4, personal communication, June 30, 2014). Three years later, an official at an international organization explains that legal hurdles remain for cross-border cooperation among resolution authorities, albeit not financial supervisors: "There are now legislative gages for supervisory information sharing. But now you want to bring in the CMG authorities that are not supervisors, that don't have a supervisory mandate. There is no legal basis for that sharing of information" (International Regulator 14, personal communication, December 19, 2017). By 2019, only authorities in the UK and Switzerland share full resolution plans and resolvability assessments with their peers abroad.

But regulators that supervise large banks around the world have made increasing use of nonlegal instruments such as MoUs to facilitate cross-border cooperation (FSB, 2019b, p. 40). In addition, the FSB has instituted an internal report system that circumvents legal obstacles to information sharing. Since 2015, FSB members from the home jurisdictions of G-SIBs provide an annual report of how large banks would fare in case of failure. This so-called Resolvability Assessment Process is confidential, and the reports are only shared with the FSB Chair. This allows the FSB to track the evolution of global SIFI risk over time in ways that are not accessible to individual financial supervisors and resolution authorities in the presence of perennial legal obstacles to information sharing.

Temporary Stay on Early Termination Rights

The third and final implementation gap is the lack of authority to impose a temporary stay on early termination rights. Modern SIFIs are entangled in a complex web of derivative contracts that transcend jurisdictional boundaries. Haldane (2010) explains, "When Lehman Brothers failed, it had almost one million open derivatives contracts – the financial equivalent of Facebook friends. Whatever the technology budget, it is questionable whether any man's mind or memory could cope with such complexity" (p. 18f). Derivative contracts contain a provision that allows a party to terminate the contract early if the counterparty defaults. In the event of a bank failure, all counterparties thus have an incentive to close out and seize the corresponding collateral before other agents do – the equivalent of a depositor run on the bank. Because large banks typically have derivatives books with trillions of dollars in notional exposure, the cost of early termination for the estate of the bank is massive, and the equivalent of a deposit protection scheme is not an option (Huertas, 2011).

The Basel Committee addressed this issue early on: "National resolution authorities should have the legal authority to temporarily delay immediate operation of contractual early termination clauses" (BCBS, 2010b, p. 2). An international regulator explains why such legal authority remains a distant possibility:

> This legal act would have to say that the United States will recognize the temporary stay ordered by whatever, the Swiss authorities on a contract governed by US law for 48 hours provided certain conditions are met. And I think that parliamentarians would really need to be educated on why this is in the national interest to recognize action of foreign authorities.
>
> *(International Regulator 14, personal communication, December 19, 2017)*

Seven years later, legislators in about half of all FSB member jurisdictions still have not given resolution authorities the legal powers to impose such a stay. And by 2019, only six FSB members note that they would rely on it in case of a SIFI failure (FSB, 2019b).

Each of the implementation gaps highlighted in the previous section is related to obstacles posed by legislators and legislation in FSB member jurisdiction. Resolution authorities are unable to engage in meaningful cooperation with their counterparts abroad because domestic legislation provides no mandate (recognition of foreign resolution procedures, cooperation agreements) or explicitly prohibits cross-border interaction (information sharing).

When asked about the outlook to complete the ending TBTF reform package in late 2017, an international regulator concludes the following:

> I'm sort of realistic and think that these legislative, legal obstacles will remain. There are many reasons for this but parliamentarians: financial system, financial stability, that is one aspect. There are other parliamentarians that think why should there be special rules, we have a bankruptcy code. They oppose close-out netting saying that it is preferring financial actors over the man of the street that is a creditor. When you're looking at legislators, there are many interests that are not aligned. This imperfect legal regime has essentially to be taken as a given.
>
> *(International Regulator 14, personal communication, December 19, 2017)*

The inferential power of the government network approach can only be assessed in comparison to competing theories of cross-border cooperation and global regulatory politics. The next section presents five theoretical approaches that could explain the development of ending TBTF reform. It extracts expectations from each approach and tests them against the empirical material. In engaging with each competing explanation, this section also traces global regulatory reform progress to its current state. The subsequent section then returns to the FSB, showing how the government network harnessed the power of soft law to galvanize cross-border cooperation against a tide of fragmentation and unilateral action in the mid-2010s.

Alternative Explanations

From a **hegemony** perspective we would expect the great powers to dominate the regulatory process in the area of ending TBTF, just like the other items of financial regulatory reform on the G20 agenda. Aligned in their interest to address negative cross-border externalities, they would be expected to develop club standard to be implemented by a group of states that is small enough to facilitate consensus and big enough to minimize the negative externalities of nonadherence outside the club (Drezner, 2007; Simmons, 2001b). Thus, timely and widespread implementation of the ending-TBTF reform package is expected where the interests of the great financial powers are aligned. Shortcomings and delays would manifest in areas where great power interests are at odds with each other.

Quaglia (2017) shows that the United States and the United Kingdom in particular drove global policy efforts on bank resolution, championing innovative domestic policy instruments such as bail-in and the single point of entry resolution strategy. The FSB Key Attributes of Effective Resolution Regimes can be understood as a new club standard in global finance. Quaglia and Spendzharova (2017, p. 6) regard bank resolution as an uncontroversial and successful area of international standard setting. But the empirical record shows that some elements of the key attributes are implemented and effective whereas others are not. While hegemonic interstate theories can explain the emergence of a global standard for bank resolution, they struggle to account for such uneven implementation.

Institutional development and corresponding regulatory capacity within **transnational bureaucracies** differ across market sectors and issue areas. Hence, the advance of regulatory reform in G-SIB identification and loss absorbency requirements might be a function of its inclusion into the greater Basel policy framework. From a transnational bureaucracy perspective, we would thus expect shortcomings and delays of the ending-TBTF reform package to manifest in areas where technocrats have not developed consensus on policy (yet). Conversely, timely and widespread implementation should occur in reform areas where technocrats have had enough time to agree on an optimal policy to address the problem.

Field research indicates that this explanation is popular among regulators:

> Basel III is a fully formed, if you like, area of international standards agreed. They've got very granular standards that have been agreed. . . . established a very consistent position across countries, but that took what 30, 40 years to achieve from the original Basel Concordat.
>
> *(International Regulator 6, personal communication, December 19, 2014)*

The proponents of this explanation argue that while the Basel Committee operates as an epistemic community that has jointly developed a global consensus on the resilience of multinational banks for decades, it has not dealt with the issues that come to the fore in bank resolution. A British regulator explains the following:

> The Basel Committee has been running since the mid-seventies. So people have to start a common language for thinking about capital or solvency of banks and they have some common language although it's less-developed on liquidity of banks. But I'm not sure if there was any common language about structural reforms. In a way, structural reform starts from looking at what structures you already have and although major internationally active banks look somewhat similar across countries, I guess there's quite a lot of difference nationally that will become important in structural reform.
>
> *(UK Regulator 1, personal communication, 2014)*

It is true that neither the Basel Committee nor any other government network has dealt with the corporate structure of global banks. The capital requirements of Basel III and its predecessors have become successful global standards in part because they are agnostic with respect to structural issues. What this argument overlooks however is that cross-border repercussions of bank failures are the very reason for the establishment of the Basel Committee. When Herstatt Bank failed in 1974, the bank left certain foreign exchange trades unsettled – a risk to foreign counterparties that is still dubbed Herstatt risk today. In order to deal with similar situations in the future, the Basel Committee was formed in the same year in order to find a consensus on the distribution of home and host country responsibilities.

Written with a typewriter in 1975, the Basel Concordat calls for a direct transfer of information between authorities as a prerequisite for supervisory cooperation:

> The Committee is aware that such transfers of information are often impossible because of banking secrecy laws in host countries; but many of its members consider that the operations of these laws should over time be modified as to permit them.
>
> *(BCBS, 1975, p. 4f)*

In other words, Basel Committee members were aware of the legal obstacles to successful cross-border cooperation over 40 years ago.

The Basel Committee did not limit itself to supervisory coordination of banks in good times. Following the fall of BCCI, a multinational bank in 1992, the BCBS issued a report on legal differences in liquidation that considers the advantages and disadvantages of a single versus separate-entity approach. Aware of the cross-border repercussions of liquidation in one jurisdiction, the Basel Committee calls on its members to cooperate in the case of bank resolution:

> Given the possibility that there could be many liquidation proceedings related to the multinational bank, as the bankruptcy progresses, it would be desirable for host supervisors to report to the home supervisor about developments in their jurisdictions, and for the home supervisor to keep other interested supervisors informed on overall developments to the extent possible.
>
> *(BCBS, 1992, p. 6)*

In other words, two decades ago, the Basel Committee has proposed firm-specific crisis management groups or supervisory colleges as a venue to improve cross-border cooperation among resolution authorities.

The BCBS went even further, proposing that regulators could sign cross-border cooperation agreements to facilitate the resolution of failing cross-border banks:

> Contractual cooperation arrangements could be entered into among the different liquidators, e.g. contractual pooling of assets and claims. An international convention or regime covering cross-border insolvencies of multinational banks could provide for such banks to be liquidated on a coordinated basis.
>
> *(BCBS, 1992, p. 14f)*

It is interesting to note that in suggesting cooperation agreements and even an international treaty, the Basel Committee of the early 1990s was bolder and more optimistic about the chances for cross-border cooperation than during the global financial crisis 20 years later. And even though the Basel Committee agreements eschew any explicit designation of a lender of last resort for international banks in favor of "calculated vagueness" (Verdier, 2013), the organization has developed a sophisticated transnational system of shared understandings and allocation of responsibilities in the event of cross-border bank failures (Alexander et al., 2006; Davies & Green, 2008).

In sum, many of the areas that are lagging in today's regulatory reform, cross-border information sharing in supervisory colleges, and cooperation agreements among regulators in particular have been part and parcel of Basel Committee deliberations for decades. In fact, it is in areas that were not part of the established consensus such as a surcharge for contribution to systemic risk that post-crisis regulatory reform has been most successful.

Another potential explanation for the lack of progress in some areas of the SIFI framework is that **redistributive concerns** impede cross-border cooperation. In the event of a bank failure, public authorities do not only provide temporary liquidity but also solvency support. Especially when a financial institution enters insolvency for non-idiosyncratic reasons, such as a wider financial crisis, the overall costs of its resolution become clear months or even years later. For example, when the US Treasury provided $700 million to distressed financial institutions under the Troubled Assets Relief Fund (TARP), few would have expected the program to close with a profit years later.

Bank resolution authorities operate as lenders of last resort that ultimately have to count on the backing of national governments with the fiscal capacity to take over the risk of debt write-downs. As James (2013) notes, "In the domestic setting, the action is justified by the claim that it restores the normal functioning of a national economy. In the international setting, it looks like taxpayers subsidizing foreigners" (p. 17). G-SIFIs have branches and subsidiaries in 44 countries on average (Carmassi & Herring, 2014), and while they are global in life, to paraphrase Lord Turner's famous words, it is unclear which government(s) pick up the corpses when they fail.

In this situation, the host authority has an incentive to seize the operational subsidiary or even branch of a failing global bank and bring its assets under custody before the home authority claims them for the resolution procedure of the parent bank. Baxter et al. (2004) foresaw much of what happened during the global financial crisis when they wrote, "When times are rough, [supervisors] will think like administrative officials, rather than judges. They will grab whatever they can" (p. 60). In similar fashion, the Basel Committee notes that even in places with a cross-border insolvency procedure, such as the European Union, "each national authority is likely to attach most weight to the pursuit of its own national interests in the management of a crisis" (BCBS, 2010b, p. 4).

Because the conditions of each individual bank failure are unpredictable, ex-ante agreements face a double time-inconsistency problem: States can neither credibly commit to refrain from bailout nor from ad hoc ring-fencing (Chari & Kehoe, 2013; Committee on International Economic Policy and Reform, 2012; Goodhart & Schoenmaker, 2009; Haldane, 2012b; Huertas, 2013). Under these circumstances, Verdier (2013) asserts, "Regulators will not believe each other's promise to turn assets over to foreign proceedings or abide by burden-sharing agreements" (p. 1454).

On the basis of these considerations, we can thus expect shortcomings and delays of the ending-TBTF reform package to manifest in areas where the costs of adherence to the global standard are unevenly distributed. Timely and widespread implementation in contrast should occur in reform areas where adjustment costs are diffuse or negligible.

There is no doubt that ending TBTF policies raise redistributive concerns, just like all other items on the G20s regulatory reform agenda. Chapter 3, for example, examined the intense negotiations among regulators in setting Basel III capital adequacy standards. The loss absorbency policies that are part of the SIFI framework gave rise to regulatory struggles along the same lines because banks in different jurisdictions face different adjustment costs. A Brazilian regulator recalls the following:

> I remember when we had the discussion regarding the systemically important global financial institutions, the G-SIFIs, the reaction of France because in the very beginning, the first lists, it had three banks and they fight a lot in order to reduce the list in order not to have those three banks in the list. And so there is a discussion at is not exclusively a technical discussion, it is a political discussion.
>
> *(Brazil Regulator 1, personal communication, 2014)*

Some, if not all banking supervisors, see G-SIFIs headquartered in their jurisdiction as a sign of strength and as a means of influence domestically and in global regulatory negotiations. A French regulator explains how this perception of banks as national champions undermines the very goal of the SIFI framework:

> Well ending too big to fail I think is not possible because those institutions are crucial, not from a political point of view but this has been an element of decision in the past for bailing them out. I mean they are of political importance too but they also are of economic importance.
>
> *(France Regulator 1, personal communication, December 2, 2014)*

In spite of these concerns, the identification of G-SIB and allocation of additional going-concern loss absorbency requirements are items on the SIFI agenda that were completed successfully within the stipulated timeframe.

Cooperative moves among supervisors cast further doubt on the explanatory power of redistributive concerns. In 2012, the regulators of the two largest financial markets and home supervisors of 12 of the world's 29 G-SIFIs outlined their intended resolution strategies in a joint white paper. The FDIC and the Bank of England agreed to opt for a single point of entry (SPE) approach to the resolution of a SIFI headquartered in their respective jurisdictions. In contrast to a multiple point of entry (MPE) approach, liquidity and solvency support flow down from the holding company, while losses are transmitted from the subsidiaries and branches upwards, for example, via the write-down of subordinated debt to their parent company (FDIC & Bank of England, 2012). Most other G-SIB home authorities have opted for an SPE strategy since.

In adopting an SPE approach, the resolution authorities commit to keeping subsidiaries open and operational when the parent company enters resolution. In essence, the home supervisor extends a guarantee to cover the losses incurred by branches and subsidiaries in all host jurisdictions. Moreover, home supervisors commit to initiate resolution procedures if a critical amount of overseas affiliates are in trouble even when the domestic parent company is still operational. This strategy is designed to succeed in "limiting contagion effects and cross-border complications" (FDIC & Bank of England, 2012, p. 2), but it is not cheap. In essence, the home supervisor needs to extend a sufficient guarantee to keep all subsidiaries open in order to discourage host supervisors from initiating their own resolution procedures. The advantage of the SPE approach thus lies not in limiting potential resolution costs but in reducing the need for cross-border cooperation to a minimum.

In sum, because resolution authorities face time inconsistency problems vis-à-vis troubled banks and their counterparts in other jurisdictions, concerns about the potential public costs of G-SIFI resolution are relevant. However, there is no evidence for a logical connection with implementation gaps in the SIFI framework. It is not a sufficient condition because significant redistributive concerns did not impede the successful completion of G-SIB identification and loss absorbency requirements. Neither is it a necessary condition because even the willingness of most home jurisdictions to cover losses abroad under the SPE approach has not led to the successful conclusion of cooperation agreements. Stuck between two evils, supervisors appear to prefer potentially costly unilateralism over the uncertainties of cross-border cooperation in the event of a crisis.

One of the most common explanations for the shortcomings of global financial reform is **regulatory capture** by private special interest groups. Indeed, evidence of industry resistance vis-à-vis reform policies such as Basel III is plentiful (see Chapter 4). Trade associations have significantly increased lobbying expenses to influence policymakers in order to reduce the anticipated costs of regulatory reform. In addition to monetary channels of influence, there is evidence of cultural capture in dealing with failing banks (S. Johnson & Kwak, 2010). The FDIC Material Loss Reviews reveal that supervisors had identified problems in 79% of failed banks years before they had to be resolved. However, regulators were reluctant to break cultural norms, fearing the opprobrium that necessary corrective actions would have entailed (Barth et al., 2012). From a regulatory capture perspective, we can thus expect shortcomings and delays of the ending-TBTF reform package to manifest in areas that encounter resistance by financial special interest groups. Timely and widespread implementation in turn would occur in reform areas that are supported or ignored by these special interest groups.

Zaring (2010, p. 108) expresses the concerns of many observers when he argues that "it is only through the Basel process of peer review and insulation from domestic lobbying pressures that United States regulators will be able to force themselves to do some of the difficult work of resolving financial institutions."

Financial trade associations have indeed significantly increased lobbying expenses to influence policymakers to reduce the anticipated costs of regulatory reform. But in order to argue that the implementation gaps of the SIFI framework are caused by regulatory capture, it is necessary to provide evidence of industry resistance. In the particular area of ending TBTF policy measures, the empirical picture does not support such claims.

In early 2011, the FSB circulated a consultative document on effective resolution of SIFIs that would provide the foundation for the Key Attributes later that year. In a surprisingly rare gesture of unity and collaboration among financial lobby organizations, the Global Financial Markets Association (GFMA), Clearing House Association, American Bankers Association, Financial Services Roundtable, Institute of International Bankers, and the Institute of International Finance (IIF) wrote a joint response letter in support of the measures proposed by the FSB. The trade associations state,

> We believe that a global regulatory consensus on these issues is critical, that the FSB's and the G-20's cooperation is necessary to achieve such consensus, and that their further support will be essential in order to translate the proposed policy measures into legislative action.
>
> *(GFMA et al., 2011, p. 3)*

The comment letter by the bank lobby does not merely voice general support for the FSB's policy work regarding ending TBTF. It expresses concern that the SIFI reform framework might stall due to legislative obstacles and prompts the FSB to push harder for legal changes in member jurisdictions:

> We urge the member countries of the G-20 to make the legislative actions recommended by the Consultative Document a stated priority, and encourage such legislative actions to be explicitly added to the implementation timeline. We also urge the FSB to conduct and publish a meaningful peer review of the degree to which countries comply with its final recommendations, as well as publish annual peer reviews to assess progress toward full implementation.
>
> *(GFMA et al., 2011, p. 3)*

This full-fledged support by private special interest groups is less surprising when considering the alternatives to globally coordinated structural measures. In 2011 several countries started planning unilateral measures to ring-fence certain banking activities without consulting government networks or other jurisdictions (see the next section). Global banks started to fear the massive adjustment costs and regulatory uncertainties a patchwork of uncoordinated structural measures would bring about (Epstein, 2017; Epstein & Rhodes, 2016). In fact, the bank lobby comment letter specifically speaks out against such unilateral policies: "We suggest that regulators be discouraged from exercising any powers to ringfence local assets or discriminate against foreign creditors. A non-discrimination rule would also enhance the goals of cross-border cooperation" (GFMA et al., 2011, p. 8).

In addition to uncoordinated structural measures, the industry also grew wary of overlapping requirements and duplication of efforts regarding recovery and resolution planning. The IIF in particular urged the FSB to strengthen its approach to crisis management groups and cooperation agreements: "Having set out a strong design for speedy and effective resolution of significant financial institutions within each jurisdiction, it should mandate – not just urge – effective cooperation among jurisdictions on cross-border resolution" (*Banks Urge Coordination on Cross-Border Clean-Ups*, 2012).

Consulting firms and legal service providers to the finance industry even saw a business opportunity in globally coordinated resolution planning. Davis Polk, a law firm, and McKinsey Co. published a report in 2011, arguing that "a best case international recovery or resolution would be a universal or at least a coordinated territorial approach, involving the home country supervisor making coordinated decisions on an international level" (Davis Polk & Wardwell LLP & McKinsey & Co, 2011). In order to facilitate cross-border coordination, the two firms offer a standardized "Master Living Will," a template for G-SIFIs that draws inspiration from the Master Agreement for OTC derivatives trades that was developed by ISDA, the number one industry association in this field.

It would be incorrect to argue that the interests of the industry are fully aligned with the FSB's SIFI framework. Lobby organizations have consistently expressed concerns about data privacy for example. In the eyes of the industry, home supervisors should only share recovery and resolution plans at a level of granularity that is necessary for coordination with host authorities. Broad-based sharing of firm-level data, trade associations worry, would increase the risk of leaks or unauthorized access (British Bankers Association, 2017; GFMA et al., 2011). Moreover, large banks have been vociferous in their opposition to the G-SIB surcharge, in addition to a more general assault on Basel III capital requirements (Masters & Braithwaite, 2011).

Nevertheless, the empirical picture shows that global banks are broadly supportive of the FSB in this particular area of the global regulatory reform agenda. Financial trade associations have not only expressed support for globally coordinated structural measures while fighting fiercely against unilateral measures in individual jurisdictions. They have also helped the FSB overcome the implementation gap regarding early termination rights.

As noted previously, legislators in many FSB jurisdictions to date have failed to provide supervisors with statutory powers to freeze derivatives contracts of failing banks. In contrast, the trade association at the center of derivatives markets, ISDA, offered help in this situation by amending the template that provides the legal foundation for most derivatives trades, the ISDA Master Agreement. In addition, the trade organization brokered an agreement among large banks that are major derivatives dealers to adopt the amended Master Agreement (T. Braithwaite & Alloway, 2014; ISDA, 2015). By 2017, 26 G-SIBs have formally adhered to ISDA's resolution stay protocol (FSB, 2017e).

By instituting changes in private transnational law governing derivatives trades, ISDA thus helped the FSB close a major implementation gap. In principle, legislators could have addressed this issue by providing supervisors with statutory powers to impose stays on termination rights in all member jurisdictions, but they failed to do so. The FSB enthusiastically welcomed the industry initiative. Mark Carney, FSB chairman at the time, stated,

> When the protocol goes live in November, it will close off much of the cross-border close-out risk that statutory stays have not been able to eliminate because their reach is limited to national borders. This is a major achievement, by the industry.
>
> *(FSB, 2014b, p. 1f)*

In sum, there is scant support for claims that shortcomings in ending TBTF policies are a product of regulatory capture. The private sector has resisted greater loss absorbency requirements, but these policies are being implemented successfully. In contrast, the FSB has found a consistent supporter in the industry regarding bank resolution policies. In an effort to increase the momentum for cross-border coordination and avoid a proliferation of unilateral structural measures, trade associations have orchestrated unison support for FSB efforts and even brokered a deal among major global banks in order to close a major implementation gap.

Fragmentation along jurisdictional lines due to **politicization** of regulatory reform is the fifth and final competing explanation for mixed reform progress to end TBTF considered here. Helleiner and Pagliari (2011) observe that as financial regulation has gained political salience in the wake of the crisis, national legislatures and state leaders have interfered in the regulatory reform agenda that was originally designed by technocrats. From this perspective, we can thus expect shortcomings and delays of the ending-TBTF reform package to manifest in areas where the executive branch of FSB member jurisdictions has taken unilateral action. Timely and widespread implementation is expected to occur in reform areas where the executive branch has followed the recommendations of government networks.

There is no shortage of evidence for this pattern. The United States has led the way in devising policies for the domestic financial sector without consulting its peers in the G20 or the FSB. A variety of structural measures from reinstating Glass-Steagall to imposing caps on bank size or market share were debated in Congress in the wake of the crisis (Sorkin, 2010; Wyatt, 2011). Eventually, legislators found consensus on the Volcker Rule. Passed into law in 2010 as part of the Dodd Frank Act (section 619), the Volcker Rule has undergone numerous changes before agreement was reached in December 2013. The rule bans banks from proprietary trading with the sole exception of US government debt instruments. The narrow scope and extraterritorial reach of its original version irritated regulators around the world (see Chapter 4), including the FSB chairman and Bank of Canada governor at the time. Carney (2012a) wrote, "If adopted as currently drafted, the Volcker Rule may limit market-making and risk-management activities by Canadian banks; limit trading in Canadian government bonds; and hinder the implementation of global initiatives to promote financial stability" (p. 3). In response to criticism from abroad, the reformulated Volcker Rule was relaxed to allow the use of debt instruments issued by foreign governments under certain circumstances (Mattingly, 2012; Thomson Reuters Accelus, 2013).

The second jurisdiction to propose structural measures without consulting the G20 or the FSB was the United Kingdom. Asked about the reasons for this unilateral move, a British regulator responds,

> There is a very strong political imperative to get something done. It was very important to a politician. A new government came in 2010, they wanted it to be clearly seen to be doing something. They created a commission to work on this and that commission naturally has a UK focus as it is created by the UK government.
>
> *(UK Regulator 1, personal communication, 2014)*

The Vickers commission presented a report on financial regulatory reform in September 2011, and its prescriptions formed the basis for the new Financial Services Act of 2012.

The Vickers Commission and its policy recommendations were designed for the United Kingdom only, but they had clear spillover effects across the Channel. Policymakers in Continental European countries started to devise and implement their own unilateral structural measures, with as little concern for cross-border coordination as their British counterparts.

A French regulator recalls,

> A real trigger for France to work on separating activities was the Vickers report. When Great Britain went for its own rule and we considered we worked a lot on this and considered it and we thought that we should do the things the other way around. They were ringfencing retail bank we wanted to ringfence market activities that we consider potentially dangerous for the stability of a bank so that's what we did and also in Germany.
>
> *(France Regulator 1, personal communication, December 2, 2014)*

Half a year after the Vickers Report was published, EU commissioner Michael Barnier convened the Liikanen Commission, which was under considerable domestic pressure to act fast. A European regulator explains,

> Liikanen was sort of left running after the field and so much time had passed until the Liikanen group was set up and then it worked. In the meantime, domestic pressures in Germany and in France and in others started growing

> considerably. People [were] saying 'why the hell – look at the Americans, look at the British. We haven't got anything.' So, they started doing something domestically.
>
> *(EU Regulator 3, personal communication, October 21, 2014)*

Published in October 2012, the Liikanen Report provides the blueprint for EU structural policies in the financial sector (European Commission, 2014; Liikanen, 2012).

A comparison between the regulatory initiatives led by Volcker, Vickers, and Liikanen reveals multiple fault lines and inconsistencies across borders (Gambacorta & van Rixtel, 2013). If the purpose of preemptive structural measures was to reduce complexity in the financial system, they have failed. A Thomson Reuters report notes, "The mismatch, overlap and underlap of the three sets of proposals is likely to create banks that are more, rather than less, complex" (Thomson Reuters Accelus, 2013, p. 34). The global hodgepodge of structural measures was further exacerbated by a new round of unilateral initiatives in subsequent years. British and American authorities announced new rules in late 2013 and early 2014, respectively, that foreign banks must establish separately capitalized corporate structures for their operations in the host country (Federal Reserve Board, 2012). The European Union started developing a similar proposal (Shearman & Sterling LLP, 2016). All three initiatives are designed to give greater autonomy to domestic authorities and to reduce the need for cross-border cooperation with foreign regulators.

The causal link between politicization and the incompleteness of the SIFI reform framework however is tenuous at best. The argument that politicians eager to show protagonism discouraged resolution authorities to share bank-related information in CMGs or dissuaded them from signing cooperation agreements with their peers abroad is unconvincing. It would be just as far-fetched to assert that domestic political pressures to rein in big banks prevented legislators from providing regulators with the powers to bail-in bank liabilities, recognize resolution actions abroad, or impose a temporary stay on termination rights.

Rather, the emergence of cooperative decentralization can be regarded as a partial response to the slowdown of global regulatory reform. Faced with the inability of regulators to overcome legislative obstacles to reform and the unwillingness of legislators to remove them, government leaders in the US and Europe resorted to unilateral measures while still repeating their intention to support the FSB-led global reform agenda at every G20 meeting.

PLAC, GLAC, TLAC – The Sound of Basel

That fragmentation along jurisdictional lines is not a cause for the slowdown of global regulatory reform becomes even clearer when analyzing the latest episode in the never-ending TBTF story. Following a devastating peer review in 2013 that highlighted the multiple obstacles to ending TBTF and faced with a proliferation of unilateral structural measures, the FSB decided to retake the initiative and speed up SIFI reform. It employs the concept of loss absorbency capacity (LAC) to failing banks for the first time in its guidance on effective resolution strategies from July 2013 (FSB, 2013c).

The concept of loss absorbency was part of regulatory debates in government networks for years, but always as a measure to increase the resilience of an operational bank (going-concern), not as a buffer to be used in the resolution of a failing one (gone concern). The Basel Committee considered the inclusion of bail-in-able debt for the G-SIB surcharge in 2011, but it discarded this option:

> Given the going-concern objective of the additional loss absorbency requirement, the Basel Committee is of the view that it is not appropriate for G-SIBs to be able to meet this requirement with instruments that only absorb losses at the point of non-viability.
>
> *(BCBS, 2011c, p. 23)*

Instead, it determined that the additional loss absorbency requirement of G-SIBs can only be met with Common Equity Tier 1 capital.

The idea of a gone-concern loss absorbing capital requirement resurfaced in the report of the Independent Commission on Banking (ICB) in the United Kingdom. The Vickers Commission recommends a so-called Primary Loss-Absorbency Capacity (PLAC) requirement for G-SIB and ring-fenced banks (Independent Commission on Banking, 2011).

Next in line was the Liikanen Commission. It recommended EU supervisors to issue what it called a Minimum Requirement for Own Funds and Eligible Liabilities (MREL) that combines going-concern and gone concern loss absorbency (Liikanen, 2012). The UK government endorsed the recommendations of the Vickers Commission in 2012 and states that MREL "broadly resembles the PLAC requirement as envisaged by the ICB" (HM Treasury, 2012, p. 34).

It is surprising that gone-concern loss absorbing requirements had not entered the FSB discourse before mid-2013, even though European member jurisdictions were in the process of implementing them. An international regulator recalls,

> It really wasn't part of the discussion until shortly before the St. Petersburg Summit, you know, that being obviously the Key Attributes had been developed by the FSB as a set of qualitative principles. We had higher loss absorbing capacity in the shape of an extra layer of ordinary capital [as] a going concern concept.
>
> *(International Regulator 6, personal communication, December 19, 2014)*

The FSB submitted a proposal to develop a new global standard for gone-concern loss-absorbing capital (GLAC) to the G20 in September 2013 in the hope that it would persuade member states to roll back unilateral measures:

> The point being, that as we get to the end of this year and make the progress we intend to, that then maps into adjustment of the resolution plans in firms

and potentially, one would hope, some adjustment in the applications of national decisions.

(H. Jones & Bruce, 2014)

The idea of GLAC (or TLAC as it was called later) is simple. Liabilities that are eligible for TLAC include subordinated unsecured debt that would count as Tier 2 capital, and more senior unsecured debt that can be understood as a new category of Tier 3 capital. G-SIBs are required to hold TLAC equivalent to 18% of risk-weighted assets on their balance sheets by 2022. In addition, the FSB requires a so-called leverage ratio exposure equivalent to 6.75% of unweighted assets by the same deadline. The FSB working group in charge of devising a global TLAC standard was composed not only of regulators but also finance ministers because governments ultimately provide the fiscal backstop that makes resolution planning credible (Pauly, 2009). The new TLAC requirements were subject to a gradual phase-in, and G-SIB headquartered in emerging market economies have until 2028 to meet global standards (FSB, 2015b). All G-SIB have met or exceeded TLAC requirements by 2020, ahead of the deadline (FSB, 2021). Figure 5.5 depicts this progress on the TBTF agenda.

If this process appears very similar to that of Basel III, it is because it is designed to be. An international regulator describes TLAC as

something that's so closely involved with Basel III. So invariably [the BCBS has] to be involved, but it's a funny relationship because 90% of what they

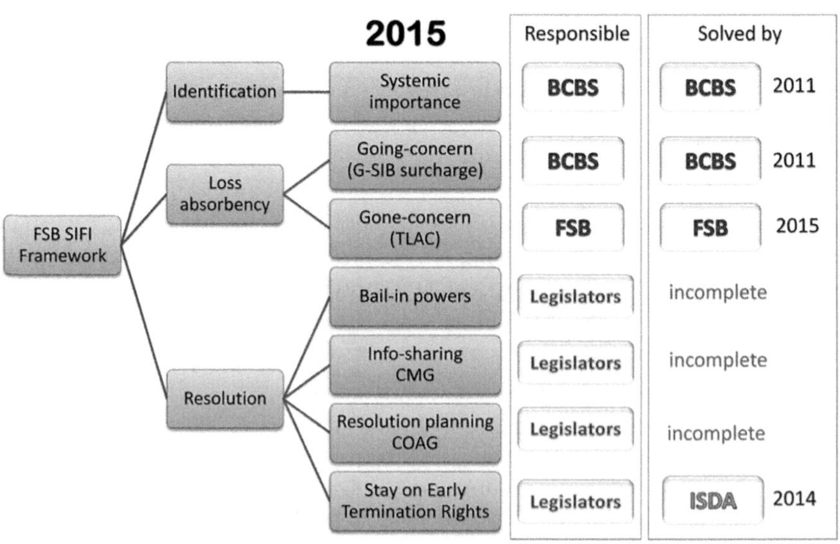

FIGURE 5.5 SIFI Framework and Progress, 2015

Source: Author's visualization

> [FSB] do, what they did anyway, [was] in some form or fashion involved in banking, and that are things on which [the BCBS is] working.
>
> *(International Regulator 5, personal communication, December 18, 2014)*

In coordinating global regulatory reform regarding the banking sector and beyond, the FSB has experimented with a variety of institutional processes and designs, such as guidance documents, thematic peer reviews, and member surveys. Yet the dismal state of ending TBTF reform in 2013 showed that the only successful and complete reform policies were those undertaken by the Basel Committee. This chapter argues that the FSB learned from the Basel Committee and mimicked its operations in channeling TLAC policies through the same institutional pathways as Basel III.

The TLAC initiative has four key advantages: First, it involves members of the executive branch in policy deliberation and design, and it circumvents legislators and legislation, the main obstacles to TBTF reform. Legal frameworks that allow for loss absorbency requirements are already in place in the US and Europe. The new global standard was subject to a consultation period but not parliamentary deliberation, and the final rules will be issued by regulatory agencies alone.

Second, the new initiative also enabled policymakers to look beyond their respective jurisdictions and engage in cross-border harmonization. As shown in the previous section, different varieties of loss absorbing requirements were recommended prior to 2014, and it was unclear whether a new standard would be congruent both with these proposals and the Basel III package. But instead of engaging in the race for a first mover advantage (as in ring-fencing policies), policymakers used a G20 finance minister and central governor meeting in September 2014 to negotiate a harmonized, common standard. A European regulator recalls the following:

> The Germans and the British and the French went to Cairns, with quite different views. . . . But they came back with a perfect joint agreement there. But that was this agreement in Cairns reached simply by a rapprochement between the British, the Americans, the Germans, the French and possibly the Chinese on the compatibility of the BRRD instruments and GLAC, which is now called TLAC.
>
> *(EU Regulator 3, personal communication, October 21, 2014)*

In contrast to the other pending items on the TBTF agenda, the new standard has served to inspire confidence and galvanize cross-border cooperation. An international regulator notes this change in the attitudes of FSB members:

> There was a growing realization that in order to reduce the risk of fragmentation, to improve the confidence of countries in cooperating with each other, and to improve their mutual confidence, we had an international framework which really could avoid taxpayers bearing some of the losses and economic

> disruption, there needed to be more of a floor to give confidence that there was actually a buffer of liabilities that could absorb the losses.
>
> *(International Regulator 6, personal communication, December 19, 2014)*

In the aftermath of the Cairns meeting, the European Banking Authority has started technical work to make MREL requirements congruent with global TLAC standards (Durand, 2014). And the German governing coalition considered delaying the implementation of its unilateral structural policies (Jennen & Comfort, 2015). Even the Fed, the organization that unilaterally implemented a subsidiarization of foreign banks in February 2014, decided to postpone its own rulemaking on long-term debt requirements until a common standard was found. A senior official of the Fed's Division of Banking Supervision and Regulation stated that the "first best outcome" is international consensus on a rule "that creates a level playing field and maximum confidence" (Tracy, 2014). The Chinese banking regulator issued preliminary "Guidelines on Improving Regulation of Systemically Important Financial Institutions" in 2018 and specific rules for recovery and resolution planning in line with the FSB Key Attributes in June 2021, after the bailout of several medium-sized financial institutions in recent years. G-SIBs headquartered in China have met TLAC requirements ahead of the implementation deadline (CBIRC, 2021; FSB, 2019b).

Third, TLAC makes it easier for resolution authorities to deal with bank complexity and to engage in cross-border resolution planning. The members of CMG are now expected to reach consensus on the trigger for debt conversion and to insert this clause in cooperation agreements. Paul Tucker argues that this will bring clarity to the work of CMGs:

> By framing the trigger for "converting" intra-group debt into equity, home and host authorities can hard-wire co-operation; or if they fail to agree on a trigger, they at least discover ex ante rather than ex post that they can't rely on each other. This would usefully give a harder edge to discussions amongst home and host authorities in supervisory and crisis-management colleges.
>
> *(P. Tucker, 2014, p. 8)*

Fourth, the new standard aims to eschew inconsistencies in domestic legislation by shifting the burden of adjustment to the banks. The final standard clarifies that "liabilities that cannot be written down or converted into equity by the relevant resolution authority without giving rise to material risk of legal challenge are not eligible for TLAC" (FSB, 2015b, p. 7). This requirement allows TLAC standards to be implemented even though legislators in some jurisdictions have failed to provide supervisors with sufficient bail-in powers, and it might serve to enlist global banks as a pressure group to lobby for corresponding legal change.

Conclusion

Ending too-big-to-fail has been an element of the G20 financial regulatory reform agenda since 2009, but over a decade later, large global banks still enjoy implicit state guarantees. Despite initial rapid advances by the Basel Committee, progress in tackling TBTF banks has been mixed. The FSB has coordinated a great amount of policy work to steer member jurisdictions in making the resolution of global banks without resorting to public bailouts a realistic endeavor, but regulators have stumbled over multiple obstacles in existing legislation. Furthermore, national legislators have not taken action to remove these obstacles, and they have often failed to provide regulators with a legal mandate to engage in the kind of cross-border cooperation that is necessary to make cross-border bank resolution credible. A new initiative by the FSB seeks to circumvent these obstacles by emulating the Basel approach to bank resilience. The TLAC approach has provided global regulatory reform with new momentum, convincing key jurisdictions to put unilateral measures on hold and engage in cross-border harmonization, and the new global standard is likely to be implemented successfully in due time. Of the five competing explanations discussed in this chapter, the politicization approach matches the empirical pattern most clearly. Three other competing explanations provide inferential leverage to make sense of parts of the reform process. From a government network perspective, both the failures in the TBTF reform package and the renewed reform momentum with the introduction of the TLAC standard become understandable.

Many caveats remain, and regulatory work to address the systemic importance of global insurers and market infrastructures is still ongoing. What the evolution of FSB work to end TBTF over the last decade has shown however is the friction between government networks and the nation state as embodied in legislation and legislators. The following chapter will explore this tension with regards to the key questions of effectiveness and legitimacy that any global governance arrangement inevitably confronts.

6

EFFECTIVENESS AND LEGITIMACY OF GOVERNMENT NETWORKS

In analyzing the uneven performance of the FSB in coordinating financial regulatory reform across the globe, the preceding chapters have highlighted the tension between government networks and parliamentarians. They have documented legislative reluctance in passive and active forms, ranging from unwillingness to endow regulators with a sufficient mandate for cross-border cooperation to the creation of new legal obstacles in post-crisis lawmaking. But while this book has engaged in a positive analysis of the legal obstacles that limit the power of the FSB and the standard setters it coordinates, it has refrained from asking a key question: Are legislators justified in their reluctance vis-à-vis government networks?

From a normative point of view, legislative unease with government networks can be a reprehensible move that undermines global efforts to bring about greater financial stability, or it can be an honorable act of resistance against the unaccountable and captured forums of global governance that fail to regulate in the interest of common citizens. The rising tension between government networks and domestic legislative bodies thus calls for a debate on the merits of transnational governance designs. Are legislators right in resisting the FSB and global networked governance in general? What are the advantages and shortcomings of government networks in dealing with global governance challenges of the 21st century?

The first step to address the normative implications of this study is to ask whether global financial governance is desirable in general. Only if the answer to this question is yes will an assessment of the dis/advantages of government networks vis-à-vis other global institutional designs merit attention. The chapter revisits the concept of Schoenmaker's financial trilemma to assess under which conditions global financial governance is desirable. It identifies scope conditions and argues that policymaking in finance and elsewhere should be subjected to strict subsidiarity, as most policy issues to date can still best be dealt with at the national or regional level.

DOI: 10.4324/9781003290001-6

The chapter then engages in a comparison of government networks and other institutional designs regarding two key quality indicators: effectiveness and legitimacy. It discusses the notion that institutional designs of governance at the national, regional, and global level face a dilemma between effectiveness and representational legitimacy. The rules that embed IGOs in international public law represent one compromise between the two, whereas the institutional design of government networks provides an alternative solution.

The first quality indicator under scrutiny is effectiveness, that is, the relationship between stated policy goals and outcomes. IGOs commonly employ hard law instruments to bolster their effectiveness, and hard law traditionalists often criticize the FSB and other government networks for their reliance on soft law instruments. The section will provide four reasons why this criticism is unwarranted. Soft law facilitates rulemaking with a speed and flexibility that can reduce regulatory arbitrage, peer review can harness the power of reputation, the incorporation of the executive branch brings political power to the table, and issue linkage can bolster compliance.

The second quality indicator, legitimacy, is arguably even more important than the first. The institutions of global economic governance have been widely criticized for being unaccountable and illegitimate. Citizens around the world have good reasons to be angry when policymakers fail to prevent devastating financial crises that devastate their livelihoods. The second half of this chapter engages with this question by first disentangling the relationship between direct elections and democratic legitimacy. It recognizes the power of electoral accountability, but it moves beyond the nation-state as an ideal type to assess global governance in the wider terms of procedural legitimacy. It argues that stakeholder inclusion and deliberative equality are the two key indicators of procedural legitimacy, and it highlights the deficiencies of the FSB and other government networks on both accounts. Furthermore, it identifies structural inequalities in three dimensions that pose significant obstacles to deliberative equality. The chapter argues that while government networks don't measure up well in deliberative equality, IGOs and the involvement of national parliaments in ratification procedures of international agreements do little to ameliorate these problems. Moreover, even at the national level, parliaments exhibit serious shortcomings in deliberative equality. This is because legislators operate on a wide thematic but narrow geographical scope. If common interest policymaking is hampered by the prevalence of special interest groups, differences in technical sophistication in policy deliberations, and differences in cross-border mobilization, parliamentarians as parochial generalists are in no position to provide countervailing measures to these inequalities.

Consequently, the chapter provides a qualified endorsement of experts. Moving beyond the existing scholarship, it proposes the creation of expert councils. In reversing the features that constrain parliamentarians, experts could be elected on a narrow issue area of global policy and with a vast geographic constituency. In this way, expert councils could potentially combine the advantages of technocratic expertise and electoral accountability.

The end of the chapter begins with a summary of the key arguments offered in this book. On the basis of the government network perspective developed throughout the chapters, it concludes with remarks on avenues towards improving the legitimacy of the FSB and other government networks, suggesting areas for further research.

Why Global Financial Governance?

Any normative assessment of the merits of government networks in financial regulation as compared to other institutional designs must first address the question of whether global financial governance is desirable at all. Schoenmaker (2011) provides a valuable point of departure for this question. The author transposes the Mundell-Fleming model of monetary autonomy to the realm of financial policies, drawing a triangle of three desirable options, only two of which can be obtained concurrently. Schoenmaker's financial trilemma is composed of financial stability, financial integration across borders, and national financial policies.

The destructive magnitude of financial crises and the repercussions they have for the real economy and unwitting households makes financial stability a highly desirable goal. But policymakers may achieve this goal in two ways: they can refrain from national financial policies and foster cross-border coordination together with financial integration, or they can ringfence their national financial markets and pursue national policy autonomy. The latter is indeed an intellectually coherent policy option that would render global financial governance unnecessary.

However, over the past half century, financial markets have integrated at a rapid pace, and cross-border flows of finance are magnitudes higher than those of goods, services, and people. Few policymakers would be willing and able to reverse financial integration to pre-globalization levels. Under such conditions, the trilemma only offers the choice between national financial policies and financial stability.

Frieden (2016) offers insight into the underlying reasons for this trade-off. He understands financial stability as a global public good. At a national level, governments seek to provide financial stability with two main instruments: a lender of last resort facility and prudential regulation. In both dimensions, governments aim to achieve protection for the national financial sector but not more, thus under-providing financial stability globally. As Frieden puts it:

> Individual national governments do not fully internalize the benefits of tighter regulation, and they may even realize significant costs if business flees for looser jurisdictions. This means that national governments, like private firms, may not have sufficient incentives to provide adequate global regulatory consistency or rigor on their own.
>
> *(Frieden, 2016, p. 37)*

Yet financial markets feature significant negative externalities: They are susceptible to panics and cross-border contagion. Moreover, market participants can take advantage of cross-border inconsistencies in financial regulation, and such regulatory arbitrage may undermine financial stability. The recurrent financial crises of the last decades have painfully demonstrated that these mechanisms are not merely hypothetical. Thus, if a return to 1950s-style national financial markets is not deemed desirable, a clear normative case for a supranational effort to internalize the externalities of global financial markets by means of regulatory cross-border harmonization can be made.

If global financial governance can be justified on the basis of cross-border externalities, it is important to be clear about the scope conditions of this justification. Anderson (2005) distinguishes between two kinds of a "common problem": one that involves cross-border interaction (e.g. loans to foreign entities) and one that occurs in several jurisdictions (e.g. debt-financed loans, leverage). The latter is not an instance of cross-border externalities and thus would not necessitate global governance arrangements. This book makes a strong case for subsidiarity: The authority of global governance institutions should be strictly confined to global issues that exhibit cross-border externalities, in finance and elsewhere.

Subsidiarity is particularly important for this study because it argues that while national parliaments are ill designed to deal with global governance problems, they are reasonably well-suited to deal with national problems. Even today, most policy challenges remain within the confines of a single nation-state, and for such issues, the institution of parliamentary democracy provides a better means of interest aggregation than any alternative. When legislators argue that their participation in the decision-making process is key to ensuring that policies are in the public interest, they are right to the extent that the area of concern is congruent with the Westphalian notion of sovereign nation-states. Few would argue that global governance arrangements can solve national problems better than national political institutions. On the other hand, whether government networks are less legitimate than national parliaments in making public interest decisions in areas fraught with cross-border externalities and global interdependence is a question that the remainder of this chapter turns to.

That there can be a trade-off between effectiveness and representation has been recognized by scholars of domestic organizations half a century ago, if not earlier. Merton (1966) distinguishes between instrumental and group-maintaining functions and points out that the tension between the two is especially high in democratic organizations. A drive towards more effective practices threatens the processes that ensure all constituents are represented, that is, internal democracy. Conversely, group-maintaining functions that are geared towards maintaining representativeness may render the organization ineffectual. Merton (1966) states, "We note that some members develop so deep a passion for democratic processes that they often forget the purposes which these processes were meant to serve" (p. 1060).

This dilemma of representation and effectiveness does not only apply to domestic organizations and governments but also to international organizations. The legal structure of IGOs is designed to achieve a compromise between both goals. They are firmly embedded in international public law. Representation is ensured by the ratification procedure: The organization and its agreements are effective only after ratification by a certain number of member states (Harland, 2004; Sands & Klein, 2001; Shaw, 2008). Effectiveness in turn is thought to follow from the fact that member states are legally bound by the agreements they make.

Some global governance scholars regard the circumvention of such legal procedures as a fundamental weakness of government networks both with regards to effectiveness and legitimacy. It is worth subjecting these arguments to scrutiny by assessing FSB performance in both dimensions, starting with effectiveness.

Effectiveness

Making legally binding commitments is an unavoidable prerequisite for the effective implementation of global policies in the eyes of many scholars. The "hard law traditionalists," as Kirton (2013) calls them, have a point. The institutional design of government networks may be suited to facilitate member agreement on a certain focal point as stylized by coordination games (Fearon, 1998; Lazer, 2005; Milner, 1997). However, as soon as redistributive issues arise (and they always do), government networks have no power to punish free riders and deal with defection issues of the Prisoners' Dilemma kind (Abbott & Snidal, 2000; Joyce, 2014; Mosley, 2009; Ötker-Robe, 2014). This may be why many scholars have regarded soft law arrangements as "an unwelcome stepchild that is tolerated when other options are unattainable" (Hafner-Burton et al., 2012, p. 73, Kirton & Trebilcock, 2016).

Davies (2014) applies this criticism to the FSB, calling it a "watchdog without teeth. It can neither instruct the other regulators what to do (or not do) nor force countries to comply with new regulations." Even Paul Martin, intellectual author of the government network that provided the foundations for the G20 summit series, called the FSB toothless (Greenwood, 2012). In a similar vein, the FSB's predecessor, FSF, was widely seen as merely a talk shop because of its lack of enforcement powers. When reconstituting it as the FSB, G20 leaders had the opportunity to give it international legal standing. That they chose not to do this is seen by some scholars as a sign that post-crisis reform failed to change the status quo. Helleiner (2014a) argues,

> The G20's failure to depart from the soft law nature of the pre-crisis governance of international financial standards in a significant way meant that the challenges in enforcing implementation and compliance remained. These challenges in fact intensified in the wake of the crisis, making the failure to innovate in a more substantial way even more significant.
>
> *(p. 150)*

As a response to the perceived shortcomings of government networks, hard law traditionalists call for an international treaty to provide global financial governance with a legal foundation (Wright, 2012). Alexander et al. (2006) call for the "institutional and legal consolidation" of regulatory standards and the establishment of a

Global Financial Governance Council. Eichengreen (2008, 2009, 2011) proposes the establishment of a World Financial Organization. Several other scholars envision a new governance systems that combine government networks with existing IGOs under an umbrella international treaty (Avgouleas, 2012; Greene & Boehm, 2011; King, 2010; Knight, 2014; Ocampo, 2014; Stiglitz, 2010).

Not oblivious to such suggestions, G20 leaders tasked the FSB with making recommendations for "strengthening the FSB's capacity, resources and governance" at the 2011 Cannes summit (FSB, 2012b). One option was to transform the board into a classic intergovernmental organization. Yet the Plenary arrived at a consensus that the FSB must remain a government network in order to operate effectively. The decision was communicated to G20 leaders at the Los Cabos summit: "The FSB considers a treaty-based inter-governmental organisation not to be an appropriate legal form at this juncture" (FSB, 2012b: pt. 11). Instead, it currently has legal personality as a mere association under Swiss law.

The institutional proposals mentioned in the preceding section are without a doubt the product of thorough consideration by experts in the field. Nevertheless, this chapter provides four reasons to argue that hard law traditionalists not only provide unfeasible alternatives to government networks such as the FSB, they also underestimate its power as an enforcement agent. First, the instruments of international public law are unsuitable for a policy environment that is driven by fast change and uncertainty. Second, the review procedures inherent in the design of the FSB can be more effective than legal obligation. Third, certain institutional innovations in the reconstitution of the FSB strengthen its enforcement powers, giving it more teeth than previous soft law arrangements. And fourth, states are entangled in the global financial system in such interdependent fashion that the mechanisms of issue linkage can be exploited to bolster enforcement.

The first reason why government networks represent a more suitable design for global financial governance is that uncertainty and rapid evolution of this policy area puts a premium on speed and flexibility. Jaime Caruana, general manager of the BIS, refers to this issue as the "regulatory uncertainty principle" (Slater, 2014). The author states,

> In a highly dynamic world, imperfect knowledge leaves regulatory design permanently in catch-up mode. . . . As soon as a rule, simple or complex, becomes a binding financial regulation, it will cause changes in financial institutions' risk management that will make it less binding and less effective.
>
> *(Caruana, 2014, p. 2f)*

Financial corporations do not only have the ability to work around financial regulation, they also have the incentive to do so (Beck et al., 2017). As Romer (2012) asserts in a paper that applies Myron's Law to financial regulation: "The technology is evolving too quickly. The scale of the markets is enormous and continues to grow. There may be no other setting in which opportunism can be so lucrative" (p. 123.).

Given the speedy operation of this feedback loop between regulators and the industry, the policymaking procedures of traditional IGOs would render financial rulemaking a hopeless endeavor (Alvarez, 2006). At the same time, the speed and flexibility needed for effective regulation insulates government networks from external control, in particular, that of member state parliaments. Paul Tucker, the Bank of England's Deputy Governor for Financial Stability, describes this tension in the following words:

> Legislators in many countries favour rules-based regulation in order to guard against the exercise of arbitrary power by unelected regulators. But a static rulebook is the meat and drink of regulatory arbitrage. And the more detailed the rules, the more rules-arbitrage is implicitly legitimized, because the rule-makers must have said precisely what they meant and no more.
>
> *(P. Tucker, 2014, p. 9)*

This debate frames financial regulation as a trade-off between arbitrage on the one hand and illegitimate rule by unaccountable regulators on the other. This is a problematic perspective however because legislative scrutiny is neither a necessary nor sufficient condition for legitimacy and because accountability can be achieved by other means, as a later section shows.

The second argument against hard law traditionalists builds on Raustiala's (2005) conceptual separation between form, substance, and structure of international agreements. The author notes that legally binding agreements often lack substance because treaty members build in generous compliance cushions to protect themselves against legal challenges (Downs et al., 1996). Alternatively, substantive agreements can be reached when legal form is replaced by a strong review structure (Posner, 2015; Sabel & Zeitlin, 2008). As shown to a greater extent in Chapter 1, the FSB peer review process leverages the role of reputation to ensure compliance among many if not all members.

The candor of FSB peer reviews and progress reports contrasts with the prevalence of vague and polished language at the G20. Even though the political headmasters of the FSB have intended to employ peer review mechanisms with the Mutual Assessment Program and a so-called "accountability report" (G20, 2013), efforts at naming and shaming fell flat under pressures to apply a diplomatic shine to G20 documents. Future research is needed to investigate the underlying reasons for the stark differences in peer review at the G20 and the FSB.

The third argument against hardening soft law arrangements in global financial governance focuses on the specific institutional innovations that distinguish the FSB from its predecessor, the FSF. Both generations of this government network have been created by state leaders, and both bring together regulators, central bankers, and representatives of the executive branch of member countries, usually finance ministry deputies. But the institutional connection between the political leadership of member countries and the government network has been strengthened tremendously since the global financial crisis. All FSB policy documents and reports mention the G20, and from 2012 onwards, they start with an explicit reference to an item of a G20 declaration. At the same time the G20 reconfirms FSB authority to pursue global regulatory reform at every leader's summit.

The tight institutional connection between government network and political leadership increases the prospects of domestic implementation in two ways. Members of the executive branch are involved both in the negotiation of G20 commitments and in their FSB-coordinated implementation. In this respect, the commonly used term "transnational regulatory networks" may be misleading exactly because government networks are comprised not only of regulators. An EU official explains the crucial difference:

> If it is just regulatory standards or supervisory standards, that all supervisors should be implementing, which are at a sub-legal or sub-parliamentary level. . . . Then, this can work out to the extent that the central bank is the supervisor, which they often are. But not uniformly. As soon as you're talking about anything that needs legal transposition: what's a central banker?
>
> *(EU Regulator 3, personal communication, October 21, 2014)*

The double involvement of government officials in the G20 and the FSB might thus make agreements harder to reach because domestic political realities reduce the interstate win-set (Odell, 2011; Putnam, 1988). But once an agreement is reached, it is more likely to be implemented than otherwise.

Another benefit of a close connection to political leadership is that it bolsters the peer review process. Normally, the social pressure that is created by naming and shaming remains confined to the group of officials in the government network (J. Braithwaite, 2011). The FSB however can escalate this pressure to the highest political level, as Mark Carney explained shortly before assuming his role as FSB Chair:

> So we're going to run formal audits, basically, of these things and one of my jobs is going to be to go back to leaders if there's an issue and call people out and say, you know: "We have a problem here. You signed this communiqué in 2009 that meant that, and you're not implementing it, and this has repercussions."
>
> *(Coyne, 2011)*

The fourth criticism of soft law government networks concerns the narrowness of the negotiation space. Verdier (2009) argues that successful international negotiations make use of issue linkages (Schelling, 1980). Financial regulators in turn, the author states, have no trade-offs to offer. The empirical picture however shows that even a relatively narrow field such as financial regulation offers space for issue linkage. This is because G20 member states are involved in a variety of international commitments in issue areas ranging from tax evasion and money laundering to relations with the Paris Club of sovereign creditors. A country that fails to comply with a substantial portion of FSB commitments has reasons to fear not only opprobrium within the FSB but also in these other forums (Argentina Regulator 2, personal communication, 2014). Conversely, a stellar compliance record in the FSB may also be of advantage in debt negotiations and other areas.

In sum, there are many reasons to believe that the critics of FSB reliance on soft law alone are overly pessimistic. Traditional hard law approaches are too cumbersome to make effective global financial regulation possible. The design of the FSB substitutes legal form with a strong review structure to ensure compliance with global standards. It represents a significant institutional improvement from the FSF, with wider membership and much tighter integration with political leadership in the G20. The review process is driven by an acceptance of candid messages among members and in public. Moreover, de facto interlinkages between the FSB and other institutions of global financial governance make it hard for laggards to assume that noncompliance will only have narrow repercussions. All the preceding reasons give a government network like the FSB an advantage vis-à-vis traditional IGOs in moving forward the global financial reform agenda. That government networks are less ineffective than IGOs however does not mean they are effective. Even when the executive branch of member countries is a supporter of regulatory reform, it faces difficulties in overcoming the challenges that legislation and legislators pose.

Legitimacy

The quality indicator for institutional design that is arguably even more important than effectiveness is legitimacy. The question of legitimacy of international institutions has attracted more attention with the rise of globalization over the last decades as these institutions take on an increasing range of responsibilities and policymaking authority that affects citizens around the world. The perceived lack of legitimacy is particularly acute with regards to the institutions of global economic governance. From the protests against the OECD's multilateral investment agreement to the outcry against IMF mismanagement of the Asian Financial Crisis and street rallies against the WTO in Seattle and elsewhere, citizens around the world have expressed their conviction that the institutions of global economic governance have a negative impact on their lives without providing them with any channel to make their voices heard (Birchfield & Freyberg-Inan, 2004; Della Porta & Tarrow, 2005; Ghimire, 2005; Juris, 2008; Marchetti, 2009; Mittelman, 2000). As the millions of people whose savings and jobs were destroyed in the series of financial crises over the past decades can attest, mismanagement of economic affairs can have immediate and devastating repercussions for people's livelihoods. Given the high stakes of international policymaking in this issue area, how do government networks compare to other institutional designs in terms of legitimacy?

This section looks at different scholarly views on whether democratic legitimacy is desirable and feasible at the international level. It moves beyond the nation-state as an ideal type and seeks to assess different institutional designs of international organizations regarding their legitimacy. Adopting a proceduralist approach and drawing from the work of Habermas, the section then identifies two yardsticks against which all organizations can be measured, namely, stakeholder inclusion and deliberative equality. It shows that government networks in general and the FSB in particular struggle to meet expectations on both accounts. At the same time, the section argues that traditional intergovernmental organizations and even national parliaments exhibit shortfalls in both dimensions as well.

Democratic Legitimacy at the International Level?

Whether international institutions of any design can carry legitimacy of the democratic kind is the subject of much debate. The field can be meaningfully divided into three approaches (Bexell et al., 2010). The first group of scholars argues that it is desirable but impossible to establish democratic legitimacy at the supranational level (Dahl, 1999). In their view, the intricate polyarchic system of voting equality, effective participation, enlightened understanding, control of the agenda, and inclusion that endows domestic institutions with democratic legitimacy cannot be reproduced outside the confines of the nation-state. Thus, global governance of any institutional design undermines national democratic sovereignty, contributing to a democratic deficit (Altvater, 1999; Tobin, 1999).

A second school of thought regards democratic legitimacy as both desirable and achievable for international institutions if they undergo democratic reforms (Held, 1995, 1999). Advances in technology and the recognition of fundamental interdependency on a global scale, scholars argue, provide the foundations for the evolution of a cosmopolitan polity that engages with global institutions similar to the way citizens do with their respective domestic institutions (Castells, 2008; Keane, 2003; Mittelman, 2000).

A third approach regards democratic legitimacy as neither feasible nor desirable. Bignami (1999, p. 451) acknowledges that "in contemporary parliamentary systems, legitimacy rests in, and government authority flows from, the directly elected chamber." But several scholars recognize that an exclusive reliance on parliamentary democracy as the source of legitimacy is misplaced (Keohane & Nye, 2003; Klijn & Skelcher, 2007). Bignami (1999) notes that the foundational thinkers of the European Union such as Monet, Spinelli, and de Gaulle shared the notion of a "supranational virtue" – a means of allowing Europeans to transform the narrow and self-destructive national interest of the past into a higher common good to the benefit of all citizens in the Union. The European Commission is not chosen in direct elections, but it has tried to substitute electoral legitimation with efforts at increasing transparency, albeit with mixed success (Héritier, 1999). While critics continue to highlight the democratic deficit inherent in the non-electoral nomination of the European Commission, voter turnout for the European Parliament has decreased significantly over the last two decades, and European citizens continue to express greater trust in the European Union than in the national governments or parliaments they can elect directly (European Commission, 2017a).

Even in parliamentary democracies, officials are held accountable by other means than electoral competition. That federal judges, regulators, and central bankers for example are not subject to popular voting procedures may not decrease the legitimacy of their offices. In these positions, accountability is achieved through hierarchical (appointment and removal by superiors) and reputational (dis/approval by peer group of experts) mechanisms (Keohane & Nye, 2003; Héritier, 2003). In a recent book on the topic, Paul Tucker (2018) takes a thorough look at the legitimacy of independent agencies. Combining academic work and a long tenure as a technocrat himself, the author echoes Keohane and Nye in making a case for professional standing and public reputation as key mechanisms to make sure unelected power holders still serve the public interest. Tucker builds on the Alesina and Tabellini (2007, 2008) model to formulate four principles for delegation that outline the scope conditions under which the outsourcing of policymaking to technocrats in independent agencies would be justified. But he stops short of taking his analysis beyond the domestic realm, arguing that "a robust bridge from the Principles to the legitimacy of international policy making would require further elaboration" (P. M. W. Tucker, 2018, p. 24).

Even though competitive elections are not synonymous with legitimacy, many observers would argue that the potential for common citizens to punish policymakers that fail to act in their interest at the voting booth represents a stronger accountability mechanism than its hierarchical or reputational alternatives. As a European legislator asserts, "*You won't tell me that the accountability that [ECB President] Draghi has is the same that I have*" (EU Legislator 1, personal communication, November 26, 2017). In line with this thinking, this book advocates for the incorporation of elected experts into the institutions of global governance.

While recognizing the power of electoral accountability, this chapter moves beyond the nation-state as an ideal type of legitimacy. It adopts a proceduralist approach to assess the legitimacy of the decision-making process in government networks in general and the FSB in particular. Academic work on trust in regulatory regimes across issue areas indicates that procedural legitimacy is a key driver of trust and compliance (Six & Verhoest, 2017).

Stakeholder Inclusion

Habermas (2015) draws on discourse theory to emphasize two conditions that must be fulfilled to attribute legitimizing force to the process of interest aggregation: inclusion and deliberation. The remainder of this section will discuss each in turn.

Inclusion of stakeholders is a central tenet of legitimacy, at the domestic as much as at the global level. In global governance, inclusion can be measured by addressing two questions: Which jurisdictions participate in the policymaking process? And which stakeholders have a say within each jurisdiction?

Legitimate global governance along the first dimension would follow what Held and Young (2009) call the equivalence principle: All jurisdictions affected by a global good (such as financial stability) or bad (such as pollution) should have a say in its provision and regulation. In this regard, financial government networks in finance have a mixed record. A few, like the network of securities regulators (IOSCO), are approaching universal membership, while others are restricted to a few high-income member states. The FSB with only 24 member jurisdictions has been criticized for excluding a large group of stakeholders, especially developing countries (E. Jones & Zeitz, 2017; E. Jones & Knaack, 2017; New Rules for Global Finance, 2014).

Over the past three decades, the international banking landscape has witnessed two dramatic shifts. First, the banking sectors of the largest developing countries became systemically important for global financial stability (BIS, 2017). We have seen a rapid cross-border expansion of banks headquartered in developing countries. This is most notable in China, which is the home jurisdiction for four of the ten largest banks on earth, with operations in over 40 countries (The Banker, 2017; FSB, 2020a). Moreover, emerging market economies account for a 20% share of the global shadow banking sector. Second, countries in the periphery have become far more interconnected to the financial core and to each other. As a result of these changes, developing countries now have a higher level of foreign bank presence than industrialized countries, making them particularly vulnerable to financial crises and regulatory changes in other jurisdictions. This heightened interconnectedness was powerfully illustrated during the GFC, which, unlike previous crises, affected all types of countries around the world (Claessens, 2017).

Nevertheless, regulatory deliberations and post-crisis rulemaking in the FSB and the standard setters it coordinates are dominated by regulators from advanced economies. While the ten developing countries that are members of the FSB and the Basel Committee have formal channels for policy input and a right to veto any decision, at least in principle, nonmember jurisdictions do not. On the face of it, nonmembers are not obliged to implement global financial standards. Yet the uneven distribution of structural power in the global financial system limits the extent to which national authorities in peripheral countries can act freely. National regulatory authorities in small countries, particularly those with nascent financial sectors, are often looking to attract international capital, maintain (or attain) investment grade ratings from international ratings agencies, and stay on good terms with International Financial Institutions. As a consequence, regulators, in conjunction with politicians and banks in peripheral countries face strong reputational and competitive incentives to adopt international financial standards. For example, only 28 jurisdictions were involved in formulating and developing the rules that comprise Basel III, but over 81 other countries report adopting it, at least in part (E. Jones & Zeitz, 2017, 2019; E. Jones, 2020).

If Basel III would fit and benefit all, wide adoption would be unproblematic and raise no legitimacy issues for standard setters. But in reality, it poses a number of implementation challenges, in particular for low and lower-middle income countries. Regulatory stringency is not necessarily one of them, as preexisting capital and liquidity requirements in developing countries are often higher than Basel standards. Instead, implementation challenges arise from deficiencies in financial infrastructure such as rating agencies, and deep and liquid stock markets, that Basel III rules rely on. Moreover, the high complexity of post-reform financial standards strains the resources of regulatory agencies in developing countries. It may also exacerbate information asymmetries between regulators and regulatees, who may have greater space for regulatory arbitrage (Beck et al., 2018; E. Jones & Knaack, 2019). A final concern is that Basel III leads to a deterioration of credit composition, raising the cost of trade finance, infrastructure financing, and loans to SME countries (Beck, 2018; Briault et al., 2018; Gobat et al., 2014; Rojas-Suarez & Muhammad, 2018). In response to the latter, the FSB commissioned a series of studies that found no significant negative impact for developing countries within the limits of data available at the time (FSB, 2017d, 2018a, 2019a).

In order to improve inclusion of stakeholders and engage with nonmember jurisdictions, the FSB established six Regional Consultative Groups (RCG) in 2010. Comprised of a total of 89 jurisdictions, these groups are designed to operate as a membrane between FSB members and nonmembers (FSB, 2012a). But doubts remain on whether that membrane is permeable or anything more than a one-way channel from the FSB to nonmembers.

The clearest case to date that casts a shadow over RCGs and the wider ability of the FSB to take developing country concerns into account is the dispute over shadow banking (McCulley, 2007) or nonbank credit intermediation (NBCI) (see also Chapter 2). Unlike banking or financial derivatives, NBCI is a heterogeneous and amorphous category. In the wake of the GFC, policymakers have advanced several partially overlapping and competing interpretative frames of how to understand this financial "non-sector," the risks and benefits it entails for the economy, and how and why to regulate it. Financial authorities from Western advanced economies have engaged in an epistemic dispute with China and several developing countries in the FSB over which interpretative frame to apply. Regulators from advanced economies took the lead in defining NBCI as shadow banking, conceiving it chiefly as a potential source of systemic risk that deserves close monitoring and control (FSB, 2011c).

China and other emerging market economies within and outside the FSB have contested this frame, arguing that NBCI also serves as a vehicle for financial development and inclusion. The People's Bank of China (PBOC) noted in its 2013 financial stability report that "as an integral part of financial market in a broad sense, shadow banking plays a positive role in facilitating social investment and financing" (PBOC, 2013, p. 199). The deputy governor of the Reserve Bank of India agreed: "In the context of developing economies, shadow banks play a gainful role in credit delivery and financial inclusion as they can facilitate credit availability to certain sectors that might otherwise have difficulty in access to credit" (Gandhi, 2014).

While significant debates between Indian and Chinese regulators on the one side and Euro-American authorities on the other on how to frame NBCI have likely occurred within the FSB, no public documentation to provide evidence is available to date. Instead, the frame dispute on shadow banking surfaced in one of the six RCG mentioned previously. Members of the RCG Asia discovered in 2013 that they share discontent with the FSB shadow banking frame. The RCG comprises regulatory authorities from 15 East Asian jurisdictions, eight of which also hold seats at the FSB. RCG members commissioned a survey, asking regulators in the region to identify nonbank financial intermediaries and report the risk profile as well as the current degree of supervisory control over the sector. A Malaysian regulator recalls the following:

> When Malaysia and Korea mooted the idea there was a consensus among all members, China and India included, to undertake this exercise. Because it provides a platform for us to share and understand what others are doing, how others are approaching this particular segment of the financial system. . . . We wanted to find out, from a developing economy perspective what are the specific factors, what are the specific methods we want to convey. This will help developing country FSB members represent the view of developing countries. Otherwise it would be pretty much be the old countries' view.
>
> *(Malaysia Regulator 2, personal communication, March 26, 2018)*

The Central Bank of Malaysia co-chaired the RCG workstream on shadow banking with the Securities and Futures Commission of Hong Kong, a well-respected high-income FSB member. Building on the survey of member jurisdictions mentioned previously, it produced a report that echoes Chinese objections to the FSB shadow banking frame. RCG members argue that nonbank financial intermediaries (NBFI) play a beneficial role in "in filling a credit void and broadening access to finance by individuals and corporations which may not otherwise benefit from access to 'traditional' sources of funding" and that "these positive attributes of NBFIs are of significant socio-economic value to most jurisdictions in the region" (FSB RCG Asia, 2014, p. 6).

The report is remarkable for two reasons. First, it openly disputes the FSB frame on shadow banking as primarily a source of risk rather than a vehicle for economic development. Second, it promotes shadow banking as a vehicle for financial inclusion and highlights the special needs of emerging and developing markets. The report explicitly states that "none of the members consider that Asia faces the same shadow banking risks as other jurisdictions such as the US or EU" (FSB RCG Asia, 2014, p. 9). In the following year, developing countries from around the world joined their Asian peers in challenging the FSB frame. In a conference organized by the Alliance for Financial Inclusion (a global network of non-OECD regulators headquartered in Kuala Lumpur) and the Russian Central Bank in Moscow, attendees declared that shadow banking regulation should take into account the financial inclusion benefits of NBCI in developing countries (Bank of Russia & Alliance for Financial Inclusion, 2015).

Just as remarkable as the RGC Asia report and the Moscow conference is the lack of response by the FSB. Its 2015 monitoring report and 2016 thematic peer review do not entertain any of the challenges put forward against the FSB frame.

The latter merely takes note of the need for the FSB to "resolve material differences of view and thereby promote greater consistency in the classification of non-bank financial entities" (FSB, 2016b, p. 6). FSB resistance to incorporating financial inclusion and developmental prerogatives is not merely a question of perceived institutional specialization around risk. The FSB shadow banking frame is informed by painful experiences of the global financial crisis, and memories of regulatory failure in Western advanced economies continue to shape the outlook of key policymakers in the FSB, as exemplified in a regulator's response to the benefits of financial inclusion:

> Securitized subprime mortgages – as a friend of mine used to say, the road to hell is paved with good intentions. They started out of a desire to improve financial inclusion, right? Where unfortunately other incentives got to work on what was originally a noble goal.
>
> *(International Regulator 6, personal communication, December 18, 2017)*

In sum, the last half-decade has witnessed a dispute of increasing alacrity over which regulatory frame is appropriate for NBCI. In spite of concerted efforts by Asian jurisdictions and developing country regulators making their voices heard through an RCG, Western regulators at the FSB have resisted adjustments to the shadow banking frame they developed in the wake of the global financial crisis (Knaack & Gruin, 2020). Thus, in spite of the creation of the RCGs over a decade ago, the FSB exhibits significant shortfalls in the inclusion of jurisdictions affected by its standard-setting.

The next question of inclusion might pose an even greater challenge: Which stakeholders within member countries should have a voice in the FSB? Financial market regulators have traditionally considered financial firms and investors as their constituency. However, as the global financial crisis made clear, even citizens that are not involved in financial markets suffer from the repercussions of a financial meltdown. Furthermore, broadening the circle of stakeholders subjects public policies to increased scrutiny. Charnovitz (2010) asserts that "transnational civil society and business should have an opportunity to participate in dialogues with regulators so that the problems of government failure can be exposed" (p. 760). An assessment of legitimacy should thus consider to what extent those affected by the policies of an organization are included in policy deliberations.

Legal scholars and political scientists have observed that government networks have started to borrow procedural designs of stakeholder involvement from the regulatory state at the national level. In particular, consultation procedures as enshrined in domestic administrative law do not only increase the legitimacy of national regulators, they are also scalable beyond the nation-state (F. E. Bignami, 1999; Kingsbury et al., 2005; Alvarez, 2006; Newman & Zaring, 2013; Stewart, 2014; McCubbins et al., 1987; Majone, 1997). Esty (2006) argues that government networks can adopt a variety of features from the administrative law toolbox, including controls on special interest influence, public hearings, structured factfinding, review mechanisms, and notice and comment procedures.

Global financial standard-setting bodies have indeed adopted several such procedures over time, including a notice and comment process of stakeholder engagement. The Basel Committee for example negotiated Basel I in 1988 in a largely secretive process. Basel II in contrast involved a five-year comment and adjustment procedure in the late 1990s and early 2000s (Zaring, 2010). The original FSB charter of 2009 contained a provision for "consultation with private sector authorities," but as a consequence of widespread criticism, it was revised in June 2012 to provide for a wider "structured process for public consultation on policy proposals" (Helleiner, 2013). According to this procedure, FSB publishes rule proposals and invites public comment letters from interested parties for a period of several weeks. At the end of the consultative period, comment letters are made public, and the government network takes comments into consideration when finalizing the rulemaking process.

In sum, in its original institutional design from 2009 or thanks to subsequent amendments, the FSB is providing avenues for participation in the regulatory process that would match the equivalence principle to some extent. But the empirical picture to date shows that only a fraction of stakeholders actually use the avenues provided to them to make their voices heard. Thus, the FSB as a government network may score lower on a measure of deliberation than inclusion.

Deliberative Equality

Deliberation, and more specifically, deliberative equality is the second procedural criterion of legitimacy under study here. Slaughter (2004) argues that a basic principle for all legitimate government networks is the inclusion of all relevant and affected parties on an equal footing. This ideal is shared by many scholars of globalization who have studied the rise of transnational civil society (Barnett & Finnemore, 1999; Berry & Gabay, 2009; Bexell et al., 2010; R. C. Carpenter & Jose, 2012; Castells, 2008; Cerny, 2010; Finnemore & Sikkink, 1998; Fraser, 2007; Glasius et al., 2004; Kaldor, 2003). Arguably, deliberative equality is harder to achieve than inclusion because the mere provision of institutional channels for the incorporation, development, and aggregation of interests is a necessary but not sufficient condition.

Mattli and Woods (2009) highlight this point by distinguishing between the demand and supply side of common interest regulation. The authors assert as follows:

> Global regulation is at great risk of capture. In part this risk is due to institutional constraints – the lack of transparency, due process, and mechanisms of accountability at the global level. Equally important, however, the risk of capture is due to weakness and unevenness of demand for robust regulation at the global level, largely because the requisite expertise and financial as well

> as organizational capacity to participate meaningfully in global regulation are not evenly distributed across affected countries or transnational non-state actors.
>
> *(p. 43)*

The process of post-crisis financial regulatory reform shows that deliberation is highly skewed in favor of advanced economies (New Rules for Global Finance, 2013, 2014). Even though representatives from major emerging market economies (EME) were at the negotiation table of the FSB and its member standard-setting bodies, observers do not qualify their influence as significant. This may be because EME regulators value domestic benefits from global standards over their influence in standard-setting process (Kempthorne, 2016; Knaack, 2017) or because rich-country regulators "form a relatively well-resourced elite network that has developed shared trust, knowledge and experience over decades" (Walter, 2016, p. 2).

While deliberative inequalities are manifest between jurisdictions, critics predominantly focus on unequal participation within countries. Kahler and Lake (2009) summarize the concerns of many scholars when they assert that "patterns of regulatory capture at the domestic level are likely to be reproduced at the global level, with the privileged actors selecting that form of global governance that locks in their control over policy" (p. 256). Baker (2009) goes one step further by arguing that government networks are fundamentally incapable of achieving deliberative equality.

> Unfortunately, 'transgovernmentalism' is entirely incompatible with deliberative equality, and it is precisely the transgovernmental characteristics and qualities of the GFA [global financial architecture] that have to be reformed and challenged if we are to arrive at anything approximating deliberative equality.
>
> *(p. 196)*

The field of stakeholders in global finance is beset with significant structural inequalities in three dimensions. The first structural inequality has been identified half a century ago. Mancur Olson (1968) recognized that the distribution of costs and benefits of a policy is a key driver of the logic of collective action. The cost of financial regulatory failure may be acute enough to spur societal action in the wake of a crisis, but the benefits of financial stability are too diffuse for civil society actors to sustain political mobilization. In contrast, the financial sector has a clear and persistent incentive to water down financial regulation. Even in the immediate aftermath of a financial crisis, the uneven distribution of costs and benefits of financial regulation undermines veritable deliberative equality.

This situation is exacerbated by Aizenman's (2009) "regulatory paradox": assessing the benefits of regulation relies on the counterfactual of "crisis avoided," whereas the cost of regulation is tangible and measurable. Due to this fundamental information asymmetry, long periods of regulatory success may actually contribute to the reduction of the perceived optimal degree of regulation.

The second structural inequality in the field of global finance lies in access to information. Sensible regulation, particularly in finance, relies on high-quality data and sophisticated methods to estimate the likely impact of a given policy. Both access to this data and the technical skills to process it in meaningful ways couldn't be more unevenly distributed. A bank lobbyist explains as follows:

> They know that they don't have the information. I mean they really, having been working in the European Commission, where do you get your information about what is going on and what will work? Who else is going to give it to you? If you talk to the Consumer Federations, those guys are chronically under-resourced. The investors equally. You know I've got a lot of time for them but they, they really do not have the resources. Who is going to give you the information? Ultimately the only people who have the information, or who can tell you exactly what's going on, are the banks.
>
> *(US Lobbyist 1, personal communication, 2012)*

In all areas of financial reform covered in this book, the finance lobby has consistently used dynamic stochastic general equilibrium models and sophisticated econometric methods to convince policymakers that proposed regulation has a devastating impact on the industry, growth, and jobs. No civil society organization in the field has sufficient technical expertise to counter these claims. As long as parliaments and civil society groups lack the technical sophistication to undertake cost-benefit analyses and quantitative impact studies, their arguments are likely to lose out against those of the private sector.

Whereas the first two structural sources of inequality exist both domestically and internationally, the third one manifests in the capacity of cross-border organization. The recognition that financial rulemaking increasingly takes place at a global level has triggered a structural transformation among financial trade associations. The few lobby organizations that existed at the global level before, such as the IIF and ISDA, received stronger financial backing from their member firms, while previously domestic organizations went global. When asked about the reasons for the establishment of a new global umbrella organization, a bank lobbyist responded as follows:

> Everybody realized in 2008 and 2009 that what was going on in the different jurisdictions ultimately related to one another. So it's to make sure that what we're advocating for in the European marketplace is consistent with what we're advocating for in the Asian marketplace, and in the American marketplace.
>
> *(US Lobbyist 3, personal communication, 2014)*

Civil society organizations in contrast have failed to establish comparable cross-border organizational structures (Landolt & Goldring, 2010). Asked about the reasons for this lack of cross-border coordination, an American activist admitted, "If we had more resources we would do a better job collaborating with our counterparts in Europe and elsewhere, but there are enough bush fires right now for us to put out, and we're largely playing defense" (US Civil Society Representative 2, personal communication, July 26, 2012). A deeper inquiry into why civil society groups in finance represent a patchwork rather than a network are beyond the scope of this work. In effect however, in the deliberation of global standards, the financial lobby tends to have greater means and incentives to speak with one voice than civil society. In sum, the global field of policy deliberation in finance is heavily tilted in favor of special interest groups in the regulated industry.

Arguably, parliamentary democracy in its current form only reinforces and exacerbates the structural inequalities that obstruct both deliberative equality and public interest policymaking in global governance. The key reason is that the work of a legislator is wide in functional yet narrow in geographical terms. Parliamentarians in most democracies are elected as generalists, expressing opinions on a wide range of policy areas. At the same time, they serve as representatives of a narrow, geographically circumscribed constituency whose boundaries are of no obvious relevance for issues of global governance.

The function of a legislator as a geographically bound generalists resonates with all three of the structural inequalities outlined in the previous section. First, the Olsonian conjecture that special interest groups have greater mobilization power and incentives holds true especially at the subnational level. When electing their local representative, it is rational for citizens to remain ignorant about policy issues that are of relevance at the global level (Keohane & Nye, 2003). An activist from the United States notes the following:

> The overriding problem that we faced and that is currently the case is that financial services unfortunately lives in the mud of enormous campaign contributions from the financial sector and complexity, which allows a Senator to view banking as a fundraising opportunity for which bad policy will not generally get him in trouble with his electorate. Nobody in Idaho is going to vote for or against Senator Crapo based on his views on margin requirements for cross-border swaps trading.
>
> *(US Civil Society Representative 2, personal communication, June 11, 2014)*

Arguably, the mobilization imbalance between civil society and special interest groups is less drastic at the national level because this is where a critical mass of citizens concerned with global governance issues may be found.

Second, legislators as generalists are not in a position to engage in the technically demanding debates that shape regulatory governance. This is a key reason why legislatures have delegated such tasks to regulatory agencies in the first place.

In order to arrive at public interest regulation, policymakers must critically assess the claims made by the regulated industry and weigh it against alternative proposals. This judgment however requires a degree of technical training and sophistication that generalists cannot afford to have.

Third, as this book has tried to show, public interest regulation of global markets requires cross-border coordination. Regulators have been trailblazers in the creation of transnational networks to facilitate such exchanges. And the engagement of members of the executive branch shows that electoral pressures and a limited time horizon per se are not unsurmountable obstacles to cross-border coordination. But unlike parliamentarians, executive representatives are not beholden to subnational constituencies, and they tend to be experts. Parliamentarians in contrast struggle to meaningfully engage with their counterparts in other jurisdictions.

In sum, deliberative equality in global governance may be obstructed by three structural imbalances: the uneven mobilization potential of civil society and special interest groups, differences in technical sophistication, and differences in cross-border cooperation. Arguably, parliamentarians are not able to redeem and may even exacerbate these existing imbalances because they are parochial generalists, fulfilling a function that is wide in scope and narrow in geography.

Consequently, this book argues in favor of a greater reliance on experts, and it advocates for the establishment of a new institution that combines functional specialization with electoral accountability.

Expert Councils – A Proposal

Placing greater authority in the hands of experts is a proposal that may be met with skepticism. The notion of technocratic paternalism has clear negative connotations, but these connotations deserve to be questioned in the light of institutional alternatives and their empirical record. Habermas summarizes much scholarly work on the democratic deficit when he argues that technocratic rule without democratic roots would have neither power nor motivation to accord sufficient weight to demands of social justice, status security, public service, and collective goods when they conflict with systemic demands of competitiveness and economic growth. The author asserts:

> Without feedback from the insistent dynamics of a political public sphere and a mobilized civil society, political management lacks the drive to use the means of democratically enacted law to redirect the profit-oriented imperatives of investment capital into socially acceptable channels in accordance with the standards of political justice.
>
> *(Habermas, 2015, p. 11)*

Openness to feedback from affected stakeholders is indeed a crucial procedural requirement for common interest regulation, and that is why inclusion is a key dimension of legitimacy for any governance arrangement. But Habermas assumes that civil society remains mobilized and insistent on common interest regulation and that technocrats have an innate bias in favor of special interest groups. At least in the field of global financial regulation, neither of these assumptions finds unequivocal empirical support.

On the one hand, half a century of empirical work on regulatory capture has demonstrated under which conditions regulatory agencies issue policies that benefit the regulated sector. Moreover, and in the realm of global financial regulation in particular, scholarship has shown how a flawed ideology among regulators, revolving doors between public service and industry jobs, and a conformity bias have contributed to regulatory failure (Barth et al., 2012; Goldbach, 2015; S. Johnson & Kwak, 2010; Laffont & Tirole, 1991; Lall, 2012; Dewatripont et al., 2010; Jelveh et al., 2018).

On the other hand, government networks may perform better than alternative governance designs. They may be instrumental in providing information necessary to improve the quality of policy deliberation and in restraining the influence of special interest factions in domestic policymaking (Keohane et al., 2009). A European legislator finds support for this argument in Basel III negotiations at the Basel Committee. He notes that "Basel is more removed from Washington and Brussels, and they take maybe a more balanced view. And since they are more removed from the battlefield they may take a more stringent view" (EU Legislator 1, personal communication, November 26, 2017). In a similar vein, Abbott and Snidal (2001, p. 366) assert, "Right or wrong, paternalism here operates in a new direction: when states cannot find domestic solutions to their problems, they turn to international forums, where a different balance of representation leads to superior policies."

What Habermas and many other observers don't envision is that technocratic paternalism in global governance is not necessarily at odds with electoral accountability. The involvement of the executive branch in government networks such as the FSB shows that electoral cycles are no impediment to transgovernmental coordination. This book argues that parliamentarians struggle to engage in the kind of cross-border exchanges that are necessary for global public interest regulation because their function is wide in scope and narrow in geography.

If this analysis has merit, a reversal of the features that constrain legislators may provide a solution. Policymakers with authority in global governance issues could, in principle, be elected in a nationwide election and on a narrow field of expertise. In the field of financial regulation, this procedure would be akin to electing a finance minister with a mandate to represent one nation in the relevant forums of global regulatory governance. The representatives of such an "expert council" would then join regulators and central bankers in regulatory deliberations in government networks. An expert council promises to harness the benefits of technocracy (technical sophistication and cross-border allegiance to an epistemic community) with those of electoral competition (direct feedback from the dynamics of a political public sphere, strong accountability).

In order to respect a strict notion of subsidiarity, expert councils would exist with an explicit mandate for global governance and only in the few policy areas where global coordination is truly necessary for the public interest. How many experts would be elected per nation-state, how many nation-states are included, and how would these elected experts relate to national governments? These and many more questions deserve further deliberations that are beyond the scope of this book.

As the preceding discussion shows, the indicators of legitimacy are in dispute. Government networks in general and the FSB in particular may offer avenues for inclusion both among countries and for stakeholders within them. Actual policy deliberation however is heavily skewed towards high-income countries, and in favor of special interest groups within these countries. Reducing between-country inequality may be achievable as regulators from developing countries gain expertise and capacity over time. The deliberative playing field among stakeholders in contrast is beset with structural inequalities that cannot be easily addressed by the institution of national parliaments. Leaving policymaking authority with financial experts in government networks after the global financial crisis maybe equivalent to trusting pilots after a series of airplane crashes. But in providing a technocratic bulwark against special interest groups, government networks may represent a more legitimate venue for global economic governance than its critics would believe. Moreover, there is no categorical reason why experts cannot be subjected to competitive elections. Instituting a council of elected experts that represent their respective nations in the forums of global governance may provide a combination of technocratic sophistication and electoral accountability.

Conclusion

This book is motivated by the harrowing experiences of the global financial crisis. The author moved to the United States for graduate studies in 2009, at a time when unemployment was sky-high, billions of pension savings were wiped out, and public squares in big cities were populated with families who had to swap their houses for tents. This crisis was the product neither of divine vengeance nor a natural calamity such as a pandemic but merely the result of reckless behavior by a few well-paid financial operators and the failure of public authorities to stop them in time. Over a decade ago, G20 leaders pledged to rewrite the rules of global finance to make sure such a crisis would never happen again. And they put the FSB in charge of coordinating global financial regulatory reform. What can we learn from this crisis and from the gap between the reform commitments of the G20 and the reality of their implementation?

The process tracing analysis presented in this book analyzed three major reform areas, all agreed upon by the same group of G20 state leaders in and around 2009. It shows the mixed track record of the FSB in implementing reform in prudential banking (Basel III), OTC derivatives, and ending TBTF. And it argues that the institutional pathway of reform is the main predictor of reform success or failure. Specifically, reform areas that are channeled through government networks see rapid and consistent completion. In contrast, in areas where legislators emerge as protagonists, financial regulatory reform stumbles into incomplete and inconsistent implementation.

Basel III is the bright success case on the post-crisis reform agenda. Even though the financial supervisors of the Basel Committee, a government network, had to change their mind about the need for macroprudential regulation in the face of their failures, they were able to craft a new, tougher, and more comprehensive global standard in a short period of time. Major banks in all G20 jurisdictions have adjusted to meet Basel III requirements, and local implementation of the global rules has been consistently implemented in all jurisdictions, with the conspicuous exception of the one jurisdiction where legislators were involved, namely, the European Union.

Reform progress in the area of OTC derivatives is mixed. In the first half of the 2010s, reform efforts were encumbered by unilateral moves by the United States and Europe, years of transatlantic bickering over extraterritorial application of rules, and slow or no advances in other G20 countries. The legal frameworks created by legislators in both jurisdictions to rule the derivatives market (Title VII of the Dodd-Frank Act and EMIR) did not empower regulators to coordinate rulemaking across borders, did not remove preexisting obstacles to cross-border cooperation, and even erected new ones, such as in the area of data sharing. In the second half of the 2010s, government networks under the FSB umbrella were able to devise globally coherent standards to govern central clearing counterparties. They have also established a unified new language to make the network of OTC derivatives trades legible. Nevertheless, fragmentation along jurisdictional borders in data reporting, trading, and clearing persists, and even after a decade of efforts, regulatory reform in this area falls short of G20 commitments.

Global efforts to end TBTF have seen mixed success too. In this area, we can see a bifurcation between global rules that make systemically important financial institutions more resilient to shocks and those that help resolve them after they fail. Cross-border cooperation in resolution continues to be hamstrung by legal obstacles that make it hard to believe any large financial institution would actually fail in an orderly fashion without requiring public support. But the FSB succeeded in creating new, globally coherent standards to make large banks more resilient and to clarify who would absorb the losses of a failing institution. In doing this, it has leveraged the power of government networks in circumventing legal obstacles and legislative involvement.

The peculiar pattern of progress and shortcomings in post-crisis global financial regulatory reform provides the empirical foundation for assessing the power of the FSB and its limits in the first decade of its existence. While the government network is able to harness a variety of soft law methods to galvanize cross-border cooperation, it is hemmed in by legal obstacles and reluctance among legislators in member jurisdictions to remove them. Institutionally constrained in their ability to engage in transnational cooperation, legislators are experiencing a loss of policymaking authority over the economy under conditions of globalization. The tension between parliaments and government networks is evident in the field of financial regulation, as this book has attempted to show. The criticism leveled against the operation of government networks in general and the FSB in particular concentrates on two dimensions: effectiveness and legitimacy. But scholarship and empirical evidence assembled in this chapter attenuate the arguments of the critics. While the FSB does not have an impressive record in terms of either effectiveness or legitimacy, there are reasons to believe that this government network performs better in both dimensions than alternative institutional designs would.

Nevertheless, government networks in general and the FSB in particular have much room for improvement, especially regarding stakeholder involvement among and within affected countries. The massive structural inequalities that pose obstacles to deliberative equality are well-known and researched. Employing the instruments of national administrative law to increase procedural legitimacy at the global level is an important first step. Nonmember jurisdictions around the world are affected by global financial rulemaking, and as the example of shadow banking shows, it is not clear to what extent their voices are heard at the FSB and the standard-setting bodies it coordinates. Moreover, government networks like the FSB may be able to take greater advantage of the administrative law tool kit to further increase the supply of avenues for stakeholder engagement. While such incremental steps can help to increase procedural legitimacy, some out-of-the-box thinking may help to boost the legitimacy of government networks like the FSB in the eyes of common citizens. An expert council along the lines of the proposal made in this chapter may help galvanize demand for public interest regulation in national public spheres. It may also help dissipate the myth that experts are removed from citizens, unaccountable, and impervious to electoral accountability. More than a decade after the outbreak of the global financial crisis, the debate on how to achieve financial stability with an effective and legitimate global governance design is still far from reaching its conclusion.

BIBLIOGRAPHY

Abbott, K. W., Keohane, R. O., Moravcsik, A., Slaughter, A.-M., & Snidal, D. (2000). The concept of legalization. *International Organization, 54*(03), 401–419.

Abbott, K. W., Levi-Faur, D., & Snidal, D. (2017). Theorizing regulatory intermediaries: The RIT model. *The ANNALS of the American Academy of Political and Social Science, 670*(1), 14–35.

Abbott, K. W., & Snidal, D. (2000). Hard and soft law in international governance. *International Organization, 54*(03), 421–456.

Abbott, K. W., & Snidal, D. (2001). International 'standards' and international governance. *Journal of European Public Policy, 8*(3), 345–370.

Abbott, K. W., & Snidal, D. (2009). The governance triangle: Regulatory standards institutions and the shadow of the state. In W. Mattli & N. Woods (Eds.), *The politics of global regulation* (pp. 44–88). Princeton University Press.

Abbott, K. W., & Snidal, D. (2010). International regulation without international government: Improving IO performance through orchestration. *The Review of International Organizations, 5*(3), 315–344.

Abdelal, R. (2006). Writing the rules of global finance: France, Europe, and capital liberalization. *Review of International Political Economy, 13*(1), 1–27.

Abrams, R. (2014, March 4). Financial regulator calls Obama budget "woefully insufficient". *New York Times DealBook.* http://dealbook.nytimes.com/2014/03/04/financial-regulator-calls-obama-budget-woefully-insufficient/

Acharya, V. V., Cooley, T. F., Richardson, M. P., & Walter, I. (2011). A bird's-eye view: The Dodd-Frank Wall Street reform and consumer protection act. In V. V. Acharya, T. F. Cooley, M. P. Richardson, & I. Walter (Eds.), *Regulating Wall Street: The Dodd-Frank Act and the new architecture of global finance* (pp. 1–32). John Wiley & Sons.

Action Aid International. (2013, July 1). *G20 derivatives letter July 2013.* http://www2.weed-online.org/uploads/g20_derivatives_letter_july_2013.pdf

Admati, A. R., DeMarzo, P. M., Hellwig, M. F., & Pfleiderer, P. C. (2011). Fallacies, irrelevant facts, and myths in the discussion of capital regulation: Why bank equity is not expensive. *MPI Collective Goods Preprint, 2010/42.* www.econstor.eu/bitstream/10419/94558/1/772021627.pdf

Admati, A. R., & Hellwig, M. F. (2013). *The bankers' new clothes: What's wrong with banking and what to do about it*. Princeton University Press.

AFME, ASIFMA, British Bankers Association, CDMG, The Clearing House, Enterprise Data Management Council, & Financial Services Roundtable. (2011). *Requirements for a global Legal Entity Identifier (LEI) solution*. www.ici.org/pdf/11_requirements_global_lei.pdf

Afonso, G., Santos, J. A., & Traina, J. (2014). Do 'Too-Big-To-Fail' banks take on more risk? *Economic Policy Review, Forthcoming*. http://papers.ssrn.com/sol3/papers.cfm?abstract_id=2420465

Aizenman, J. (2009). *Financial crisis and the paradox of under- and over-regulation* (Working Paper No. 15018). National Bureau of Economic Research. www.nber.org/papers/w15018

Alesina, A., & Tabellini, G. (2007). Bureaucrats or politicians? Part I: A single policy task. *American Economic Review, 97*(1), 169–179.

Alesina, A., & Tabellini, G. (2008). Bureaucrats or politicians? Part II: Multiple policy tasks. *Journal of Public Economics, 92*(3–4), 426–447.

Alexander, K., Dhumale, R., & Eatwell, J. (2006). *Global governance of financial systems: The international regulation of systemic risk*. Oxford University Press.

Alexander, L. (2008, June 5). Centralised counterparties could lessen systemic risk. *Financial Times*. www.ft.com/intl/cms/s/0/29d1f72a-329a-11dd-9b87-0000779fd2ac.html#axzz3Q45WrFsl

Allen & Overy LLP. (2020). *Brexit and its impact on the cleared derivatives markets: A primer*. www.google.com/url?sa=t&rct=j&q=&esrc=s&source=web&cd=&cad=rja&uact=8&ved=2ahUKEwjjoZLy0PTxAhVlMlkFHbfTCBsQFjAAegQIAxAD&url=https%3A%2F%2Fwww.fia.org%2Fsites%2Fdefault%2Ffiles%2F2020-07%2FFIA_WP_Brexit%2520Round-up.pdf&usg=AOvVaw0IwwI5FZXUAr556fj2GBUS

Allen, B., Chan, K. K., Milne, A., & Thomas, S. (2012). Basel III: Is the cure worse than the disease? *International Review of Financial Analysis, 25*, 159–166. https://doi.org/10.1016/j.irfa.2012.08.004

Allison, G. T., & Halperin, M. H. (1972). Bureaucratic politics: A paradigm and some policy implications. *World Politics, 24*(S1), 40–79.

Altvater, E. (1999). The democratic order, economic globalization, and ecological restrictions – On the relation of material and formal democracy. In I. Shapiro (Ed.), *Democracy's edges* (pp. 41–62). Cambridge University Press.

Alvarez, J. E. (2006). International organizations: Then and now. *The American Journal of International Law, 100*(2), 324–347.

Anderson, K. (2005). *Squaring the circle? Reconciling sovereignty and global governance through global government networks*. JSTOR. www.jstor.org/stable/4093380

Angelini, F. (2021, April 21). Solving the EMIR reporting data quality problem. *Kaizen Reporting*. www.kaizenreporting.com/solving-the-emir-reporting-data-quality-problem/

Aosaki, M. (2013). *Implementation of Basel III: Economic impacts and policy challenges in the United States, Japan, and the European Union*. http://fsi.stanford.edu/sites/default/files/Implementation_Basel_III_Aosaki.pdf

Argentina Regulator 2. (2014). *Interview, Buenos Aires, 10 Sep 2014* [Personal communication].

Arner, D. (2011). Adaptation and resilience in global financial regulation. *North Carolina Law Review, 89*, 101.

Avgouleas, E. (2012). *Governance of global financial markets: The law, the economics, the politics*. Cambridge University Press.

Axelrod, R., & Hamilton, W. D. (1981). The evolution of cooperation. *Science, 211*(4489), 1390–1396.

Axelrod, R., & Keohane, R. O. (1985a). Achieving cooperation under anarchy: Strategies and institutions. *World Politics*, *38*(1), 226–254.

Axelrod, R., & Keohane, R. O. (1985b). Achieving cooperation under anarchy: Strategies and institutions. *World Politics*, *38*(1), 226–254.

Ba, S. (2010). *中国金融大未来 (China's great financial future)*. Huawen Publishers.

Bach, D., & Newman, A. L. (2007). The European regulatory state and global public policy: Micro-institutions, macro-influence. *Journal of European Public Policy*, *14*(6), 827–846.

Bach, D., & Newman, A. L. (2010). Transgovernmental networks and domestic policy convergence: Evidence from insider trading regulation. *International Organization*, *64*(03), 505–528.

Bach, D., & Newman, A. L. (2014). Domestic drivers of transgovernmental regulatory cooperation. *Regulation & Governance*, *8*(4), 395–417.

Backer, L. C. (2011). Private actors and public governance beyond the state: The multinational corporation, the Financial Stability Board, and the global governance order. *Indiana Journal of Global Legal Studies*, *18*(2), 751–802.

Bair, S. (2012). *Bull by the horns: Fighting to save Main Street from Wall Street and Wall Street from itself* (1st ed.). Free Press.

Baker, A. (2009). Deliberative equality and the transgovernmental politics of the global financial architecture. *Global Governance: A Review of Multilateralism and International Organizations*, *15*(2), 195–218.

Baker, A. (2010). Restraining regulatory capture? Anglo-America, crisis politics and trajectories of change in global financial governance. *International Affairs*, *86*(3), 647–663.

Baker, A. (2013a). The gradual transformation? The incremental dynamics of macroprudential regulation. *Regulation & Governance*, 7(4), 417–434.

Baker, A. (2013b). The new political economy of the macroprudential ideational shift. *New Political Economy*, *18*(1), 112–139.

Bank of Russia, & Alliance for Financial Inclusion. (2015). *The Moscow resolution on financial inclusion and shadow banking*. www.afi-global.org/publications/1987/The-Moscow-Resolution-on-Financial-Inclusion-and-Shadow-Banking

Banks urge coordination on cross-border clean-ups. (2012, June 7). http://in.reuters.com/article/2012/06/07/banks-iif-livingwills-idINL5E8H69LV20120607

Barker, A., & Masters, B. (2012a, January 22). Paris and Berlin seek to dilute bank rules. *Financial Times*. www.ft.com/intl/cms/s/0/7f8485a8-4500-11e1-a719-00144feabdc0.html?siteedition=intl#axzz2wQIYflwL

Barker, A., & Masters, B. (2012b, May 1). EU set for clash on banking rules. *Financial Times*. www.ft.com/intl/cms/s/0/0d630b52-938e-11e1-8ca8-00144feab49a.html#axzz3J2cmtNXJ

Barnett, M. N., & Finnemore, M. (1999). The politics, power, and pathologies of international organizations. *International Organization*, *53*(04), 699–732.

Barnewall, M. (2009, April 18). *What happened to American sovereignty at G-20?* www.newswithviews.com/Barnewall/marilyn103.htm

Barnier, M. (2013, April 18). *Letter to US Treasury Secretary Lew regarding cross-border OTC derivatives regulation*. www.fsa.go.jp/inter/etc/20130419-1/01.pdf

Barth, J. R., Caprio, G., & Levine, R. (2012). *Guardians of finance: Making regulators work for us* (1st ed., 1st Printing ed.). The MIT Press.

Baxter Jr, T. C., Hansen, J. M., & Sommer, J. H. (2004). Two cheers for territorality: An essay on international bank insolvency law. *American Bankruptcy Law Journal*, *78*, 57.

Bayoumi, T. (2017). *Unfinished business: The unexplored causes of the financial crisis and the lessons yet to be learned*. Yale University Press.

BCBS. (1975). *Report on the supervision of banks' foreign establishments (Concordat)*. www.bis.org/publ/bcbs00a.pdf

BCBS. (1992). *The insolvency liquidation of a multinational bank*. www.bis.org/publ/bcbs10c.pdf

BCBS. (1996). *Amendment to the capital accord to incorporate market risks*. www.bis.org/publ/bcbs119.htm

BCBS. (2004). *Basel II: International convergence of capital measurement and capital standards: A revised framework*. www.bis.org/publ/bcbs107.htm

BCBS. (2009). *Strengthening the resilience of the banking sector*. Bank for International Settlements. www.bis.org/publ/bcbs164.pdf

BCBS. (2010a). *An assessment of the long-term economic impact of stronger capital and liquidity requirements*. Bank for International Settlements. www.bis.org/publ/bcbs173.pdf?noframes=1

BCBS. (2010b). *Report and recommendations of the cross-border bank resolution group*. www.bis.org/publ/bcbs169.pdf

BCBS. (2010c). *Results of the comprehensive quantitative impact study*. www.bis.org/publ/bcbs186.pdf

BCBS. (2011a). *Basel III: A global regulatory framework for more resilient banks and banking systems*. Bank for International Settlements. www.bis.org/publ/bcbs189.pdf

BCBS. (2011b). *Resolution policies and frameworks – Progress so far*. www.bis.org/publ/bcbs200.pdf

BCBS. (2011c). *Global systemically important banks: Assessment methodology and the additional loss absorbency requirement*. www.bis.org/publ/bcbs207.pdf

BCBS. (2012a). *Basel III monitoring report No. 1*. www.bis.org/publ/bcbs217.pdf

BCBS. (2012b). *Basel III regulatory consistency assessment programme*. www.bis.org/publ/bcbs216.htm

BCBS. (2012c). *Basel III monitoring report No. 2*. www.bis.org/publ/bcbs231.pdf

BCBS. (2013a). *Basel III monitoring report No. 3*. www.bis.org/publ/bcbs243.pdf

BCBS. (2013b). *Basel III regulatory consistency assessment (Level 2). Assessment of Basel III regulations – Singapore*. www.bis.org/bcbs/implementation/l2_sg.htm

BCBS. (2013c). *Basel III regulatory consistency assessment (Level 2). Assessment of Basel III regulations – Switzerland*. www.bis.org/bcbs/implementation/l2_ch.htm

BCBS. (2013d). *Report to G20 Leaders on monitoring implementation of Basel III regulatory reforms*. Bank for International Settlements. www.bis.org/publ/bcbs260.pdf

BCBS. (2013e). *Basel III monitoring report no. 4*. www.bis.org/publ/bcbs262.pdf

BCBS. (2013f). *Regulatory Consistency Assessment Programme (RCAP), Assessment of Basel III regulations – China*. Bank for International Settlements. www.bis.org/bcbs/implementation/l2_cn.pdf

BCBS. (2013g). *Regulatory Consistency Assessment Programme (RCAP) – Assessment of Basel III regulations in Brazil*. www.bis.org/bcbs/implementation/l2_br.htm

BCBS. (2014a). *Regulatory Consistency Assessment Programme (RCAP) – Assessment of Basel III regulations – United States of America*. www.bis.org/bcbs/publ/d301.pdf

BCBS. (2014b). *Basel III monitoring report No. 5*. www.bis.org/publ/bcbs278.pdf

BCBS. (2014c). *Regulatory Consistency Assessment Programme (RCAP) – Assessment of Basel III regulations in Australia*. www.bis.org/bcbs/implementation/l2_au.htm

BCBS. (2014d). *Regulatory Consistency Assessment Programme (RCAP) – Assessment of Basel III regulations in Canada*. www.bis.org/bcbs/implementation/l2_ca.htm

BCBS. (2014e). *Basel III monitoring report no. 6*. www.bis.org/publ/bcbs289.pdf

BCBS. (2014f). *Seventh progress report on adoption of the Basel regulatory framework*. www.bis.org/publ/bcbs290.pdf

BCBS. (2014g). *Regulatory Consistency Assessment Programme (RCAP) – Assessment of Basel III regulations – European Union.* www.bis.org/bcbs/publ/d300.pdf

BCBS. (2015a). *Regulatory Consistency Assessment Programme (RCAP) – Assessment of Basel III risk-based capital regulations – Hong Kong SAR.* www.bis.org/bcbs/publ/d313.htm

BCBS. (2015b). *Regulatory Consistency Assessment Programme (RCAP) – Assessment of Basel III risk-based capital regulations – Mexico.* www.bis.org/bcbs/publ/d315.htm

BCBS. (2015c). *Regulatory Consistency Assessment Programme (RCAP) – Assessment of Basel III risk-based capital regulations – India.* www.bis.org/bcbs/publ/d320.htm

BCBS. (2015d). *Regulatory Consistency Assessment Programme (RCAP) – Assessment of Basel III risk-based capital regulations – South Africa.* www.bis.org/bcbs/publ/d322.htm

BCBS. (2016a). *Regulatory Consistency Assessment Programme (RCAP) Assessment of Basel III risk-based capital regulations – Russia.* www.bis.org/bcbs/publ/d357.pdf

BCBS. (2016b). *Basel III monitoring report.* www.bis.org/bcbs/publ/d378.pdf

BCBS. (2016c). *Regulatory Consistency Assessment Programme (RCAP) – Assessment of Basel III risk-based capital regulations – Argentina.* www.bis.org/bcbs/publ/d382.htm

BCBS. (2016d). *Regulatory Consistency Assessment Programme (RCAP) – Assessment of Basel III risk-based capital regulations – Korea.* www.bis.org/bcbs/publ/d380.htm

BCBS. (2016e). *Eleventh progress report on adoption of the Basel regulatory framework.* www.bis.org/bcbs/publ/d388.pdf

BCBS. (2016f). *RCAP – Assessment of Basel III risk-based capital regulations – Indonesia.* www.bis.org/bcbs/publ/d394.pdf

BCBS. (2017a). *Thirteenth progress report on adoption of the Basel regulatory framework.* www.bis.org/bcbs/publ/d418.pdf

BCBS. (2017b). *Basel III: Finalising post-crisis reforms.* www.bis.org/bcbs/publ/d424.pdf

BCBS. (2020a). *Basel III – Implementation.* www.bis.org/bcbs/publ/d510.pdf

BCBS. (2020b). *Eighteenth progress report on adoption of the Basel regulatory framework.* www.bis.org/bcbs/publ/d506.htm

Bearce, D. H., & Bondanella, S. (2007). Intergovernmental organizations, socialization, and member-state interest convergence. *International Organization, 61*(04), 703–733.

Beck, T. (2018, May). Basel III & emerging markets: Effects on capital market development and the real economy. *Center For Global Development.* www.cgdev.org/blog/basel-iii-unintended-consequences-emerging-markets-and-developing-economies-part-5-effects

Beck, T., Carletti, E., & Goldstein, I. (2017). Financial regulation in Europe: Foundations and challenges. In L. Matyas, R. Blundell, E. Cantillon, B. Chizzolini, M. Ivaldi, W. Leininger, R. Marimon, & F. Steen (Eds.), *Economics without borders: Economic research for European policy challenges.* Cambridge University Press.

Beck, T., Jones, E., & Knaack, P. (2018, October 15). Basel standards and developing countries: A difficult relationship. *VoxEU.Org.* https://voxeu.org/article/basel-standards-and-developing-countries

Bennett, A., & Elman, C. (2007). Case study methods in the international relations subfield. *Comparative Political Studies, 40*(2), 170–195.

Berg, S. V., & Horrall, J. (2008). Networks of regulatory agencies as regional public goods: Improving infrastructure performance. *The Review of International Organizations, 3*(2), 179–200.

Berman, P. S. (2004). From international law to law and globalization. *Columbia Journal of Transnational Law, 43,* 485.

Bermann, G. A. (1992). Regulatory cooperation with counterpart agencies abroad: The FAA's aircraft certification experience. *Law and Policy in International Business, 24,* 669–782.

Bernstein, M. H. (1955). *Regulating business by independent commission*. Princeton University Press.

Berry, C., & Gabay, C. (2009). Transnational political action and 'global civil society' in practice: The case of Oxfam. *Global Networks*, *9*(3), 339–358.

Bexell, M., Tallberg, J., & Uhlin, A. (2010). Democracy in global governance: The promises and pitfalls of transnational actors. *Global Governance: A Review of Multilateralism and International Organizations*, *16*(1), 81–101.

Biermann, F., Abbott, K., Andresen, S., Bäckstrand, K., Bernstein, S., Betsill, M. M., Bulkeley, H., Cashore, B., Clapp, J., Folke, C., Gupta, A., Gupta, J., Haas, P. M., Jordan, A., Kanie, N., Kluvánková-Oravská, T., Lebel, L., Liverman, D., Meadowcroft, J., . . . Zondervan, R. (2012). Navigating the Anthropocene: Improving earth system governance. *Science*, *335*(6074), 1306–1307. https://doi.org/10.1126/science.1217255

Bignami, F. (2004). Transgovernmental networks vs. democracy: The case of the European information privacy network. *Michigan Journal of International Law*, *26*, 807.

Bignami, F. E. (1999). Democratic deficit in European community rulemaking: A call for notice and comment in comitology. *Harvard International Law Journal*, 451.

Birchfield, V., & Freyberg-Inan, A. (2004). Constructing opposition in the age of globalization: The potential of ATTAC. *Globalizations*, *1*(2), 278–304.

BIS. (2012). *Annual report. 82nd*. Bank for International Settlements.

BIS. (2013). *Macroeconomic impact assessment of OTC derivatives regulatory reforms report*. www.bis.org/publ/othp20.htm

BIS. (2014a, May 8). *Derivatives statistics*. www.bis.org/statistics/derstats.htm

BIS. (2014b). *BIS 84th annual report*. www.bis.org/publ/arpdf/ar2014e.pdf

BIS. (2017). *Consolidated banking statistics*. www.bis.org/statistics/consstats.htm

Blustein, P. (2012). *How global watchdogs missed a world of trouble*. CIGI. www.cigionline.org/sites/default/files/no.5_0.pdf

Bostrom, N. (2013). Existential risk prevention as global priority. *Global Policy*, *4*(1), 15–31.

Bostrom, N. (2017a). Strategic implications of openness in AI development. *Global Policy*, *8*(2), 135–148.

Bostrom, N. (2017b). *Superintelligence*. Dunod.

Bostrom, N., Dafoe, A., & Flynn, C. (2020). Public policy and superintelligent AI: A vector field approach. In S. M. Liao (Ed.), *The ethics of artificial intelligence* (pp. 293–326). Oxford University Press.

Braithwaite, J. (2011). The essence of responsive regulation. *UBCL Review*, *44*, 475.

Braithwaite, T. (2010, July 20). FDIC chief warns over capital standards. *Financial Times*. www.ft.com/intl/cms/s/0/40271298-9428-11df-a3fe-00144feab49a.html#axzz2wQIYflwL

Braithwaite, T., & Alloway, T. (2014, October 7). Banks rewrite derivatives rules to cope with future crisis. *Financial Times*. www.ft.com/intl/cms/s/0/aeb57e26-4e6d-11e4-bfda-00144feab7de.html?siteedition=intl#axzz3HAJZdMzB

Braithwaite, T., & Mackenzie, M. (2013, September 26). US rules 'endanger' derivatives reforms. *Financial Times*. www.ft.com/intl/cms/s/0/dda5f480-26c4-11e3-bbeb-00144feab7de.html#axzz35CwYJiRF

Brazil Regulator 1. (2014). *Interview, São Paulo, 30 Sep 2014* [Personal communication].

Brewer III, E., & Jagtiani, J. (2013). How much did banks pay to become Too-Big-To-Fail and to become systemically important? *Journal of Financial Services Research*, *43*(1), 1–35.

Breyer, S. G. (1993). *Breaking the vicious circle: Toward effective risk regulation*. Harvard University Press.

Briault, C., Feyen, E., Gonzalez Del Mazo, I., Kwok Chung Yee, B., Rademacher, J., & Skamnelos, I. (2018). Cross-border spillover effects of the g20 financial regulatory reforms: Results from a pilot survey. *World Bank Policy Research Working Paper, 8300.*

British Bankers Association. (2017). *Written evidence to the UK Treasury Committee regarding legislative proposals to amend EU prudential requirements.* http://data.parliament.uk/writtenevidence/committeeevidence.svc/evidencedocument/treasury-committee/capital-and-resolution/written/48261.pdf

Brooks, S. M., & Kurtz, M. J. (2012). Paths to financial policy diffusion: Statist legacies in Latin America's globalization. *International Organization, 66*(01), 95–128.

Brown, E. (2014, December 13). The global bankers' coup: "Bail-in" and the shadowy financial stability board. *Global Research.* www.globalresearch.ca/the-global-bankers-coup-bail-in-and-the-shadowy-financial-stability-board/5419698

Broz, L., & Hawes, M. (2006). US domestic politics and International Monetary Fund policy. In D. G. Hawkins, D. A. Lake, D. L. Nielson, & M. J. Tierney (Eds.), *Delegation and agency in international organizations* (1st ed., pp. 77–106). Cambridge University Press.

Brummer, C. (2010). Why soft law dominates international finance – and not trade. *Journal of International Economic Law, 13*(3), 623–643.

Brummer, C. (2012). *Soft law and the global financial system: Rule making in the 21st century.* Cambridge University Press.

Brummer, C. (2014). *Minilateralism: How trade alliances, soft law and financial engineering are redefining economic statecraft.* Cambridge University Press.

Brunnermeier, M., De Gregorio, J., Eichengreen, B., & El-Erian, M. (2012). *Banks and cross-border capital flows: Policy challenges and regulatory responses.* Brookings. www.brookings.edu/%7E/media/research/files/reports/2012/9/ciepr/09%20ciepr%20banking%20capital%20flows

Brunsden, J. (2013, November 21). EU says Gensler swaps rule clashes with trans-Atlantic pact – Bloomberg. *Bloomberg.* www.bloomberg.com/news/2013-11-21/eu-says-gensler-swaps-rule-clashes-with-trans-atlantic-pact.html

Bruszt, L., & McDermott, G. A. (2012). Integrating rule takers: Transnational integration regimes shaping institutional change in emerging market democracies. *Review of International Political Economy, 19*(5), 742–778.

Bulkeley et al., H. (2014). *Transnational climate change governance.* Cambridge University Press.

Büthe, T., & Mattli, W. (2011). *New global rulers: The privatization of regulation in the world economy.* Princeton University Press.

Calomiris, C. W. (2013). Reforming banks without destroying their productivity and value. *Journal of Applied Corporate Finance, 25*(4), 14–20. https://doi.org/10.1111/jacf.12037

Campbell-Verduyn, M., & Porter, T. (2014). Experimentalism in European Union and global financial governance: Interactions, contrasts, and implications. *Journal of European Public Policy, 21*(3), 408–429.

Cao, X. (2012). Global networks and domestic policy convergence: A network explanation of policy changes. *World Politics, 64*(03), 375–425.

Cardenas, S. (2003). Transgovernmental activism: Canada's role in promoting national human rights commissions. *Human Rights Quarterly, 25*(3), 775–790.

Carmassi, J., & Herring, R. J. (2014). *Corporate structures, transparency and resolvability of global systemically important banks.* www.systemicriskcouncil.org/wp-content/uploads/2015/01/Carmassi-Herring_Corporate-Structures-Transparency-and-Resolvability-of-G-SIBs.pdf

Carney, M. (2012a, February 13). *Bank of Canada submits comments to U.S. regulators regarding Joint Proposal on Prohibitions and Restrictions on Proprietary Trading.* www.bankofcanada.ca/wp-content/uploads/2012/02/volcker_rule_130212.pdf

Carney, M. (2012b). *Letter to G20 Finance Ministers and Central Bank governors*. www.financialstabilityboard.org/publications/r_120420a.pdf

Carney, M. (2014a). *Letter to G20 Finance Ministers and Central Bank governors*. www.financialstabilityboard.org/publications/r_140222.pdf

Carney, M. (2014b, November 17). *The future of financial reform*. www.bankofengland.co.uk/publications/Documents/speeches/2014/speech775.pdf

Carpenter, D. (2004). Protection without capture: Product approval by a politically responsive, learning regulator. *American Political Science Review*, *98*(4), 613–631.

Carpenter, D. (2013). Detecting and measuring capture. In D. Carpenter & D. A. Moss (Eds.), *Preventing regulatory capture: Special interest influence and how to limit it*. Cambridge University Press.

Carpenter, D., Grimmer, J., & Lomazoff, E. (2010). Approval regulation and endogenous consumer confidence: Theory and analogies to licensing, safety, and financial regulation. *Regulation & Governance*, *4*(4), 383–407.

Carpenter, R. C., & Jose, B. (2012). Transnational issue networks in real and virtual space: The case of women, peace and security. *Global Networks*, *12*(4), 525–543.

Caruana, J. (2014, June 4). *Financial regulation, complexity and innovation*. www.bis.org/speeches/sp140604.pdf

Castells, M. (1997). *The power of identity*. Blackwell.

Castells, M. (1998). *End of millennium*. Blackwell.

Castells, M. (2000). *The rise of the network society* (2nd ed.). Blackwell.

Castells, M. (2004). Informationalism, networks, and the network society: A theoretical blueprint. In *The network society: A cross-cultural perspective* (pp. 3–45). Edward Elgar.

Castells, M. (2008). The new public sphere: Global civil society, communication networks, and global governance. *The Annals of the American Academy of Political and Social Science*, *616*(1), 78–93.

Castells, M. (2009). *Communication power*. Oxford University Press.

CBIRC. (2021). *Interim measures for the implementation of the recovery and resolution plans of banking and insurance institutions (银行保险机构恢复和处置计划实施暂行办法)*. www.cbirc.gov.cn/cn/view/pages/ItemDetail.html?docId=989402&itemId=928&generaltype=0

CCBA. (2012). *Regulatory capital rules*. www.communitybankers.org/docs/CCBA%20Basel%20III%20Final.pdf

Cerny, P. G. (2010). *Rethinking world politics: A theory of transnational neopluralism*. Oxford University Press.

Cetorelli, N., McAndrews, J., & Traina, J. (2014). *Evolution in bank complexity*. http://papers.ssrn.com.libproxy.usc.edu/sol3/papers.cfm?abstract_id=2421367

CFTC. (2012a). *Cross-border application of swaps provisions* [FragLibs]. www.cftc.gov/LawRegulation/DoddFrankAct/Rulemakings/Cross-BorderApplicationofSwapsProvisions/index.htm

CFTC. (2012b). *Swap data recordkeeping and reporting requirements: Pre-enactment and transition swaps*. www.federalregister.gov/documents/2012/06/12/2012-12531/swap-data-recordkeeping-and-reporting-requirements-pre-enactment-and-transition-swaps

CFTC. (2013a, July 11). *The European Commission and the CFTC reach a common path forward on derivatives* [PressRelease]. www.cftc.gov/PressRoom/PressReleases/pr6640-13

CFTC. (2013b). *Federal register: Interpretive guidance and policy statement regarding compliance with certain swap regulations*. www.cftc.gov/ucm/groups/public/@newsroom/documents/file/federalregister071213b.pdf

CFTC. (2013c, December 20). *Statement of dissent by commissioner Scott D. O' Malia on comparability determinations* [Speech and Testimony]. www.cftc.gov/PressRoom/SpeechesTestimony/omaliastatement122013

CFTC, & SEC. (2012). *Joint report on international swap regulation.* www.cftc.gov/ucm/groups/public/@swaps/documents/file/dfstudy_isr_013112.pdf

Chari, V. V., & Kehoe, P. J. (2013). *Bailouts, time inconsistency, and optimal regulation.* National Bureau of Economic Research. www.nber.org/papers/w19192

Charnovitz, S. (2010). Addressing government failure through international financial law. *Journal of International Economic Law, 13*(3), 743–761.

Chayes, A., & Chayes, A. H. (1993). On compliance. *International Organization, 47*(02), 175–205.

Chey, H. (2016). International financial standards and emerging economies since the global financial crisis. In C. R. Henning & A. Walter (Eds.), *Global financial governance confronts the rising powers* (pp. 211–236). CIGI.

Chon, G. (2013, December 4). CFTC sued by trade groups over swaps rules. *Financial Times.* www.ft.com/intl/cms/s/0/0f998b74-5d1a-11e3-a558-00144feabdc0.html#axzz36tfBPVKP

Chwieroth, J. (2007). Neoliberal economists and capital account liberalization in emerging markets. *International Organization, 61*(02), 443–463.

Chwieroth, J. M., & Walter, A. (2017). Banking crises and politics: A long-run perspective. *International Affairs, 93*(5), 1107–1129.

Claessens, S. (2017). Global banking: Recent developments and insights from research. *Review of Finance, 21*(4), 1513–1555.

Cline, W. R. (2017). *The right balance for banks: Theory and evidence on optimal capital requirements.* Peterson Institute for International Economics.

Cocheo, S. (2017, November 8). Fresh air at Federal Reserve? *Banking Exchange.* www.bankingexchange.com/news-feed/item/7163-fresh-air-at-federal-reserve?Itemid=259

Coffee, J. C. (2014). *Extraterritorial financial regulation. Why E.T. can't come home* (SSRN Scholarly Paper ID 2347556). Social Science Research Network. http://papers.ssrn.com/abstract=2347556

Cohen, B. H., & Scatigna, M. (2014). *Banks and capital requirements: Channels of adjustment.* BIS Working Papers 443. www.bis.org/publ/work443.pdf

Comizio, G. (2013, March 7). *Fed introduces Dodd-Frank enhanced prudential supervision, early remediation rules for foreign banking organizations.* www.bna.com/early-remediation-rules-for-fbos/

Committee on International Economic Policy and Reform. (2012). *Banks and cross-border capital flows: Policy challenges and regulatory responses.* Brookings. www.brookings.edu/~/media/research/files/reports/2012/9/ciepr/09-ciepr-banking-capital-flows.pdf

Conconi, P., Facchini, G., & Zanardi, M. (2012). Fast-track authority and international trade negotiations. *American Economic Journal: Economic Policy, 4*(3), 146–189.

Conconi, P., Facchini, G., Steinhardt, M. F., & Zanardi, M. (2020). The political economy of trade and migration: Evidence from the US Congress. *Economics & Politics, 32*(2), 250–278.

Cooley, T. F., & Walter, I. (2011). The architecture of financial regulation. In V. V. Acharya, T. F. Cooley, M. P. Richardson, & I. Walter (Eds.), *Regulating Wall Street: The Dodd-Frank Act and the new architecture of global finance* (pp. 35–50). John Wiley & Sons.

Cooper, A. F. (2010). The G20 as an improvised crisis committee and/or a contested 'steering committee' for the world. *International Affairs, 86*(3), 741–757.

Cortell, A., & Peterson, S. (2006). Dutiful agents, rogue actors, or both? Staffing, voting rules, and slack in the WHO and WTO. In D. G. Hawkins, D. A. Lake, D. L. Nielson, & M. J. Tierney (Eds.), *Delegation and agency in international organizations* (pp. 255–280). Cambridge University Press.

Cotton, T., Crapo, M., Toomey, P., Perdue, D., Tillis, T., & Kennedy, J. (2018, January 18). *Letter to President Trump FSB*. www.cotton.senate.gov/files/documents/180118_Letter_to_President_Trump_FSB_VF_Signatures.pdf

Coyne, A. (2011, December 5). In conversation: Mark Carney. *Macleans.Ca*. www.macleans.ca/general/on-europes-crisis-%ef%ac%81ghting-in%ef%ac%82ation-and-his-new-job-heading-the-financial-stability-board/

CPMI, & IOSCO. (2014). *Recovery of financial market infrastructures*. www.bis.org/cpmi/publ/d121.htm

CPMI, & IOSCO. (2017). *Resilience of central counterparties (CCPs): Further guidance on the PFMI*. www.bis.org/cpmi/publ/d163.htm

CPMI, & IOSCO. (2018). *Framework for supervisory stress testing of central counterparties (CCPs)*. www.bis.org/cpmi/publ/d176.htm

CPSS, & IOSCO. (2012a). *Principles for financial market infrastructures (PFMI)*. www.bis.org/cpmi/info_pfmi.htm

CPSS, & IOSCO. (2012b). *Report on OTC derivatives data reporting and aggregation requirements*. www.bis.org/cpmi/publ/d100.pdf

CPSS, & IOSCO. (2013). *Authorities' access to trade repository data*. www.bis.org/cpmi/publ/d110.pdf

Crabb, J. C. V. M., & Holt, P. M. (1989). *Invitation to struggle: Congress, the president, and foreign policy* (3rd ed.). CQ Press.

Crow, D. (2020, March 11). Treasury puts back deadline for divestiture of RBS shares by one year. *Financial Times*. www.ft.com/content/0a3b3c1e-63b1-11ea-a6cd-df28cc3c6a68

Crum, B., & Fossum, J. E. (2009). The multilevel parliamentary field: A framework for theorizing representative democracy in the EU. *European Political Science Review*, *1*(2), 249–271.

Culpepper, P. D., & Reinke, R. (2014). Structural power and bank bailouts in the United Kingdom and the United States. *Politics & Society*, 0032329214547342.

Dafoe, A. (2018). Global politics and the governance of artificial intelligence. *Journal of International Affairs*, *72*(1), 121–126.

Dahl, R. A. (1999). Can international organizations be democratic? A skeptic's view. In I. Shapiro & C. Hacker-Cordon (Eds.), *Democracy's edges* (pp. 19–36). Cambridge University Press.

Damro, C. (2006). Transatlantic competition policy: Domestic and international sources of EU-US cooperation. *European Journal of International Relations*, *12*(2), 171–196. https://doi.org/10.1177/1354066106064506

Davies, H. (2014, October 16). *The spider of finance*. Project Syndicate. www.project-syndicate.org/commentary/financial-stability-board-impact-by-howard-davies-2014-10

Davies, H., & Green, D. (2008). *Global financial regulation: The essential guide*. John Wiley & Sons.

Davis Polk. (2012). *U.S. Basel III capital proposed rules and market risk final rule: Out with the old, in with the new*. www.davispolk.com/download.php?file=sites/default/files/files/Publication/1dd53468-02fe-448d-844d-89ff416619d5/Preview/PublicationAttachment/b36a2a4a-d3a1-44e6-a5ee-73a2710d950c/061212_US_Basel_3_Bank_Capital.pdf

Davis Polk & Wardwell LLP, & McKinsey & Co. (2011). *Credible living wills: The first generation*. www.davispolk.com/Credible-Living-WillsThe-First-Generation-04-26-2011/

Della Porta, D., & Tarrow, S. G. (2005). *Transnational protest and global activism*. Rowman & Littlefield. https://books.google.es/books?hl=es&lr=&id=o3E7rF6WgKwC&oi=fnd&

pg=PR9&dq=della+Porta+Tarrow&ots=4xrKoXCYlm&sig=ShXIggcDiRJu5sof1xi0IU9kSTE

DeMeritt, J. H. (2012). International organizations and government killing: Does naming and shaming save lives? *International Interactions*, *38*(5), 597–621.

Dempsey, G. (2017). *Three developments concerning EU-US cross-border swaps*. www.lexology.com/library/detail.aspx?g=375e00e9-3558-4080-8f8b-fc6c6db5a45d

Destler, I. M. (1986). Protecting Congress or protecting trade? *Foreign Policy*, *62*, 96–107.

Dewatripont, M., Rochet, J.-C., & Tirole, J. (2010). *Balancing the banks: Global lessons from the financial crisis*. Princeton University Press.

Dicken, P. (2007). *Global shift, fifth edition: Mapping the changing contours of the world economy* (5th Edition ed.). The Guilford Press.

Directive 2014/59/EU of the European Parliament and of the Council, no. 2014/59/EU (2014). http://eur-lex.europa.eu/legal-content/EN/TXT/PDF/?uri=CELEX:32014L0059&from=EN

Djankov, S., La Porta, R., Lopez-de-Silanes, F., & Shleifer, A. (2002). The regulation of entry. *The Quarterly Journal of Economics*, *117*(1), 1–37.

Dodd-Frank Wall Street Reform and Consumer Protection Act, no. Pub. L. No. 111–203 (2010).

Donnelly, S. (2012). Institutional change at the top: From the financial stability forum to the financial stability board. In R. Maynte (Ed.), *Crisis and control: Institutional change in financial market regulation* (pp. 263–278). Campus.

Dorn, N. (2012). Render unto caesar: EU financial market regulation meets political accountability. *Journal of European Integration*, *34*(3), 205–221.

Downs, G. W., & Jones, M. A. (2002). Reputation, compliance, and international law. *The Journal of Legal Studies*, *31*(31), 395–3114. https://doi.org/10.1006/340405

Downs, G. W., Rocke, D. M., & Barsoom, P. N. (1996). Is the good news about compliance good news about cooperation? *International Organization*, *50*(03), 379–406.

Draghi, M. (2010, June 24). *FSB Chair letter to G20 Leaders*. www.financialstabilityboard.org/wp-content/uploads/r_100627a.pdf?page_moved=1

Drezner, D. W. (2007). *All politics is global*. Princeton University Press.

Drezner, D. W., & McNamara, K. R. (2013). International political economy, global financial orders and the 2008 financial crisis. *Perspectives on Politics*, *11*(1), 155–166.

Duffield, J. S. (2003). The limits of "Rational design". *International Organization*, *57*(02), 411–430.

Durand, H. (2014, November 28). Europe strives for consistency as MREL consultation begins. *Reuters*. www.reuters.com/article/2014/11/28/banks-capital-idUSL6N0TI2KG20141128

EBA. (2016). *Report on SMEs and SME supporting factor*. www.eba.europa.eu/documents/10180/1359456/EBA-Op-2016-04++Report+on+SMEs+and+SME+supporting+factor.pdf

ECON committee of the European Parliament. (2014). *Reaction to the opinion of the Basel Committee on CRD IV*. www.europarl.europa.eu/news/en/press-room/20141205IPR82904/reaction-to-the-opinion-of-the-basel-committee-on-crd-4

Ehrlich, S. D. (2007). Access to protection: Domestic institutions and trade policy in democracies. *International Organization*, *61*(03), 571–605.

Eichengreen, B. (2008). Not a new Bretton Woods but a new Bretton Woods process. In B. Eichengreen & R. Baldwin (Eds.), *What G20 leaders must do to stabilise our economy and fix the financial system* (pp. 25–29). Centre for Economic Policy Research. http://voxeu.org/sites/default/files/file/G20_Summit%20vox.pdf

Eichengreen, B. (2011, May). *Reforming the international financial architecture, 2011 edition.* Annual Research Conference, Bank of Korea, Seoul. http://eml.berkeley.edu/~eichengr/Reforming_Intl_Arch_2011_Ed.pdf

Eichengreen, B. J. (2009). *Out of the box thoughts about the International Financial Architecture.* International Monetary Fund.

Elkins, Z., Guzman, A. T., & Simmons, B. (2008). Competing for capital: The diffusion of bilateral investment treaties, 1960–2000. *University of Illinois Law Review*, 265.

Elkins, Z., & Simmons, B. (2005). On waves, clusters, and diffusion: A conceptual framework. *The Annals of the American Academy of Political and Social Science*, *598*(1), 33–51.

Elliott, D. (2009). *Quantifying the effects on lending of increased capital requirements.* Brookings Institution. www.brookings.edu/~/media/research/files/papers/2009/9/24%20capital%20elliott/0924_capital_elliott.pdf

Engelen, E., Erturk, I., Froud, J., Johal, S., Leaver, A., Moran, M., Nilsson, A., & Williams, K. (2011). *After the great complacence: Financial crisis and the politics of reform.* Oxford University Press.

Epstein, R. A. (2017). *Banking on markets: The transformation of bank-state ties in Europe and beyond.* Oxford University Press.

Epstein, R. A., & Rhodes, M. (2016). States ceding control: Explaining the shift to centralized bank supervision in the Eurozone. *Journal of Banking Regulation*, *17*(1–2), 90–103.

ESMA. (2014). *Q&A – implementation of the regulation (EU) no 648/2012 on OTC derivatives, central counterparties and trade repositories (EMIR).* www.lexology.com/library/detail.aspx?g=292c0579-6590-4fc5-aa96-92019b52bd54

ESMA. (2020). *Issues affecting EMIR and SFTR reporting following the end of the UK transition period on 31 December 2020.* www.esma.europa.eu/sites/default/files/library/esma74-362-881_statement_brexit_emir_and_sftr_data.pdf

Estache, A., & Wren-Lewis, L. (2009). Toward a theory of regulation for developing countries: Following Jean-Jacques Laffont's lead. *Journal of Economic Literature*, *47*(3), 729–770.

Esty, D. C. (2006). Good governance at the supranational scale: Globalizing administrative law. *The Yale Law Journal*, 1490–1562.

EU. (2008). *Memorandum of understanding on co-operation between the Financial Supervisory Authorities, Central Banks and Finance Ministries of the EU on cross-border financial stability.* www.ecb.europa.eu/pub/pdf/other/mou-financialstability2008en.pdf

EU Civil Society Representative 2. (2017). *Interview, Oxford, 19 May 2017* [Personal communication].

EU Legislator 1. (2017, November 26). *Interview, Brussels, 26 Nov 2017* [Personal communication].

EU Regulator 3. (2014, October 21). *Interview, Brussels, 21 Oct 2014* [Personal communication].

EU Regulator 6. (2014, November 14). *Interview, Brussels, 14 Nov 2014* [Personal communication].

Eurofi. (2014). *Cross-border implementation and global consistency of OTC derivatives and banking requirements.* www.eurofi.net/wp-content/uploads/2014/03/2014_Cross_Border_and_Gloabal_consistency_OTC_derivatives_Athens.pdf

European Commission. (2012). *Comment for proposed rule 77 FR 41213.* http://comments.cftc.gov/PublicComments/ViewComment.aspx?id=58431

European Commission. (2014, January 29). *Structural reform of the EU banking sector.* http://europa.eu/rapid/press-release_IP-14-85_en.htm

European Commission. (2017a). *Standard Eurobarometer 88.* http://ec.europa.eu/commfrontoffice/publicopinion/index.cfm/Survey/getSurveyDetail/instruments/STANDARD/surveyKy/2143

European Commission. (2017b). *EMIR equivalence decision for derivatives transactions in the United States*. https://ec.europa.eu/info/sites/info/files/171013-press-release-emir-cftc_en.pdf

European Commission. (2017c). *Implementing decision 2017/2238 on the equivalence of the legal and supervisory framework applicable to designated contract markets and swap execution facilities in the United States of America*. http://eur-lex.europa.eu/legal-content/EN/TXT/PDF/?uri=CELEX:32017D2238&from=EN

European Commission. (2021). *No 648/2012 equivalence decisions*. ec.europa.eu/info/sites/info/files/business_economy_euro/banking_and_finance/documents/emir-equivalence-decisions_en.pdf

European Parliament. (2016). *Report on the EU role in the framework of international financial, monetary and regulatory institutions and bodies – A8–0027/2016*. www.europarl.europa.eu/sides/getDoc.do?pubRef=-//EP//TEXT+REPORT+A8-2016-0027+0+DOC+XML+V0//EN

Falleti, T. G. (2006). Theory-guided process-tracing in comparative politics: Something old, something new. *Newsletter of the Organized Section in Comparative Politics of the American Political Science Association*, *17*(1), 9–14.

Farrell, H., & Newman, A. L. (2010). Making global markets: Historical institutionalism in international political economy. *Review of International Political Economy*, *17*(4), 609–638.

Farrell, H., & Newman, A. L. (2015). Structuring power: Business and authority beyond the nation state. *Business and Politics*, *17*(3), 527–552.

Farrell, H., & Newman, A. L. (2019). Weaponized interdependence: How global economic networks shape state coercion. *International Security*, *44*(1), 42–79.

FCIC. (2011). *The financial crisis inquiry report*. http://fcic-static.law.stanford.edu/cdn_media/fcic-reports/fcic_final_report_full.pdf

FDIC, & Bank of England. (2012). *Resolving globally active, systemically important, financial institutions*. www.fdic.gov/about/srac/2012/gsifi.pdf

Fearon, J. D. (1998). Bargaining, enforcement, and international cooperation. *International Organization*, *52*(02), 269–305.

Federal Reserve Board. (2012, December). *Proposed rules to strengthen the oversight of U.S. operations of foreign banks*. www.federalreserve.gov/newsevents/press/bcreg/20121214a.htm

Federal Reserve Board. (2014, February 18). *Federal Reserve Board approves final rule strengthening supervision and regulation of large U.S. bank holding companies and foreign banking organizations*. www.federalreserve.gov/newsevents/press/bcreg/20140218a.htm

Fernandez, R., & Rodrik, D. (1991). Resistance to reform: Status quo bias in the presence of individual-specific uncertainty. *The American Economic Review*, 1146–1155.

Finance Watch. (2012). *Position paper on CRD IV/CRR*. www.finance-watch.org/ifile/Publications/Reports/Finance-Watch-CRD-IV-Position-Paper.pdf

Financial CHOICE Act of 2016. (2016). Testimony of Jeb Hensarling. www.congress.gov/bill/114th-congress/house-bill/5983

FINMA. (2018). *Finanzmarktregulierung: Hängige Vorhaben (Stand und Ausblick)*. www.finma.ch/de/~/media/finma/dokumente/dokumentencenter/myfinma/5finma/finanzmarktregulierung-vorhaben.pdf?la=de

Finnemore, M., & Sikkink, K. (1998). International norm dynamics and political change. *International Organization*, *52*(04), 887–917.

Flanagan, T. (2014, September 25). Global LEI foundation takes reins. *Markets Media*. www.marketsmedia.com/global-lei-foundation-takes-reins/

Flandreau, M., & Flores, J. H. (2012). The peaceful conspiracy: Bond markets and international relations during the Pax Britannica. *International Organization*, *66*(2), 211–241.

Fligstein, N. (1996). Markets as politics: A political-cultural approach to market institutions. *American Sociological Review*, 656–673.

France Regulator 1. (2014, December 2). *Interview, Paris, 2 Dec 2014* [Personal communication].

Fraser, N. (2007). Transnationalizing the public sphere: On the legitimacy and efficacy of public opinion in a post-Westphalian world. *Theory, Culture & Society*, *24*(4), 7–30.

Frieden, J. (2016). The governance of international finance. *Annual Review of Political Science*, *19*(1), 33–48. https://doi.org/10.1146/annurev-polisci-053014-031647

Friedman, J. (2011). *Engineering the financial crisis: Systemic risk and the failure of regulation* (1st ed.). University of Pennsylvania Press.

FSB. (2009). *FSB charter*. www.financialstabilityboard.org/wp-content/uploads/r_090925d.pdf?page_moved=1

FSB. (2010a). *Reducing the moral hazard posed by systemically important financial institutions*. www.financialstabilityboard.org/wp-content/uploads/r_101111a.pdf?page_moved=1

FSB. (2010b). *Implementing OTC derivatives market reforms* (1st progress report.). www.financialstabilityboard.org/publications/r_101025.pdf

FSB. (2010c). *Progress since the Washington summit in the implementation of the G20 recommendations for strengthening financial stability*. FSB. www.financialstabilityboard.org/publications/r_101111b.pdf

FSB. (2011a). *OTC derivatives market reforms: Progress report on implementation*. FSB. www.financialstabilityboard.org/publications/r_111011b.pdf

FSB. (2011b). *A coordination framework for monitoring the implementation of agreed G20/FSB financial reforms*. www.financialstabilityboard.org/publications/r_111017.pdf

FSB. (2011c). *Shadow banking: Strengthening oversight and regulation. recommendations of the financial stability board*. www.financialstabilityboard.org/publications/r_111027a.pdf

FSB. (2011d). *Policy measures to address systemically important financial institutions*. www.financialstabilityboard.org/wp-content/uploads/r_111104bb.pdf?page_moved=1

FSB. (2012a). *Current membership of the FSB regional consultative groups*. www.fsb.org/wp-content/uploads/rcg.pdf

FSB. (2012b). *FSB Charter with revised Annex*. www.financialstabilityboard.org/wp-content/uploads/FSB-Charter-with-revised-Annex-FINAL.pdf

FSB. (2012c). *Identifying the effects of regulatory reforms on emerging market and developing economies: A review of potential unintended consequences*. www.financialstabilityboard.org/wp-content/uploads/r_120619e.pdf

FSB. (2012d). *Resolution of systemically important financial institutions – progress report*. www.financialstabilityboard.org/wp-content/uploads/r_121031aa.pdf?page_moved=1www.financialstabilityboard.org/publications/r_121031aa.pdf

FSB. (2012e). *Policy framework for strengthening oversight and regulation of shadow banking entities – consultative document*. www.fsb.org/wp-content/uploads/r_121118a.pdf

FSB. (2013a). *Peer review report on resolution regimes*. www.financialstabilityboard.org/wp-content/uploads/r_130411a.pdf

FSB. (2013b). *Implementing the FSB key attributes of effective resolution regimes – how far have we come?* www.financialstabilityboard.org/publications/r_130419b.pdf

FSB. (2013c). *Recovery and resolution planning for SIFI: Guidance on Developing Effective Resolution Strategies*. www.financialstabilityboard.org/wp-content/uploads/r_130716b.pdf?page_moved=1

FSB. (2013d). *OTC derivatives market reforms – sixth progress report on implementation*. www.financialstabilityboard.org/publications/r_130902b.pdf

FSB. (2013e). *Monitoring note on the effects of regulatory reforms on emerging market and developing economies*. www.financialstabilityboard.org/publications/r_130912.pdf

FSB. (2014a). *Feasibility study on approaches to aggregate OTC derivatives data*. www.financialstabilityboard.org/wp-content/uploads/r_140919.pdf

FSB. (2014b). *FSB welcomes industry initiative to remove cross-border close-out risk*. www.financialstabilityboard.org/wp-content/uploads/pr_141011.pdf

FSB. (2014c). *Monitoring note on the effects of regulatory reforms on emerging market and developing economies*. www.financialstabilityboard.org/wp-content/uploads/Monitoring-the-effects-of-reforms-on-EMDEs.pdf

FSB. (2014d). *OTC derivatives market reforms – eight progress report on implementation*. www.financialstabilityboard.org/wp-content/uploads/r_141107.pdf

FSB. (2015a). *Peer review on trade reporting*. www.financialstabilityboard.org/wp-content/uploads/Peer-review-on-trade-reporting.pdf

FSB. (2015b). *Principles on loss-absorbing and recapitalisation capacity of G-SIBs in resolution*. www.fsb.org/wp-content/uploads/TLAC-Principles-and-Term-Sheet-for-publication-final.pdf

FSB. (2016a). *Second thematic review on resolution regimes*. www.fsb.org/wp-content/uploads/Second-peer-review-report-on-resolution-regimes.pdf

FSB. (2016b). *Thematic review on the implementation of the FSB policy framework for shadow banking entities*. Financial Stability Board. www.fsb.org/wp-content/uploads/Shadow-banking-peer-review.pdf

FSB. (2016c). *Resilience through resolvability – moving from policy design to implementation: 5th progress report on resolution*. www.fsb.org/wp-content/uploads/Resilience-through-resolvability-%E2%80%93-moving-from-policy-design-to-implementation.pdf

FSB. (2017a). *Policy recommendations to address structural vulnerabilities from asset management activities*. www.fsb.org/2017/01/policy-recommendations-to-address-structural-vulnerabilities-from-asset-management-activities/

FSB. (2017b). *Global shadow banking monitoring report 2016*. www.fsb.org/wp-content/uploads/global-shadow-banking-monitoring-report-2016.pdf

FSB. (2017c). *OTC derivatives 12th progress report*. www.fsb.org/wp-content/uploads/P290617-2.pdf

FSB. (2017d). *Implementation and effects of the G20 financial regulatory reforms: Third annual report*. www.fsb.org/2017/07/implementation-and-effects-of-the-g20-financial-regulatory-reforms-third-annual-report/

FSB. (2017e). *Ten years on – taking stock of post-crisis resolution reforms*. www.fsb.org/2017/07/ten-years-on-taking-stock-of-post-crisis-resolution-reforms/

FSB. (2017f). *Guidance on central counterparty resolution and resolution planning*. www.fsb.org/2017/07/guidance-on-central-counterparty-resolution-and-resolution-planning-2/

FSB. (2018a). *Evaluation of the effects of financial regulatory reforms on infrastructure finance*. www.fsb.org/2018/11/evaluation-of-the-effects-of-financial-regulatory-reforms-on-infrastructure-finance/

FSB. (2018b). *Global shadow banking monitoring report 2017*. www.fsb.org/wp-content/uploads/P050318-1.pdf

FSB. (2018c). *Resolution report: "Keeping the pressure up"*. www.fsb.org/2018/11/fsb-2018-resolution-report-keeping-the-pressure-up/

FSB. (2018d). *Trade reporting legal barriers: Follow-up of 2015 peer review recommendations*. www.fsb.org/2018/11/trade-reporting-legal-barriers-follow-up-of-2015-peer-review-recommendations/

FSB. (2019a). *Evaluation of the effects of financial regulatory reforms on small and medium-sized enterprise (SME) financing: Consultation report*. www.fsb.org/2019/06/evaluation-of-the-effects-of-financial-regulatory-reforms-on-small-and-medium-sized-enterprise-sme-financing-consultation-report/

FSB. (2019b). *Thematic peer review on bank resolution planning*. www.fsb.org/2019/04/thematic-peer-review-on-bank-resolution-planning/

FSB. (2020a). *List of global systemically important banks (G-SIBs)*. www.fsb.org/2020/11/2020-list-of-global-systemically-important-banks-g-sibs/

FSB. (2020b). *Implementation and effects of the G20 financial regulatory reforms: 2020 annual report*. www.fsb.org/2020/11/implementation-and-effects-of-the-g20-financial-regulatory-reforms-2020-annual-report/

FSB. (2020c). *OTC derivatives market reforms: 2020 note on implementation progress*. www.fsb.org/2020/11/otc-derivatives-market-reforms-2020-note-on-implementation-progress/

FSB. (2021). *Evaluation of the effects of too-big-to-fail reforms*. www.fsb.org/2021/03/evaluation-of-the-effects-of-too-big-to-fail-reforms-final-report/

FSB, & BCBS. (2011). *Assessment of the macroeconomic impact of higher loss absorbency for global systemically important banks, October 2011*. www.bis.org/publ/bcbs202.pdf

FSB, IMF, & BIS. (2009). *Guidance to assess the systemic importance of financial institutions, markets and instruments: Initial considerations*. www.financialstabilityboard.org/wp-content/uploads/r_091107c.pdf?page_moved=1

FSB RCG Asia. (2014). *Report on shadow banking*. Financial Stability Board Regional Consultative Group Asia. www.fsb.org/wp-content/uploads/r_140822c.pdf

FSF. (2008a). *Report of the financial stability forum on enhancing market and institutional resilience*. www.financialstabilityboard.org/wp-content/uploads/r_0804.pdf?page_moved=1

FSF. (2008b). *Report of the FSF on enhancing market and institution resilience: Follow-up on implementation*. www.financialstabilityboard.org/wp-content/uploads/pr_081009f.pdf?page_moved=1

FSF. (2009a). *Report of the financial stability forum on enhancing market and institutional resilience*. www.financialstabilityboard.org/wp-content/uploads/r_0904d.pdf?page_moved=1

FSF. (2009b). *FSF principles for cross-border cooperation on crisis management*. www.financialstabilityboard.org/wp-content/uploads/r_0904c.pdf

FSI. (2014). *FSI survey – Basel II, 2.5 and III implementation*. www.bis.org/fsi/fsiop2014.pdf

Füglister, K. (2012). Where does learning take place? The role of intergovernmental cooperation in policy diffusion. *European Journal of Political Research, 51*(3), 316–349.

G14, Managed Funds Association, & SIFMA. (2011). *Letter to OTC derivatives supervisors group*. www.newyorkfed.org/newsevents/news/markets/2011/SCL0331.pdf

G20. (2008). *Declaration of the summit on financial markets and the world economy, Washington DC*. www.g20.utoronto.ca/2008/2008declaration1115.html

G20. (2009a). *Declaration on strengthening the financial system*. www.treasury.gov/resource-center/international/g7-g20/Documents/London%20April%202009%20Fin_Deps_Fin_Reg_Annex_020409_-_1615_final.pdf

G20. (2009b). *G20 action plan for recovery and reform*. www.g20.utoronto.ca/summits/2009london.html

G20. (2009c). *Leaders' statement: The Pittsburgh summit*. www.g20.utoronto.ca/2009/2009communique0925.html

G20. (2010a). *The G20 Toronto summit declaration*. www.g20.utoronto.ca/2010/to-communique.html

G20. (2010b). *The G20 Seoul summit declaration*. www.g20.utoronto.ca/2010/g20seoul.pdf

G20. (2013). *Saint Petersburg accountability report on G20 development commitments.* https://g20.org/wp-content/uploads/2014/12/Saint%20Petersburg%20Accountability%20Report%20on%20G20%20Development%20Commitments_0.pdf

G20. (2015). *Antalya summit leaders communiqué.* www.g20.utoronto.ca/2015/151116-communique.pdf

G20. (2017). *Hamburg action plan.* www.g20.utoronto.ca/2017/2017-g20-hamburg-action-plan.html

Gadinis, S. (2013). The financial stability board: The new politics of international financial regulation. *Texas International Law Journal, 48*, 157–325.

Gadinis, S. (2015). Three pathways to global standards: Private, regulator, and ministry networks. *American Journal of International Law, 109*(1), 1–57.

Gambacorta, L., & van Rixtel, A. (2013). *Structural bank regulation initiatives: Approaches and implications* (BIS Working Papers No. 412). www.bis.org/publ/work412.pdf

Gandhi, R. (2014, August). Danger posed by shadow banking systems to the global financial system: The Indian case. In *Address at the Indian council for research on international economic relations conference on governance and development: Views from G20 Countries, Mumbai* (Vol. 21).

GAO. (1986). *International coordination of bank supervision: The record to date.* [Report to the Chairmen, House Committee on Banking, Finance and Urban Affairs and Senate Committee on Banking, Housing and Urban Affairs]. www.gao.gov/assets/150/144034.pdf

Gensler, G., & Barnier, M. (2010). *Joint statement by CFTC Chairman Gary Gensler and European Commissioner Michel Barnier on the financial reform agenda.* www.cftc.gov/PressRoom/PressReleases/pr5905-10

GFMA, The Clearing House, ABA, Financial Services Roundtable, IIB, & IIF. (2011). *Comments to the FSB on effective resolution of systemically important financial institutions.* www.gfma.org/Initiatives/Cross-Border-Resolution/GFMA-and-Other-Associations-Submit-Comments-to-the-FSB-on-Effective-Resolution-of-Systemically-Important-Financial-Institutions/

Ghimire, K. B. (2005). The contemporary global social movements: Emergent proposals, connectivity and development implications. *Civil Society and Social Movements Programme Paper.* www.unrisd.org/80256B3C005BCCF9/(httpAuxPages)/F0F8C2DF84C2FB2DC1257088002BFBD9/$file/ghimire.pdf

Gibson, M. (2013). *Testimony by Michael S. Gibson, director, division of banking supervision and regulation on cross-border resolution.* www.federalreserve.gov/newsevents/testimony/gibson20130515a.htm

Gilardi, F. (2005). The institutional foundations of regulatory capitalism: The diffusion of independent regulatory agencies in Western Europe. *The Annals of the American Academy of Political and Social Science, 598*(1), 84–101.

Gilardi, F., Jordana, J., & Levi-Faur, D. (2006). *Regulation in the age of globalization: The diffusion of regulatory agencies across Europe and Latin America.* http://papers.ssrn.com/sol3/papers.cfm?abstract_id=960739

Gill, S. (1992). Economic globalization and the internationalization of authority: Limits and contradictions. *Geoforum, 23*(3), 269–283.

Glasius, M., Lewis, D., & Seckinelgin, H. (Eds.). (2004). *Exploring civil society: Political and cultural contexts.* Routledge.

Gobat, J., Yanase, M., & Maloney, J. (2014). The net stable funding ratio: Impact and issues for consideration. *IMF Working Papers, 14*(106), 1. https://doi.org/10.5089/9781498346498.001

Goldbach, R. (2015). Asymmetric influence in global banking regulation: Transnational harmonization, the competition state, and the roots of regulatory failure. *Review of International Political Economy, 22*(6), 1087–1127.

Goldstein, J., Kahler, M., Keohane, R. O., & Slaughter, A.-M. (2000). Introduction: Legalization and world politics. *International Organization, 54*(03), 385–399.

Goodhart, C. (2011). *The Basel committee on banking supervision: A history of the early years 1974–1997*. Cambridge University Press.

Goodhart, C., & Avgouleas, E. (2014). *A critical evaluation of Bail-ins as bank recapitalisation mechanisms*. http://papers.ssrn.com/sol3/Papers.cfm?abstract_id=2478647

Goodhart, C., & Schoenmaker, D. (2009). Fiscal burden sharing in cross-border banking crises. *International Journal of Central Banking, 5*(1), 141–165.

Gordon, S. C., & Hafer, C. (2005). Flexing muscle: Corporate political expenditures as signals to the bureaucracy. *American Political Science Review, 99*(02), 245–261.

Goulding, W., & Nolle, D. E. (2012). *Foreign banks in the U.S.: A primer*. Board of Governors of the Federal Reserve System. www.federalreserve.gov/pubs/ifdp/2012/1064/ifdp1064.pdf

Gourevitch, P. (1978). The second image reversed: The international sources of domestic politics. *International Organization, 32*(04), 881–912.

Gravelle, M., & Pagliari, S. (2018). Global markets, national toolkits: Extraterritorial derivatives rule-making in response to the global financial crisis. In E. Helleiner, S. Pagliari, & I. Spagna (Eds.), *Governing the world's biggest market: The politics of derivatives regulation after the 2008 crisis* (pp. 82–106). Oxford University Press.

Greene, E. F., & Boehm, J. L. (2011). Limits of name-and-shame in international financial regulation, the. *Cornell Law Review, 97*, 1083.

Greene, E. F., & Potiha, I. (2012). Examining the extraterritorial reach of Dodd – Frank's Volcker rule and margin rules for uncleared swaps – A call for regulatory coordination and cooperation. *Capital Markets Law Journal*, kms026.

Greenwood, J. (2012, January 13). Global financial watchdog toothless, Martin says. *Financial Post*. http://business.financialpost.com/news/fp-street/global-financial-watchdog-toothless-martin-says

Greenwood, J., & Roederer-Rynning, C. (2015). The "Europeanization" of the Basel process: Financial harmonization between globalization and parliamentarization. *Regulation & Governance, 9*(4), 325–338. https://doi.org/10.1111/rego.12063

Griffith-Jones, S., Helleiner, E., & Woods, N. (2010). The financial stability board: An effective fourth pillar of global economic governance? *CIGI Special Report, 2*. http://dspace.cigilibrary.org/jspui/handle/123456789/28801

Grody, A. (2014, August 12). LEI + COU = GLEIS. *Wall Street & Technology*. www.wallstreetandtech.com/security/lei-+-cou – gleis-/a/d-id/1297916

Grossman, G. M., & Helpman, E. (1994). Protection for sale. *American Economic Review, 84*(4), 833–850.

Grossman, G. M., & Helpman, E. (2001). *Special interest politics*. MIT.

Gruin, J., Knaack, P., & Xu, J. (2018). Tailoring for development: China's post-crisis influence in global financial governance. *Global Policy, 9*(4), 467–478.

Guerrera, F., & Pimlott, D. (2010, October 25). Pandit and King clash over Basel III. *Financial Times*. www.ft.com/intl/cms/s/0/1d392ba0-e071-11df-99a3-00144feabdc0.html?siteedition=intl#axzz2QuntezGQ

Haas, P. M. (1989). Do regimes matter? Epistemic communities and Mediterranean pollution control. *International Organization, 43*(03), 377–403.

Habermas, J. (2015). *The lure of technocracy* (1st ed.). Polity Press.

Hafner-Burton, E. M., Victor, D. G., & Lupu, Y. (2012). Political science research on international law: The state of the field. *American Journal of International Law, 106*(1), 47–97.

Haldane, A. (2010). The $100 billion question. *Journal of Regulation and Risk North Asia, 2*, 101–122.

Haldane, A. (2012a). The dog and the frisbee. *Speech presented at the Federal Reserve Bank of Kansas City's Jackson hole economic policy symposium.* www.thebrokenwindow.net/papers/a/ah.pdf

Haldane, A. (2012b). *On being the right size.* www.bankofengland.co.uk/publications/Documents/speeches/2012/speech615.pdf

Haldane, A. (2014, October 29). *Managing global finance as a system.* www.bankofengland.co.uk/publications/Documents/speeches/2014/speech772.pdf

Haldane, A., Ali, R., & Nahai-Williamson, P. (2012). *Towards a common financial language.* www.bankofengland.co.uk/news/2012/march/towards-a-common-financial-language-speech-by-andy-haldane

Hall, P. A. (2006). Systematic process analysis: When and how to use it. *European Management Review, 3*(1), 24–31.

Hall, P. A., & Soskice, D. W. (2001). *Varieties of capitalism: The institutional foundations of comparative advantage.* Oxford University Press.

Hanson, S. G., Kashyap, A. K., & Stein, J. C. (2011). A macroprudential approach to financial regulation. *The Journal of Economic Perspectives*, 3–28.

Hardy, D. (2012). *Bank capitalization as a signal.* http://papers.ssrn.com.libproxy.usc.edu/sol3/papers.cfm?abstract_id=2135991

Harland, D. (2004). Legitimacy and effectiveness in international administration. *Global Governance, 10*(1), 15–19.

Harper, C. (2010, August 8). Crash of 2015 Won't wait for regulators to rein in Wall Street. *Bloomberg Business.* www.bloomberg.com/news/articles/2010-08-09/crash-of-2015-won-t-wait-for-regulators-to-buckle-wall-street-safety-belts

Hawkins, D. G., Lake, D. A., Nielson, D. L., & Tierney, M. J. (2006). Delegation under anarchy: States, international organizations, and principal-agent theory. In D. G. Hawkins, D. A. Lake, D. L. Nielson, & M. J. Tierney (Eds.), *Delegation and agency in international organizations* (1st ed., pp. 3–38). Cambridge University Press.

Hawkins, J., & Turner, P. (2001). International financial reform: Regulatory and other issues. In *International financial contagion* (pp. 431–460). Springer. http://link.springer.com.libproxy.usc.edu/chapter/10.1007/978-1-4757-3314-3_16

Held, D. (1995). *Democracy and the global order.* Cambridge University Press.

Held, D. (1999). The transformation of political community: Rethinking democracy in the context of globalization. In I. Shapiro (Ed.), *Democracy's edges* (pp. 84–111). Cambridge University Press.

Held, D., & Young, K. L. (2009). *Global financial governance: Principles of reform.* http://eprints.lse.ac.uk/43602/1/The%20world%20crisis_%20global%20financial%20governance(lsero).pdf

Helleiner, E. (2010). What role for the new financial stability board? The politics of international standards after the crisis. *Global Policy, 1*(3), 282–290.

Helleiner, E. (2011). Reining in the market: Global governance and the regulation of derivatives. In D. H. Claes & C. H. Knutsen (Eds.), *Governing the global economy: Politics, institutions and economic development* (pp. 131–150). Routledge.

Helleiner, E. (2013). FSB governance. In New Rules for Global Finance (Ed.), *Global financial governance & impact Report* (pp. 12–21). www.new-rules.org/storage/documents/global_financial_governance__impact%20report_2013%20.pdf

Helleiner, E. (2014a). *The status quo crisis: Global financial governance after the 2008 financial meltdown.* Oxford University Press.

Helleiner, E. (2014b). Towards cooperative decentralization? The post-crisis governance of global OTC derivatives. In T. Porter (Ed.), *Transnational financial regulation after the crisis* (p. 132). Routledge.

Helleiner, E. (2014c). Out from the shadows: Governing over-the-counter derivatives after the 2007–2008 financial crisis. In J. Best & A. Gheciu (Eds.), *The return of the public in global governance* (pp. 70–94). Cambridge University Press.

Helleiner, E. (2018). Positioning for stronger limits? The politics of regulating commodity derivatives markets. In E. Helleiner, S. Pagliari, & I. Spagna (Eds.), *Governing the world's biggest market: The politics of derivatives regulation after the 2008 crisis* (pp. 199–225). Oxford University Press.

Helleiner, E., & Pagliari, S. (2011). The end of an era in international financial regulation? A postcrisis research agenda. *International Organization, 65*(01), 169–200.

Helleiner, E., Pagliari, S., & Spagna, I. (Eds.). (2018). *Governing the world's biggest market: The politics of derivatives regulation after the 2008 crisis*. Oxford University Pres.

Hellwig, M. (2010). *Capital regulation after the crisis: Business as usual?* Max Planck Institute for Research on Collective Goods. www.coll.mpg.de/pdf_dat/2010_31online.pdf

Heltman, J. (2015, February 24). Warren sharply criticizes fed staff over Dodd-Frank views. *American Banker*. www.americanbanker.com/news/law-regulation/warren-sharply-criticizes-fed-staff-over-dodd-frank-views-1072900-1.html

Henisz, W. J., & Mansfield, E. D. (2006). Votes and vetoes: The political determinants of commercial openness. *International Studies Quarterly, 50*(1), 189–212.

Héritier, A. (1999). Elements of democratic legitimation in Europe: An alternative perspective. *Journal of European Public Policy, 6*(2), 269–282.

Héritier, A. (2003). Composite democracy in Europe: The role of transparency and access to information. *Journal of European Public Policy, 10*(5), 814–833.

Herring, R. J. (2011). The capital conundrum. *EBR Advisory Board, Rome, March 25th*. www.betterregulation.com/external/Herring%20paper.pdf

Hinckley, B. (1994). *Less than meets the eye: Foreign policy making and the myth of the assertive Congress*. University of Chicago Press.

Hirschman, A. (1945). *National power and the structure of foreign trade*. Univ. of California Press.

HM Treasury. (2012). *Banking reform: Delivering stability and supporting a sustainable economy*. www.gov.uk/government/uploads/system/uploads/attachment_data/file/32556/whitepaper_banking_reform_140512.pdf

Ho, D. E. (2002). Compliance and international soft law: Why do countries implement the Basle accord? *Journal of International Economic Law, 5*(3), 647–688.

Hoenig, T. (2013, April). *Basel III capital: A well-intended illusion*. Remarks by FDIC Vice Chairman Thomas M. Hoenig to the International Association of Deposit Insurers 2013 Research Conference in Basel, Switzerland. www.fdic.gov/news/news/speeches/spapr0913.html

Holmquist, J. (2009). *EU-US cooperation in financial markets regulation in times of crisis*. http://ec.europa.eu/internal_market/speeches/docs/2009/090401-jh-financial-services-roundtable-speech.pdf

Holzinger, K., Knill, C., & Sommerer, T. (2008). Environmental policy convergence: The impact of international harmonization, transnational communication, and regulatory competition. *International Organization, 62*(04), 553–587.

Horsman, M., & Marshall, A. (1994). *After the nation-state: Citizens, tribalism and the new world disorder*. HarperCollins.

Howarth, D., & Quaglia, L. (2013). Banking on stability: The political economy of new capital requirements in the European Union. *Journal of European Integration, 35*(3), 333–346.

Howarth, D., & Quaglia, L. (2016). The 'ebb and flow' of transatlantic regulatory cooperation in banking. *Journal of Banking Regulation, 17*(1–2), 21–33. https://doi.org/10.1057/jbr.2015.21

Huertas, T. (2011, March). Barriers to resolution. *Draft for Discussion, London School of Economics Workshop on Bail-Ins.*

Huertas, T. (2013). The case for bail-ins. *The Bank Recovery and Resolution Directive.* http://fic.wharton.upenn.edu/fic/papers/12/12-17.pdf

Hughes, J. P., & Mester, L. J. (2013). Who said large banks don't experience scale economies? Evidence from a risk-return-driven cost function. *Journal of Financial Intermediation, 22*(4), 559–585.

Huntington, S. P. (1952). The Marasmus of the ICC: The commission, the railroads, and the public interest. *The Yale Law Journal, 61*(4), 467–509.

ICBA. (2012). *Regulatory capital.* www.icba.org/our-positions-a-z/regulatory-capital-basel-iii-and-the-standardized-approach

Igan, D., & Lambert, T. (2019). *Bank lobbying: Regulatory capture and beyond* (IMF Working Paper No. 19/171). IMF. www.imf.org/en/Publications/WP/Issues/2019/08/09/Bank-Lobbying-Regulatory-Capture-and-Beyond-45735

IIF. (2011). *The cumulative impact on the global economy of changes in the financial regulatory framework.* www.iif.com/press/press+203.php

IMF. (2010a). *A fair and substantial contribution by the financial sector: Final report for the G-20.* www.imf.org/external/np/g20/pdf/062710b.pdf

IMF. (2010b). *Resolution of cross-border banks – a proposed framework for enhanced coordination.* IMF. www.imf.org/external/np/pp/eng/2010/061110.pdf

IMF. (2012). *From bail-out to bail-in: Mandatory debt restructuring of systemic financial institutions* [Staff Discussion Note 12/03]. www.imf.org/external/pubs/ft/sdn/2012/sdn1203.pdf

IMF. (2014). *Global financial stability report.* IMF. www.imf.org/external/pubs/ft/gfsr/2014/01/pdf/text.pdf

Independent Commission on Banking. (2011). *Final report.* http://webarchive.nationalarchives.gov.uk/20131003105424/https:/hmt-sanctions.s3.amazonaws.com/ICB%20final%20report/ICB%2520Final%2520Report%5B1%5D.pdf

Institute of International Finance. (2011). *The cumulative impact on the global economy of changes in the financial regulatory framework.* IIF. www.iif.com/download.php?id=oXT67gHVBJk=

International Insurance Capital Standards Accountability Act of 2015 (2015). Testimony of Dean Heller & John Tester. www.congress.gov/bill/114th-congress/senate-bill/1086/text

International Regulator 5. (2014, December 18). *Interview, Basel, 18 Dec 2014* [Personal communication].

International Regulator 6. (2014, December 19). *Interview, Basel, 19 Dec 2014* [Personal communication].

International Regulator 6. (2017, December 18). *Interview, Basel, 18 Dec 2017* [Personal communication].

International Regulator 14. (2017, December 19). *Interview, Basel, 19 Dec 2017* [Personal communication].

International Regulator 17. (2017, December 19). *Interview, Basel, 19 Dec 2017* [Personal communication].

ISDA. (2011a). *ISDA leads industry effort to establish commodity derivatives trade repository.* https://www2.isda.org/attachment/MjkxOQ==/press032511.html

ISDA. (2011b). *ISDA announces commodity derivatives trade repository selection.* https://www2.isda.org/attachment/MzIwNg==/CommodityRepositorySelection.pdf

ISDA. (2015, November 12). *Major banks sign relaunched ISDA resolution stay protocol.* http://www2.isda.org/news/major-banks-sign-relaunched-isda-resolution-stay-protocol

ISDA, GFMA, EBF, AIMA, FOA, IMA, LEBA, & WMBA. (2011, July 5). *Letter to Commissioner Barnier and Secretary Geithner on extra-territoriality.* http://www2.isda.org/

attachment/MzU4Ng==/05-%20JT_associations_letter_re_extra_territoriality_5_july_FINAL_approved.pdf

James, H. (2013). *International cooperation and central banks*. www.cigionline.org/sites/default/files/vol.1.pdf

James, S. C., & Lake, D. A. (1989). The second face of hegemony: Britain's repeal of the Corn Laws and the American Walker Tariff of 1846. *International Organization, 43*(01), 1–29.

Jay, J. (1788). Federalist paper number LXIV. In A. Hamilton, J. Madison, & J. Jay (Eds.), *The federalist papers*. J.P. Lippincott & Co.

Jelveh, Z., Kogut, B., & Naidu, S. (2018). *Political language in economics*. Columbia Business School Research Paper, 14–57.

Jenik, I., & Duff, S. (2021). *Regulatory sandboxes: A practical guide for policy makers*. CGAP. www.cgap.org/research/slide-deck/regulatory-sandboxes-practical-guide-policy-makers

Jennen, B., & Comfort, N. (2015, March 12). Merkel coalition said near bank-structure law delay deal. *Bloomberg.Com*. www.bloomberg.com/news/articles/2015-03-12/merkel-coalition-said-near-bank-structure-law-delay-deal

Johnson, K. N. (2011). Things fall apart: Regulating the credit default swap commons. *University of Colorado Law Review, 82*, 167–258.

Johnson, S., & Kwak, J. (2010). *13 bankers: The Wall Street takeover and the next financial meltdown*. Pantheon Books.

Jones, E. (2014). *Global banking standards and low income countries: Helping or hindering effective regulation?* (Global Economic Governance Programme Working Paper No. 91). Blavatnik School of Government.

Jones, E. (Ed.). (2020). *The political economy of bank regulation in developing countries: Risk and reputation*. Oxford University Press.

Jones, E., & Knaack, P. (2017). *The future of global financial regulation* (No. 127; Global Economic Governance Programme Working Paper). Blavatnik School of Government.

Jones, E., & Knaack, P. (2019). Global financial regulation: Shortcomings and reform options. *Global Policy*. https://doi.org/10.1111/1758-5899.12656

Jones, E., & Zeitz, A. O. (2017). The limits of globalizing basel banking standards. *Journal of Financial Regulation, 3*(1), 89–124.

Jones, E., & Zeitz, A. O. (2019). Regulatory convergence in the financial periphery: How interdependence shapes regulators' decisions. *International Studies Quarterly, 63*(4), 908–922.

Jones, H. (2012, February 5). ET, the new alien scaring global markets. *Reuters*. www.reuters.com/article/2012/02/05/us-financial-regulation-et-idUSTRE8140DV20120205

Jones, H. (2014, February 10). EU rules to light up derivatives markets set for shaky start. *Reuters*. www.reuters.com/article/2014/02/10/europe-derivatives-idUSL5N0LA3XY20140210

Jones, H., & Bruce, A. (2014, March 31). FSB's Carney says to crack too-big-to-fail bank barriers by December. *Reuters*. www.reuters.com/article/2014/03/31/us-g20-fsb-carney-idUSBREA2U1EV20140331

Jopson, B., & Binham, C. (2015, April 28). Republicans attack new global insurance rules. *Financial Times*. www.ft.com/content/b1229cb8-edc6-11e4-90d2-00144feab7de

Jordana, J. (2017). Transgovernmental networks as regulatory intermediaries: Horizontal collaboration and the realities of soft power. *The ANNALS of the American Academy of Political and Social Science, 670*(1), 245–262.

Jordana, J., & Levi-Faur, D. (2005). The diffusion of regulatory capitalism in Latin America: Sectoral and national channels in the making of a new order. *The Annals of the American Academy of Political and Social Science, 598*(1), 102–124.

Jordana, J., Levi-Faur, D., & i Marin, X. F. (2011). The global diffusion of regulatory agencies: Channels of transfer and stages of diffusion. *Comparative Political Studies*, *44*, 1343–1369. https://doi.org/10.1177/0010414011407466

Joyce, J. P. (2014, December 8). The G20 and the (non)pursuit of financial stability. *EconoMonitor*. www.economonitor.com/blog/2014/12/the-g20-and-the-nonpursuit-of-financial-stability/

Judge, D., & Earnshaw, D. (2008). *The European parliament: Leadership and 'followership'*. Oxford University Press.

Juris, J. S. (2008). *Networking futures: The movements against corporate globalization*. Duke University Press. https://books.google.es/books?hl=es&lr=&id=D0E-kpwGeeYC&oi=fnd&pg=PR7&dq=juris+networking+future&ots=QIsmyrTZ4B&sig=b5GffNDv7fvLN4rVszRoYB09-Jc

Kaczmarek, S. C., & Newman, A. L. (2011). The long arm of the law: Extraterritoriality and the national implementation of foreign bribery legislation. *International Organization*, *65*(04), 745–770.

Kahler, M., & Lake, D. A. (2003). Globalization and governance. In M. Kahler & D. A. Lake (Eds.), *Governance in a global economy: Political authority in transition* (pp. 1–32). Princeton University Press.

Kahler, M., & Lake, D. A. (2009). Economic integration and global governance: Why so little supranationalism?". In W. Mattli & N. Woods (Eds.), *The politics of global regulation* (pp. 243–275). Princeton University Press.

Kaldor, M. (2003). *Global civil society: An answer to war* (1st ed.). Polity.

Kapstein, E. (1989). Resolving the regulator's dilemma: International coordination of banking regulations. *International Organization*, *43*(2), 323–347.

Kapstein, E. (1992). Between power and purpose: Central bankers and the politics of regulatory convergence. *International Organization*, *46*(1), 265–287.

Kashyap, A., Stein, J. C., & Hanson, S. G. (2010). *An analysis of the impact of "substantially heightened" capital requirements on large financial institutions*. www.hbs.edu/faculty/Pages/item.aspx?num=41199

Kastner, S. L., & Rector, C. (2003). International regimes, domestic veto-players, and capital controls policy stability. *International Studies Quarterly*, *47*(1), 1–22.

Keane, J. (2003). *Global civil society?* http://onlinelibrary.wiley.com/doi/10.1111/j.1478-9299.2004.004_7.x/full

Kempthorne, D. (2016). China's role in financial standard setting after the 2007–2009 financial crisis: The case of Basel III and shadow banking reform. In D. Lombardi & H. Wang (Eds.), *Enter the dragon: China in the international financial system* (pp. 353–384). CIGI Press.

Kent, A. (2007). *Beyond compliance: China, international organizations, and global security*. Stanford University Press.

Keohane, R. O. (1984). *After Hegemony: Cooperation and discord in the world political economy*. Princeton University Press.

Keohane, R. O. (1997). International relations and international law: Two optics. *Harvard International Law Journal*, *38*, 487.

Keohane, R. O., Macedo, S., & Moravcsik, A. (2009). Democracy-enhancing multilateralism. *International Organization*, *63*(01), 1–31.

Keohane, R. O., & Nye, J. S. (1977). *Power and interdependence: World politics in transition*. Little, Brown.

Keohane, R. O., & Nye, J. S. (2003). Redefining accountability for global governance. In M. Kahler & D. A. Lake (Eds.), *Governance in a global economy: Political authority in transition* (pp. 386–412). Princeton University Press.

Kharas, H., & Lombardi, D. (2012). *The group of twenty: Origins, prospects and challenges for global governance*. Brookings Institutions. www.brookings.edu/research/the-group-of-twenty-origins-prospects-and-challenges-for-global-governance/

Kiff, J., Gullo, A., Hillier, C., & Papapaschalis, P. (2022). Applying the central clearing mandate: Different options for different markets. *IMF Working Papers, 2022*(014), 1. https://doi.org/10.5089/9781616359232.001

Kindleberger, C. P. (1973). *The world in depression: 1929–1939*. University of California Press.

King, M. (2010, January 19). *Speech at the University of Exeter*. www.bankofengland.co.uk/speech/2010/mervyn-king-speech-at-the-university-of-exeter

Kingsbury, B., Krisch, N., & Stewart, R. B. (2005). The emergence of global administrative law. *Law and Contemporary Problems, 68*(3/4), 15–61.

Kirton, J. J. (2013). *G20 governance for a globalized world*. Ashgate Publishing, Ltd.

Kirton, J. J., & Trebilcock, M. J. (2016). *Hard choices, soft law: Voluntary standards in global trade, environment and social governance* (1st ed.). Routledge.

Kissinger, H. A., Schmidt, E., & Huttenlocher, D. (2021). *The age of AI: And our human future* (1st ed.). Little, Brown and Company.

Klijn, E.-H., & Skelcher, C. (2007). Democracy and governance networks: Compatible or not? *Public Administration, 85*(3), 587–608.

Knaack, P. (2015). Innovation and deadlock in global financial governance: Transatlantic coordination failure in OTC derivatives regulation. *Review of International Political Economy, 22*(6), 1217–1248.

Knaack, P. (2017). An unlikely champion of global finance: Why is China exceeding international banking standards? *Journal of Current Chinese Affairs, 46*(2), 41–79.

Knaack, P. (2018). A web without a center: Fragmentation in the OTC derivatives trade reporting system. In E. Helleiner, S. Pagliari, & I. Spagna (Eds.), *Governing the world's biggest market: The politics of derivatives regulation after the 2008 crisis* (pp. 226–256). Oxford University Press.

Knaack, P., & Gruin, J. (2017). *From shadow banking to digital financial inclusion: Regulatory framework contestation between China and the FSB* (GEG Working Paper 2017/134). Blavatnik School of Government.

Knaack, P., & Gruin, J. (2020). From shadow banking to digital financial inclusion: China's rise and the politics of epistemic contestation within the financial stability board. *Review of International Political Economy*. www.tandfonline.com/doi/abs/10.1080/09692290.2020.1772849

Knaack, P., & Katada, S. N. (2013). Fault lines and issue linkages at the G20: New challenges for global economic governance. *Global Policy, 4*(3), 236–246.

Knight, M. (2014). *Reforming the global architecture of financial regulation: The G20, the IMF and the FSB* (No. 42; CIGI Papers). CIGI. http://eprints.lse.ac.uk/61213/1/SP-6%20CIGI.pdf

Koremenos, B. (2008). When, what, and why do states choose to delegate? *Law and Contemporary Problems*, 151–192.

Koremenos, B., Lipson, C., & Snidal, D. (2001). The rational design of international institutions. *International Organization, 55*(04), 761–799.

Krasner, S. D. (1976). State power and the structure of international trade. *World Politics, 28*(3), 317–347.

Krasner, S. D. (2011). Changing state structures: Outside in. *Proceedings of the National Academy of Sciences, 108*(Supplement 4), 21302–21307.

Laffont, J.-J., & Tirole, J. (1991). The politics of government decision-making: A theory of regulatory capture. *The Quarterly Journal of Economics, 106*(4), 1089–1127.

Lall, R. (2012). From failure to failure: The politics of international banking regulation. *Review of International Political Economy, 19*, 609–638.

Lall, R. (2014). Timing as a source of regulatory influence: A technical elite network analysis of global finance. *Regulation & Governance*, n/a-n/a. https://doi.org/10.1111/rego.12050

Lall, R. (2015). Timing as a source of regulatory influence: A technical elite network analysis of global finance. *Regulation & Governance, 9*(2), 125–143.

Landolt, P., & Goldring, L. (2010). Political cultures and transnational social fields: Chileans, Colombians and Canadian activists in Toronto. *Global Networks, 10*(4), 443–466.

Lavelle, K. C. (2011). *Legislating international organization: The US Congress, the IMF, and the World Bank*. Oxford University Press.

Lazer, D. (2005). Regulatory capitalism as a networked order: The international system as an informational network. *The Annals of the American Academy of Political and Social Science, 598*(1), 52–66.

Levi-Faur, D. (2005). The global diffusion of regulatory capitalism. *The Annals of the American Academy of Political and Social Science, 598*(1), 12–32.

Li, Y.-W. V. (2018). Power plays from the fringe: East Asian responses to derivatives regulatory reform. In E. Helleiner, S. Pagliari, & I. Spagna (Eds.), *Governing the world's biggest market: The politics of derivatives regulation after the 2008 crisis* (pp. 107–136). Oxford University Press.

Liikanen, E. (2012). *High-level Expert Group on reforming the structure of the EU banking sector.* http://indice.astrid-online.it/rassegna/Rassegna-213/08-10-2012/EU-Banking-sector_High-level-group_Liikanen-Report_02_10_12.pdf

Lima de Carvalho, T. (2011). A Regulação do Mercado Financeiro e a Necessária Intervenção Estatal na Autonomia Privada. *Revista Da Procuradoria-Geral Do Banco Central, 5*(2), 77–108.

Lindsay, J. M. (1994). Congress, foreign policy, and the new institutionalism. *International Studies Quarterly, 38*(2), 281–304. https://doi.org/10.2307/2600978

Lipson, C. (1984). International cooperation in economic and security affairs. *World Politics, 37*(1), 1–23. https://doi.org/10.2307/2010304

Lockwood, E. (2015). Predicting the unpredictable: Value-at-risk, performativity, and the politics of financial uncertainty. *Review of International Political Economy, 22*(4), 719–756.

Lockwood, E. (2018). The politics and practices of central clearing in OTC derivatives markets. In E. Helleiner, S. Pagliari, & I. Spagna (Eds.), *Governing the world's biggest market: The politics of derivatives regulation after the 2008 crisis* (pp. 168–198). Oxford University Press.

Mahoney, J., & Thelen, K. (2010). A theory of gradual institutional change. In J. Mahoney & K. Thelen (Eds.), *Explaining institutional change: Ambiguity, agency, and power* (pp. 1–37). Cambridge University Press.

Majone, G. (1997). From the positive to the regulatory state: Causes and consequences of changes in the mode of governance. *Journal of Public Policy, 17*(02), 139–167.

Major, A. (2012). Neoliberalism and the new international financial architecture. *Review of International Political Economy, 19*(4), 536–561.

Malaysia Regulator 2. (2018, March 26). *Interview, Kuala Lumpur, 26 March 2018* [Personal communication].

Mansfield, E. D., Milner, H. V., & Pevehouse, J. C. (2007). Vetoing co-operation: The impact of veto players on preferential trading arrangements. *British Journal of Political Science, 37*(03), 403–432.

Marchetti, R. (2009). Mapping alternative models of global politics. *International Studies Review, 11*(1), 133–156.

Martin, L. (2006). Distribution, information, and delegation to international organizations: The case of IMF conditionality. In D. G. Hawkins, D. A. Lake, D. L. Nielson, & M. J. Tierney (Eds.), *Delegation and agency in international organizations* (1st ed., pp. 140–164). Cambridge University Press.

Martin, L. L. (2000). *Democratic commitments: Legislatures and international cooperation*. Princeton University Press. https://books.google.co.uk/books?hl=es&lr=&id=DEY9iCo6_3IC&oi=fnd&pg=PP2&dq=lisa+martin+democratic+commitments&ots=mbuzl6DLEu&sig=FbsDhxstJ90xTEUPvYhkP_PY7TI

Masters, B., & Braithwaite, T. (2011, October 2). Tighter rules on capital: Bankers versus Basel. *Financial Times*. www.ft.com/cms/s/0/852fe7a4-eb4b-11e0-9a41-00144feab49a.html#axzz3LPFll5eR

Matthew, R. A., & Zacher, M. W. (1995). Liberal international theory: Common threads, divergent strands. In C. Kegley (Ed.), *Controversies in international relations theory: Realism and the neoliberal challenge* (pp. 107–150). St. Martin's.

Mattingly, C. H. B. (2012, February 14). Volcker rule faces critics as effective date nears. *Bloomberg.Com*. www.bloomberg.com/news/articles/2012-02-14/u-s-volcker-rule-faces-harsh-global-critics-months-before-it-takes-effect

Mattli, W., & Woods, N. (2009). In whose benefit? Explaining regulatory change in global politics. In W. Mattli & N. Woods (Eds.), *The politics of global regulation* (pp. 1–43). Princeton University Press.

McAndrews, J., Morgan, D. P., Santos, J. A., & Yorulmazer, T. (2014). What makes large bank failures so messy and what to do about it? *Economic Policy Review, Forthcoming*. http://papers.ssrn.com.libproxy.usc.edu/sol3/papers.cfm?abstract_id=2422440

McCubbins, M. D., Noll, R. G., & Weingast, B. R. (1987). Administrative procedures as instruments of political control. *Journal of Law, Economics, & Organization*, *3*(2), 243–277.

McCulley, P. A. (2007, September). Teton reflections. *Pacific Investment Management Company LLC*. www.pimco.com:443/insights/economic-and-market-commentary/global-central-bank-focus/teton-reflections

McHenry, P. (2017, January 31). *Letter to Janet Yellen on participation in international forums*. https://fortunedotcom.files.wordpress.com/2017/02/mchenry.pdf

McKeen-Edwards, H., & Porter, T. (2013). *Transnational financial associations and the governance of global finance: Assembling wealth and power*. Routledge.

Menkin, C. (2014). *Five banks hold more than 44% of US industry's assets*. http://seekingalpha.com/instablog/388783-christopher-menkin/3527595-five-banks-hold-more-than-44-percent-of-us-industrys-assets

Merton, R. K. (1966). Dilemmas of democracy in the voluntary association. *AJN The American Journal of Nursing*, *66*(5), 1055–1061.

Meseguer, C. (2005). Policy learning, policy diffusion, and the making of a new order. *The Annals of the American Academy of Political and Social Science*, *598*(1), 67–82.

Meseguer, C., & Gilardi, F. (2009). What is new in the study of policy diffusion? *Review of International Political Economy*, *16*(3), 527–543.

Milner, H. V. (1992). International theories of cooperation among nations. *World Politics*, *44*(3), 466–496.

Milner, H. V. (1997). *Interests, institutions, and information: Domestic politics and international relations*. Princeton University Press.

Milner, H. V., & Rosendorff, B. P. (1997). Democratic politics and international trade negotiations: Elections and divided government as constraints on trade liberalization. *Journal of Conflict Resolution*, *41*(1), 117–146.

Mitrany, D. (1944). *A working peace system: An argument for the functional development of international organization*. Oxford University Press.

Mittelman, J. H. (2000). *The globalization syndrome: Transformation and resistance*. Princeton University Press. https://books.google.es/books?hl=es&lr=&id=f4oRx8vKYlAC&oi=fnd&pg=PP2&dq=Mittelman+globalization+syndrome&ots=nSo9vUqNdp&sig=DnQPMxZSXARF42_Z-Fw7fffuFzQ

Modigliani, F., & Miller, M. H. (1958). The cost of capital, corporation finance and the theory of investment. *The American Economic Review*, *48*(3), 261–297.

Moschella, M., & Tsingou, E. (2013). The financial crisis and the politics of reform: Explaining incremental change. In M. Moschella & E. Tsingou (Eds.), *Great expectations, slow transformations: Incremental change in in post-crisis regulation* (pp. 1–33). ECPR Press.

Mosley, L. (2009). Private governance for the public good? Exploring private sector participation in global financial regulation. In H. V. Milner & A. Moravcsik (Eds.), *Power, interdependence, and nonstate actors in world politics* (pp. 126–146). Princeton University Press.

Mügge, D. (2014). Europe's regulatory role in post-crisis global finance. *Journal of European Public Policy*, *21*(3), 316–326.

Mügge, D., & Stellinga, B. (2015). The unstable core of global finance: Contingent valuation and governance of international accounting standards. *Regulation & Governance*, *9*(1), 47–62.

Mukherjee, B., Yadav, V., & Béjar, S. (2013). Electoral particularism, bank concentration, and capital account liberalization in developing democracies. *Comparative Political Studies*, 0010414013488551.

Murphy, C. (1994). *International organization and industrial change: Global governance since 1850. Europe and the international order*. Oxford University Press.

Myers, S. C., & Majluf, N. S. (1984). Corporate financing and investment decisions when firms have information that investors do not have. *Journal of Financial Economics*, *13*(2), 187–221.

Myerson, R. (2013). *Rethinking the principles of bank regulation: A review of Admati and Hellwig's Bankers' new clothes*. http://home.uchicago.edu/~rmyerson/research/newcloth.pdf

Naím, M. (2009, June 22). Minilateralism. *Foreign Policy*. www.foreignpolicy.com/articles/2009/06/18/minilateralism?wp_login_redirect=0

Nathan, J. A., & Oliver, J. K. (1994). *Foreign policy making and the American political system*. Johns Hopkins University Press.

Naughton, B. (2017). The regulatory storm: A surprising turn in financial policy. *China Leadership Monitor*, *53*. www.hoover.org/sites/default/files/research/docs/clm53bn.pdf

Navaretti, G. B., & Venables, A. J. (2006). *Multinational firms in the world economy*. Princeton University Press.

Newman, A. L. (2008). Building transnational civil liberties: Transgovernmental entrepreneurs and the European data privacy directive. *International Organization*, *62*(1), 103–130. https://doi.org/10.1017/S0020818308080041

Newman, A. L., & Bach, D. (2014). The European Union as hardening agent: Soft law and the diffusion of global financial regulation. *Journal of European Public Policy*, *21*(3), 430–452.

Newman, A. L., & Posner, E. (2011). International interdependence and regulatory power: Authority, mobility, and markets. *European Journal of International Relations*, *17*(4), 589–610.

Newman, A. L., & Posner, E. (2015). Putting the EU in its place: Policy strategies and the global regulatory context. *Journal of European Public Policy*, *22*(9), 1316–1335.

Newman, A. L., & Posner, E. (2016). Transnational feedback, soft law, and preferences in global financial regulation. *Review of International Political Economy*, *23*(1), 123–152.

Newman, A. L., & Posner, E. (2018). *Voluntary disruptions: International soft law, finance, and power.* Oxford University Press.

Newman, A. L., & Zaring, D. T. (2013). *Regulatory networks: Power, legitimacy, and compliance.*

New Rules for Global Finance. (2013). *Global financial governance & impact report.* www.new-rules.org/storage/documents/global_financial_governance__impact%20report_2013%20.pdf

New Rules for Global Finance. (2014). *Global financial governance & impact report.* www.new-rules.org/storage/global_financial_governance_and_impact_report_2014.pdf

Nye, J. S., & Keohane, R. O. (1971). Transnational relations and world politics: An introduction. *International Organization, 25*(03), 329–349.

Oatley, T. (2011). The reductionist gamble: Open economy politics in the global economy. *International Organization, 65*(02), 311–341.

Oatley, T., & Nabors, R. (1998). Redistributive cooperation: Market failure, wealth transfers, and the Basle Accord. *International Organization, 52*(01), 35–54.

Oatley, T., & Winecoff, W. K. (2012). The domestic rooting of financial regulation in an era of global capital markets. In *Research handbook on hedge funds, private equity and alternative investments.* Edward Elgar Publishing.

Ocampo, J. A. (2014). *Reforming the international monetary and financial architecture.* Friedrich Ebert Stiftung. http://library.fes.de/pdf-files/iez/global/10900.pdf

Odell, J. (2011). Negotiation and bargaining. *Handbook of International Relations, 2.*

ODRG. (2013). *Report on agreed understandings to resolving cross-border conflicts, inconsistencies, gaps and duplicative requirements.* www.cftc.gov/ucm/groups/public/@newsroom/documents/file/odrgreport.pdf

ODRG. (2014, August 12). *Barriers to reporting to trade repositories.* www.esma.europa.eu/system/files/letter_to_fsb_08122014.pdf

OFR. (2010). *Statement on legal entity identification for financial contracts.* www.treasury.gov/initiatives/Documents/OFR-LEI_Policy_Statement-FINAL.PDF

Oliveira Santos, A., & Elliott, D. (2012). *Estimating the costs of financial regulation.* IMF Staff Discussion Notes SDN/12/11. www.imf.org/external/pubs/ft/sdn/2012/sdn1211.pdf

Olson, M. (1968). *The logic of collective action: Public goods and the theory of groups.* Harvard University Press.

Ōmae, K. (1995). *The end of the nation state: The rise of regional economies.* Simon and Schuster. https://books.google.es/books?hl=es&lr=&id=nJMxSo05yuwC&oi=fnd&pg=PR7&dq=ohmae+nation+state&ots=DgCu5KtNG4&sig=9XRXT4TTWkc16d5zymYaD0P6Lpk

Onaran, Y. (2012, February 23). Bank Lobby widened Volcker rule, inciting foreign outrage. *Bloomberg.* www.bloomberg.com/news/2012-02-23/banks-lobbied-to-widen-volcker-rule-before-inciting-foreigners-against-law.html

Ötker-Robe, I. (2014). *Global risks and collective action failures: What can the international community do?* IMF Working Paper 14/195. www.imf.org/external/pubs/ft/wp/2014/wp14195.pdf

Ötker-Robe, I., Narain, A., Ilyina, A., & Surti, J. (2011). *The too-important-to-fail conundrum: Impossible to ignore and difficult to resolve.* IMF Staff Discussion Note 11/12. www.imf.org/external/pubs/ft/sdn/2011/sdn1112.pdf

Ötker-Robe, I., Pazarbasioglu, C., di Perrero, A. B., Iorgova, S., Kışınbay, T., Le Leslé, V., Melo, F., Podpiera, J., Sacasa, N., & Santos, A. (2010). *Impact of regulatory reforms on large and complex financial institutions.* www.imf.org/external/pubs/ft/spn/2010/spn1016.pdf

Pagliari, S. (2013a). A wall around Europe? The European regulatory response to the global financial crisis and the turn in transatlantic relations. *Journal of European Integration*, *35*(4), 391–408.

Pagliari, S. (2013b). Governing financial stability: The financial stability board as the emerging pillar in global economic governance. In M. Moschella & K. Weaver (Eds.), *Handbook of global economic governance*. Routledge.

Pagliari, S. (2018). The second half: Interest group conflicts and coalitions in the implementation of the Dodd-Frank act derivatives rules. In E. Helleiner, S. Pagliari, & I. Spagna (Eds.), *Governing the world's biggest market: The politics of derivatives regulation after the 2008 crisis* (pp. 137–167). Oxford University Press.

Pagliari, S., & Wilf, M. (2018). How novel are post-crisis international financial reforms? A text-based approach. *Forthcoming*.

Pagliari, S., & Young, K. L. (2014). Leveraged interests: Financial industry power and the role of private sector coalitions. *Review of International Political Economy*, *21*(3), 575–610.

Passmore, W., & von Hafften, A. H. (2017). Are Basel's capital surcharges for global systemically important banks too small? *FEDS Notes*, *2017*(1859). https://doi.org/10.17016/2380-7172.1859

Pastor, R. A. (1982). *Congress and the politics of US foreign economic policy, 1929–1976* (Vol. 5). University of California Press.

Pauly, L. W. (2008). Financial crisis management in Europe and beyond. *Contributions to Political Economy*, *27*(1), 73–89.

Pauly, L. W. (2009). The old and the new politics of international financial stability. *JCMS: Journal of Common Market Studies*, *47*(5), 955–975.

Pauly, L. W. (2010). The financial stability board in context. In S. Griffith-Jones, E. Helleiner, & N. Woods (Eds.), *The financial stability board: An effective fourth pillar of global economic governance?* (pp. 13–18). Centre for International Governance Innovation.

PBOC. (2013). *China financial stability report 2013*. People's Bank of China.

Peltzman, S. (1976). Toward a more general theory of regulation. *Journal of Law and Economics*, *19*(2), 211–240.

Persaud, A. (2010). The locus of financial regulation: Home versus host. *International Affairs*, *86*(3), 637–646.

Peterson, P. E. (1994). The president's dominance in foreign policy making. *Political Science Quarterly*, *109*(2), 215–234.

Pierson, P. (1993). When effect becomes cause: Policy feedback and political change. *World Politics*, *45*(04), 595–628.

Pigou, A. C. (1920). *The economics of welfare* (4th ed.). Macmillan and Co.

Piketty, T. (2014). *Capital in the 21st century*. Harvard College.

Polanyi, K. (1944). *The great transformation: Economic and political origins of our time*. Rinehart.

Porter, T. (2010). Risk models and transnational governance in the global financial crisis: The cases of Basel II and credit rating agencies. In E. Helleiner, S. Pagliari, & H. Zimmermann (Eds.), *Global finance in crisis: The politics of international regulatory change* (pp. 56–73). Routledge.

Posner, E. (2009). Making rules for global finance: Transatlantic regulatory cooperation at the turn of the millennium. *International Organization*, *63*(04), 665–699.

Posner, E. (2015). International financial regulatory cooperation: An experimentalist turn? In J. Zeitlin (Ed.), *Extending experimentalist governance?: The European Union and transnational regulation* (pp. 196–226). OUP Oxford.

Posner, E. (2018). Financial regulatory cooperation: Coordination of derivatives markets. In E. Helleiner, S. Pagliari, & I. Spagna (Eds.), *Governing the world's biggest market: The politics of derivatives regulation after the 2008 crisis* (pp. 54–81). Oxford University Press.

Posner, E., & Véron, N. (2010). The EU and financial regulation: Power without purpose? *Journal of European Public Policy*, *17*(3), 400–415.

Protard, M. (2010, January 29). French banks lobby politicians over Basel concerns. *Reuters*. www.reuters.com/article/2010/01/29/france-banks-credit-idUSLDE60R2N520100129

Public Citizen. (2012). *Forgotten lessons of deregulation: Rolling back Dodd-Frank's derivatives rules would repeat a mistake that led to the financial crisis*. www.citizen.org/documents/forgotten-lessons-of-deregulation-derivatives-report.pdf

Putnam, R. D. (1988). Diplomacy and domestic politics: The logic of two-level games. *International Organization*, *42*(03), 427–460.

Puzzanghera, J. (2009, September 8). CFTC's farm roots complicate reform efforts. *Los Angeles Times*. http://articles.latimes.com/2009/sep/08/business/fi-financial-reform8

Quaglia, L. (2012). The 'old' and 'new' politics of financial services regulation in the European Union. *New Political Economy*, *17*(4), 515–535.

Quaglia, L. (2014a). The sources of European Union influence in international financial regulatory fora. *Journal of European Public Policy*, *21*(3), 327–345.

Quaglia, L. (2014b). *The European Union and global financial regulation*. Oxford University Press.

Quaglia, L. (2017). The political economy of post-crisis international standards for resolving financial institutions. *New Political Economy*, *22*(5), 595–609.

Quaglia, L. (2019). The politics of state compliance with international "soft law" in finance. *Governance*, *32*(1), 45–62.

Quaglia, L. (2021). *The politics of regime complexity in international derivatives regulation*. Oxford University Press.

Quaglia, L., & Spendzharova, A. (2017). Post-crisis reforms in banking: Regulators at the interface between domestic and international governance. *Regulation & Governance*, *11*(4), 422–437.

Quaglia, L., & Spendzharova, A. (2021a). Regime complexity and managing financial data streams: The orchestration of trade reporting for derivatives. *Regulation & Governance*. https://doi.org/10.1111/rego.12377

Quaglia, L., & Spendzharova, A. (2021b). Disentangling derivatives: International policy reforms concerning central counterparties. *Journal of Economic Policy Reform*, *0*(0), 1–17. https://doi.org/10.1080/17487870.2021.1942874

Rajan, R. G. (2006). Has finance made the world riskier? *European Financial Management*, *12*(4), 499–533.

Raustiala, K. (2002). The architecture of international cooperation: Transgovernmental networks and the future of international law. *Virginia Journal of International Law*, *43*(1), 1–92.

Raustiala, K. (2005). Form and substance in international agreements. *American Journal of International Law*, *99*, 581–614.

Reddy, Y. V. (2012). Financial crisis and financial intermediation: Asking different questions. In O. J. Blanchard, D. Romer, M. Spence, & J. Stiglitz (Eds.), *In the wake of the crisis* (pp. 83–89). MIT Press.

Regulation (EU) No 648/2012 of the European Parliament and of the Council on OTC derivatives, central counterparties and trade repositories, no. 648/2012 (2012). http://eur-lex.europa.eu/legal-content/EN/TXT/PDF/?uri=CELEX:32012R0648&from=EN

Regulation (EU) 2019/834 of the European Parliament and of the Council of 20 May 2019 amending Regulation (EU) No 648/2012, 32019R0834, EP, CONSIL, OJ L (2019). http://data.europa.eu/eli/reg/2019/834/oj/eng

Regulations from the Executive in Need of Scrutiny Act of 2017. (2017). Testimony of Doug Collins. www.congress.gov/bill/115th-congress/house-bill/26

Regulatory Accountability Act of 2017. (2017). Testimony of Bob Goodlatte. www.congress.gov/bill/115th-congress/house-bill/5

Reinhart, C. M., & Rogoff, K. (2009). *This time is different: Eight centuries of financial folly.* Princeton University Press.

Reisenbichler, A. (2015). The domestic sources and power dynamics of regulatory networks: Evidence from the financial stability forum. *Review of International Political Economy, 22*(5), 996–1024.

Restuccia, A. (2015, December 12). The one word that almost sank the climate talks. *Politico.* http://politi.co/1NWeZ3w

Rickards, J. (2016). *Road to ruin.* Penguin Books.

Riles, A. (2011). *Collateral knowledge: Legal reasoning in the global financial markets.* University of Chicago Press.

Rixen, T. (2013). Why reregulation after the crisis is feeble: Shadow banking, offshore financial centers, and jurisdictional competition. *Regulation & Governance,* 7(4), 435–459.

Rochet, J.-C. (2010). The future of banking regulation. In M. Dewatripont, J.-C. Rochet, & J. Tirole (Eds.), *Balancing the banks: Global lessons from the financial crisis* (pp. 78–106). Princeton University Press.

Rodrik, D. (2009, March 12). A Plan B for global finance. *The Economist.* www.economist.com/node/13278147

Roemer-Mahler, A. (2013). Business conflict and global politics: The pharmaceutical industry and the global protection of intellectual property rights. *Review of International Political Economy, 20*(1), 121–152.

Roig-Franzia, M. (2009, May 26). Brooksley Born, the Cassandra of the derivatives crisis. *The Washington Post.* www.washingtonpost.com/wp-dyn/content/article/2009/05/25/AR2009052502108.html

Rojas-Suarez, L., & Muhammad, D. (2018, May). Basel III & unintended consequences for emerging markets and developing economies – part 2: Effects on trade finance. *Center For Global Development.* www.cgdev.org/blog/basel-iii-unintended-consequences-emerging-markets-and-developing-economies-part-2-effects

Romer, D. (2012). Process, responsibility, and Myron's law. In O. J. Blanchard, D. Romer, M. Spence, & J. E. Stiglitz (Eds.), *In the wake of the crisis: Leading economists reassess economic policy* (pp. 111–126). MIT Press.

Rosamond, B. (2000). *Theories of European integration.* St. Martin's Press.

Rosenau, J. (2005). Globalization and governance: Bleak prospects for sustainability. In A. Pfaller & M. Lerch (Eds.), *Challenges of globalization: New trends in international politics and society* (pp. 201–216). Transaction Publishers.

Rothfus, K. (2017, January 17). Yellen exchange on SIFI designations yields more questions than answers [Text]. *The Hill.* http://thehill.com/blogs/congress-blog/economy-budget/314583-yellen-exchange-on-sifi-designations-yields-more-questions

Rubin, G. T. (2018, January 22). Trump team keeps approach to global financial rules, for now. *Dow Jones Newswires.* www.foxbusiness.com/features/2018/01/22/trump-team-keeps-approach-to-global-financial-rules-for-now.html

Ruggie, J. G. (1982). International regimes, transactions, and change: Embedded liberalism in the postwar economic order. *International Organization, 36*(02), 379–415.

S.68–117th Congress (2021–2022): Regulations from the executive in need of scrutiny act of 2021. (2021). Testimony of Paul Rand. www.congress.gov/bill/117th-congress/senate-bill/68/text

Sabel, C. F., & Zeitlin, J. (2008). Learning from difference: The new architecture of experimentalist governance in the EU. *European Law Journal, 14*(3), 271–327.

Sands, P., & Klein, P. (2001). *Bowett's law of international institutions.* Sweet & Maxwell.

Santos, J. A. (2014). Evidence from the bond market on banks 'too-big-to-fail' subsidy. *Economic Policy Review, 20*(2), 1–11.

Schachter, O. (1998). The decline of the nation-state and its implications for international law. *Columbia Journal of Transnational Law, 36*, 7.

Schelling, T. C. (1980). *The strategy of conflict.* Harvard University Press.

Schneider, H. (2010a, September 13). Regulators meeting in Switzerland agree on new global rules to strengthen banks. *The Washington Post.* www.washingtonpost.com/wp-dyn/content/article/2010/09/12/AR2010091201864.html

Schneider, H. (2010b, September 14). Industry warms to proposed global banking rules. *The Washington Post.* www.washingtonpost.com/wp-dyn/content/article/2010/09/13/AR2010091306437.html

Schoenmaker, D. (2011). The financial trilemma. *Economics Letters, 111*(1), 57–59.

Schwartz, O. (2019, November 25). In 2016, Microsoft's racist chatbot revealed the dangers of online conversation. *IEEE Spectrum.* https://spectrum.ieee.org/in-2016-microsofts-racist-chatbot-revealed-the-dangers-of-online-conversation

Seabrooke, L. (2006). The bank for international settlements. *New Political Economy, 11*(1), 141–149.

Seabrooke, L. (2014). Epistemic arbitrage: Transnational professional knowledge in action. *Journal of Professions and Organization, 1*(1), 49–64.

Seabrooke, L., & Henriksen, L. F. (2017). Issue control in transnational professional and organizational networks. *Professional Networks in Transnational Governance*, 3–24.

Sell, S. K. (2010). The rise and rule of a trade-based strategy: Historical institutionalism and the international regulation of intellectual property. *Review of International Political Economy, 17*(4), 762–790.

Sell, S. K., & Prakash, A. (2004). Using ideas strategically: The contest between business and NGO networks in intellectual property rights. *International Studies Quarterly, 48*(1), 143–175.

Shaw, M. N. (2008). *International law.* Cambridge University Press.

Shearman & Sterling LLP. (2016). *Implications for Non-EU banking groups of the EU's new intermediate holding company proposals.* www.shearman.com/en/newsinsights/publications/2016/12/implications-non-eu-banking-groups-of-new-proposal

Sheets, N. (2017). *Race to the top: The case for the financial stability board.* Peterson Institute for International Economics. https://piie.com/system/files/documents/pb17-12.pdf

Sheng, A., & Soon, N. C. (2016). *Shadow banking in China: An opportunity for financial reform.* John Wiley & Sons.

Shipkevich, F. (2011, October 25). ECB fights CFTC on Dodd-Frank extra-territorial overreach. *CFTC LAW | Forex, Futures and Derivatives Regulatory News.* www.cftclaw.com/2011/10/ecb-fights-cftc-doddfrank-extraterritorial-overreach/

Siegert, C., & Willison, M. (2015). *Estimating the extent of the 'too big to fail' problem – A review of existing approaches* (Financial Stability Paper No. 32). Bank of England. www.bankofengland.co.uk/financialstability/Documents/fpc/fspapers/fs_paper32.pdf

SIFMA, ISDA, & IIB. (2013). *SIFMA, ISDA and IIB file lawsuit challenging commodity futures trading commission's cross-border rule.* www.sifma.org/newsroom/2013/sifma,-isda-

and-iib-file-lawsuit-challenging-commodity-futures-trading-commission_s-cross-border-rule/

Simmons, B. A. (2001a). The international politics of harmonization: The case of capital market regulation. *International Organization, 55*(03), 589–620.

Simmons, B. A. (2001b). The international politics of harmonization: The case of capital market regulation. *International Organization, 55*(3), 589–620.

Simmons, B. A., Dobbin, F., & Garrett, G. (2008). *The global diffusion of markets and democracy.* Cambridge University Press. https://books.google.es/books?hl=es&lr=&id=FCMc7f-RuPEC&oi=fnd&pg=PR1&dq=simmons+2008+policy+diffusin&ots=uhzMdVLNo6&sig=qs21mXjvhmLXH_TRT8Oe9jroglY

Singer, A. D. (2010). Uncertain leadership: The US regulatory response to the global financial crisis. In E. Helleiner, S. Pagliari, & H. Zimmermann (Eds.), *Global finance in crisis: The politics of international regulatory change.* (pp. 93–120). Routledge.

Singer, D. A. (2004). Capital rules: The domestic politics of international regulatory harmonization. *International Organization, 58*(3), 531–565.

Singer, D. A. (2007). *Regulating capital: Setting standards for the international financial system.* Cornell University Press.

Six, F., & Verhoest, K. (Eds.). (2017). *Trust in regulatory regimes.* Edward Elgar Publishing.

Skidmore, D. (1995). The business of international politics. *Mershon International Studies Review, 39*(2), 246–254. https://doi.org/10.2307/222753

Slater, S. (2014, June 4). Bank regulation issues seen settled in 6 months -UK finance minister. *Reuters.* www.reuters.com/article/2014/06/04/banking-iif-regulations-idUSL6N0OL4XT20140604

Slaughter, A.-M. (2004). *A new world order.* Princeton University Press.

Sorkin, A. R. (2010, November 28). Looking back on too big to fail. *Foreign Policy.* http://foreignpolicy.com/2010/11/28/looking-back-on-too-big-to-fail/

Spagna, I. (2018). Becoming the world's biggest market: OTC derivatives before the global financial crisis of 2008. In E. Helleiner, S. Pagliari, & I. Spagna (Eds.), *Governing the world's biggest market: The politics of derivatives regulation after the 2008 crisis* (pp. 27–53). Oxford University Press.

Standish, M. (2012). *"Examining the impact of the Volcker rule on markets, businesses, investors and job creation" – Testimony before the U.S. House of Representatives Subcommittee on Financial Institutions and Consumer Credit.* http://c.ymcdn.com/sites/www.iib.org/resource/resmgr/imported/IIB%20Mark%20Standish%20Testimony%20HFSC%20011812.pdf

Stanton, T. H. (2012). *Why some firms thrive while others fail: Governance and management lessons from the crisis.* Oxford University Press, USA.

Stephenson, E., & Lynch, S. N. (2013, May 21). U.S. Treasury's Lew says foreign officials too critical on swaps rules. *Reuters.* www.reuters.com/article/2013/05/21/treasury-lew-swaps-idUSL2N0E21I720130521

Stewart, R. B. (2014). Remedying disregard in global regulatory governance: Accountability, participation, and responsiveness. *American Journal of International Law, 108*(2), 211–270.

Stigler, G. J. (1971). The theory of economic regulation. *The Bell Journal of Economics and Management Science, 2*(1), 3–21.

Stiglitz, J. E. (2010). *The Stiglitz report: Reforming the international monetary and financial systems in the wake of the global crisis.* The New Press.

Strange, S. (1996). *The retreat of the state: The diffusion of power in the world economy.* Cambridge University Press.

Tarullo, D. K. (2008). *Banking on Basel: The future of international financial regulation.* Peterson Institute.

The Banker. (2017). *Top 1000 world banks 2017*. www.thebanker.com/Top-1000

Thiemann, M. (2014). In the shadow of Basel: How competitive politics bred the crisis. *Review of International Political Economy*, *21*, 1203–1239. https://doi.org/10.1080/09692290.2013.860612

Thompson, L. (2015, January 27). Commit to removing legal barriers to data-sharing. *Financial Times*. www.ft.com/intl/cms/s/0/1044772a-a58d-11e4-8636-00144feab7de.html#axzz3PyyUbeMk

Thomson Reuters Accelus. (2013). *The state of regulatory reform 2014*. http://accelus.thomsonreuters.com/sites/default/files/GRC00751-web.pdf

Tirole, J. (2010). Lessons from the crisis. In M. Dewatripont, J.-C. Rochet, & J. Tirole (Eds.), *Balancing the banks: Global lessons from the financial crisis*. Princeton University Press.

Titman, S. (2002). The Modigliani and Miller theorem and the integration of financial markets. *Financial Management*, *31*(1), 101–115.

Tobin, J. (1999). A comment on Dahl's skepticism. In I. Shapiro (Ed.), *Democracy's edges* (pp. 37–40). Cambridge University Press.

Tomz, M. (2012). *Reputation and international cooperation: Sovereign debt across three centuries*. Princeton University Press.

Tracy, R. (2014, June 10). Fed's long-term debt rule may slip to 2015. *WSJ Blogs – MoneyBeat*. http://blogs.wsj.com/moneybeat/2014/06/10/feds-long-term-debt-rule-may-slip-to-2015/

Tsebelis, G. (2002). *Veto players: How political institutions work*. Princeton University Press.

Tsingou, E. (2010). Regulatory reactions to the global credit crisis: Analyzing a policy community under stress. In E. Helleiner, S. Pagliari, & H. Zimmermann (Eds.), *Global finance in crisis. The politics of international regulatory change*. (pp. 21–36). Routledge.

Tsingou, E. (2015). Transnational veto players and the practice of financial reform. *The British Journal of Politics & International Relations*, *17*(2), 318–334.

Tucker, P. (2013, May 20). *Resolution and future of finance*. INSOL International World Congress. www.bankofengland.co.uk/publications/Documents/speeches/2013/speech658.pdf

Tucker, P. (2014). *Regulatory reform, stability, and central banking*. www.brookings.edu/~/media/research/files/papers/2014/01/16%20regulatory%20reform%20stability%20central%20banking%20tucker/16%20regulatory%20reform%20stability%20central%20banking%20tucker.pdf

Tucker, P. M. W. (2018). *Unelected power: The quest for legitimacy in central banking and the regulatory state*. Princeton University Press.

Turner, A. (2012). Optimal financial intermediation: Why more isn't always better. In O. J. Blanchard, D. Romer, M. Spence, & J. Stiglitz (Eds.), *In the wake of the crisis* (pp. 101–110). MIT Press.

UK Regulator 1. (2014). *Interview, London, 12 Dec 2014* [Personal communication].

UK Regulator 3. (2017). *Interview, London, 2 Aug 2017* [Personal communication].

UK Regulator 5. (2017, November 7). *Interview, London, 7 Nov 2017* [Personal communication].

Underhill, G. R., & Zhang, X. (2008). Setting the rules: Private power, political underpinnings, and legitimacy in global monetary and financial governance. *International Affairs*, *84*(3), 535–554.

US banks must boost capital under leverage rule. (2014, April 9). *The Economist*. www.eiu.com/industry/article/291712413/us-banks-must-boost-capital-under-leverage-rule/2014-04-09

US Civil Society Representative 2. (2012, July 26). *Interview, Washington DC, 26 Jul 2012* [Personal communication].

US Civil Society Representative 2. (2014, June 11). *Interview, Washington DC, 11 Jun 2014* [Personal communication].

US Department of the Treasury. (2017, February 23). *Readout of secretary Mnuchin's meeting with Mark Carney, Governor of the Bank of England (BOE) and Chair of the Financial Stability Board (FSB).* www.treasury.gov/press-center/press-releases/Pages/sm0013.aspx

US House Committee on Financial Services. (2014a, May 9). *Letter to U.S. members of the Financial Stability Board.* http://financialservices.house.gov/uploadedfiles/05-09-14_jh-letter.pdf

US House Committee on Financial Services. (2014b). *Hearing: Examining the dangers of the FSOC's designation process and its impact on the U.S. financial system* (No. 113–79). http://financialservices.house.gov/uploadedfiles/113-79.pdf

US Legislature Aide. (2012, July 27). *Interview, Washington DC, 27 Jul 2012* [Personal communication].

US Lobbyist 1. (2012). *Interview, Washington DC, 23 Jul 2012* [Personal communication].

US Lobbyist 2. (2014, June 18). *Interview, Washington DC, 18 Jun 2014* [Personal communication].

US Lobbyist 3. (2014). *Interview, Washington DC, 15 Oct 2014* [Personal communication].

US Regulator 1. (2012, July 23). *Interview, Washington DC, 23 July 2012* [Personal communication].

US Regulator 1. (2014, June 16). *Interview, Washington DC, 16 Jun 2014* [Personal communication].

US Regulator 4. (2014, June 30). *Interview, Washington DC, 30 Jun 2014* [Personal communication].

US Treasury. (2009, September 24). *Press briefing by treasury secretary Tim Geithner on the G20 meeting*. Press release, U.S. Department of the Treasury, Pittsburgh.

Verdier, P.-H. (2009). Transnational regulatory networks and their limits. *Yale Journal of International Law, 34*, 113.

Verdier, P.-H. (2013). The Political Economy of International Financial Regulation. *Indiana Law Journal, 88*, 1405.

Vickers, J. (2017). *Written evidence to the UK Treasury Committee regarding legislative proposals to amend EU prudential requirements.* http://data.parliament.uk/writtenevidence/committeeevidence.svc/evidencedocument/treasury-committee/capital-and-resolution/written/48205.pdf

Viñals, J., & Fiechter, J. (2010). *The making of good supervision: Learning to say "no"* [IMF Staff Discussion Note SPN/10/18]. IMF.

Wade, R. H. (2011). Emerging world order? From multipolarity to multilateralism in the G20, the World Bank, and the IMF. *Politics & Society, 39*(3), 347–378.

Wallace, T. (2016, April 29). *RBS plunges to a £1bn loss on bailout-era costs.* The Telegraph. www.telegraph.co.uk/business/2016/04/29/rbs-plunges-to-a-1bn-loss-on-bailout-era-costs/

Wallison, P., & Gallagher, D. (2015, March 19). How foreigners became America's financial regulators. *Wall Street Journal.* www.wsj.com/articles/peter-wallison-and-daniel-gallagher-how-foreigners-became-americas-financial-regulators-1426806547

Walsh, J. (2012). *Testimony of acting comptroller of the currency before the US senate committee on banking, housing, and urban affairs.* www.occ.gov/news-issuances/congressional-testimony/2012/pub-test-2012-50-written.pdf

Walter, A. (2008). *Governing finance: East Asia's adoption of international standards.* Cornell University Press.

Walter, A. (2016). Emerging countries and Basel III: Why is engagement still low? In C. R. Henning & A. Walter (Eds.), *Global financial governance confronts the rising powers* (pp. 179–210). CIGI.

Warmbrodt, Z. (2017, November 22). Democrats split over support for GOP-led bank bill. *Politico*. http://politi.co/2A2TsYY

Way, C. R. (2005). Political insecurity and the diffusion of financial market regulation. *The Annals of the American Academy of Political and Social Science, 598*(1), 125–144.

Weber, R. H., & Staiger, D. N. (2014). Financial stability board: Mandate and implementation of its systemic risks standards. *International Journal of Financial Studies, 2*(1), 82–102.

WEED. (2013). *MiFID2: Set to fail on food speculation*. http://www2.weed-online.org/uploads/mifid_loopholes_briefing_april_2013.pdf

Weyland, K. (2007). *Bounded rationality and policy diffusion: Social sector reform in Latin America*. Princeton University Press.

White, G. (1993). Towards a political analysis of markets. *Ids Bulletin, 24*(3), 4–11.

White, W. R. (1997). International agreements in the area of banking and finance: Accomplishments and outstanding issues. In *Regulation and supervision of financial institutions in the NAFTA countries and beyond* (pp. 48–81). Springer.

Whytock, C. A. (2005). A rational design theory of transgovernmentalism: The case of EU-US merger review cooperation. *Boston University International Law Journal, 23*, 1.

Wintour, P. (2012, January 31). Fred Goodwin stripped of knighthood. *The Guardian*. www.theguardian.com/business/2012/jan/31/fred-goodwin-stripped-of-knighthood

Wishart, J. B. C. (2014, March 20). EU reaches deal on bank-failure bill after marathon talks. *Bloomberg.Com*. www.bloomberg.com/news/articles/2014-03-20/eu-lawmakers-said-to-reach-provisional-deal-on-bank-bill

Wright, D. (2012, December 10). *Remarks by the secretary general of IOSCO*. The Atlantic Council, Washington, DC. www.iosco.org/library/speeches/pdf/20121210-Wright-David.pdf

Wriston, W. B. (1993). The twilight of sovereignty. *The Fletcher Forum of World Affairs, 17*, 117.

Wu, W. (2017, April 27). Regulatory storm hits China amid shadow banking fears. *South China Morning Post*. www.scmp.com/news/china/economy/article/2090932/regulatory-storm-hits-chinas-banks-xi-pushes-better-risk-controls

Wyatt, E. (2011, January 18). Panel begins to set rules to govern financial system. *The New York Times*. www.nytimes.com/2011/01/19/business/19rules.html

Xinhua. (2016, April 26). Xi Jinping presides over 40th Politburo Collective Study Session; Emphasizes that financial liveliness and stability is economic liveliness and stability, and that finance work must be done well and financial security maintained (习近平在中共中央政治局第四十次集体学习时强调; 金融活经济活 金融稳经济稳; 做好金融工作 维护金融安). *Xinhua News*. www.xinhuanet.com//politics/2017-04/26/c_1120879349.htm

Yan, Q., & Li, J. (2014). *Research on China's shadow banking regulation (中国影子银行监管研究)* (第1版). Renmin University of China Publishing House 中国人民大学出版社.

Yazbek, O. (2009). *Regulação do Mercado Financeiro e de Capitais*. Campus – Grupe Elsevier.

Young, K. (2014). Losing abroad but winning at home: European financial industry groups in global financial governance since the crisis. *Journal of European Public Policy, 21*(3), 367–388.

Young, K. (2016). Tying hands and cutting ties: Explaining the divergence between the EU and the US in global banking reform since the crisis. *Journal of Banking Regulation, 17*(1–2), 46–59.

Young, K. L. (2012). Transnational regulatory capture? An empirical examination of the transnational lobbying of the Basel Committee on Banking Supervision. *Review of International Political Economy, 19*(4), 663–688.

Zaring, D. (1998). International law by other means: The twilight existence of international financial regulatory organizations. *Texas International Law Journal, 33*, 281–330.

Zaring, D. (2010). A lack of resolution. *Emory Law Journal, 60*, 97.

Zaring, D. (2015). Financial reform's internationalism. *Emory Law Journal, 65*, 1255.

Zaring, D. (2016, December 2). Regulation without borders comes under fire in Washington. *The New York Times*. www.nytimes.com/2016/12/02/business/dealbook/regulation-without-borders-comes-under-fire-in-washington.html

INDEX

Note: Page locators in **bold** indicate a table. Page locators in *italics* indicate a figure.

For Product Safety Concerns and Information please contact our EU representative GPSR@taylorandfrancis.com Taylor & Francis Verlag GmbH, Kaufingerstraße 24, 80331 München, Germany

Batch number: 10725798

Printed by Printforce, the Netherlands